The UGLY Scarred Dishonest Face of Poor Old Miserable UNCLE SAM!

(A Memorial Day Legacy!)

By
The Worldwide People's Revolution!®

Book 054

(The Front Cover shows a Photo of an Imaginary Picture of "Uncle Sam," who was Inviting Young Men to Join the United States Army for the Purpose of Murdering other Ignorant Innocent Young Men, whereby the Edomites could Gain Trillions of Dollars at their Expenses! Provable Truths only ask for Fair Hearings.)

Copyright, Dedication and Introduction

By our Selected King's Chief Editor,
Dr. Samuel Walker Edison, Ph.D., MA, BS, and QC!

ISBN-13: 978-1718-8156-29
ISBN-10: 1718-8156-2X

00-01 [_] This Inspired Book is COPYRIGHTED AD 2018, by **The Worldwide People's Revolution!®**

00-02 [_] All Rights are Reserved for **"The Great Worldwide TELEVISED Court HEARING!"** No Portion of this Inspired Book shall be Reproduced by any Means for Sale without Written Permission from **The Worldwide People's Revolution!®** However, with that Permission, anyone in the World has the Right to Reproduce Exact Copies of this Book, and Sell them for a Reasonable Profit, and KEEP 90% of the Net Profits for their own Prosperity: because our Selected King only wants 10% of the Net Profits for the Construction of: **"The Great World TEMPLE of PEACE!"** (See Book 017.)

00-03 [_] We received the following E-mail Letter (minus the Verse Numbers and [_] Boxes) from an Avid Reader, which is now Published, Worldwide: because of its Great Value to Mankind, and its Controversial Words of Provable Truths. Please read it Carefully with a Capital C. Please Check any Boxes with an X, if you Agree with such Statements. Thank you. (Use a Highlighter to Draw Attention to your Greater Points of Interest.)

Brother John McArdle, my Prayer for Peace —

00-04 [_] Thank you for Hosting the *Washington Journal* this morning. You did the best that you could do with a Limited education, and I had to weep for nearly 3 whole hours over it, and am still not fully recovered from it: because the Tears well up in my eyes, just to Think about it, and also Think about you and the billions of young People who can hardly Relate with the Awfulness of those Hateful Gory Unnecessary Wars, or else they might be Capitalizing Awful, Gory, and Hateful in their own Thoughtful Minds.

00-05 [_] As one of your Callers explained, and as you "red" from some newspaper, Words are Inadequate to Describe the Horrors of Wars, much less the Depressing Thoughts that Flood the Minds of the Victims of Capitalism, Communism, Socialism, Fascism, and ISIS Insanity, who have been caught up in the Snares and Traps of Ignorant Lying Politicians, who should not Legally Qualify to be Leaders in such High Offices, until they have "Served" at least one Year in a Combat Simulator in some Hateful Bloody Gory War, if not in a Real War, just to Reduce the Chances of them Voting for another Murderous War at Home or Abroad.

00-06 [_] It is the 2016 Memorial Day, whereby the *Washington Journal* has somewhat Honored the 58,307+ Victims of Vietnam, who Lost their Lives in Vain, and Caused no less than 3 Million

Vietnamese to Lose their Lives, none of whom Uncle Sam has ever Apologized to: because they are all Dead, even though their Lives were Equally as Precious to them as ours are to us, who are now lying in their Cold Silent Graves, each of whom would no doubt like to Telephone the *Washington Journal,* and give to us a Piece of their own Minds, whose only Voices are those of Grieved Friends and Relatives, who must now Speak Up for them and the Millions more who have Suffered the Fates of the Victims of Capitalism, Communism, Socialism, Fascism, and any other Isms that have brought about all such MADNESS as the Mountains of TRASH, and the Endless WARS! Yes, each of those Victims would naturally have a whole book to write about themselves, and how they were Greatly Deprived of the Good Things in Life, who Sacrificed their Lives for nothing, and all in Vain, unless we have now Learned our Lessons, as Good Students of Superior Nolij. ("Knowledge" seems to have a lot of unnecessary extra letters, as if the word were dragged out of some Barbarian Dictionary from Ancient Times. Therefore, if you discover "mis-speld werdz" here, try to Appreciate the Superior Spelling. Thank you.)

00-07 [_] So, Thanks to that Evil Capitalist Empire across the Great Sea from Vietnam, which Empire gained several hundred Billion dollars by going to War in Vietnam, we now have to Weep every Memorial Day for our Losses, which Pathetic Fact none of your Callers got around to Mentioning this Day of Mourning: beCause their Minds were no doubt Swallowed Up by Deeper Depressive Personal Thoughts, you might say, who each have their own Sad Stories to tell to the nearby Trees and Weeds that might be Listening to them in the Forests and Brier Patches behind Abandoned Factories in Detroit, Michigan, for Example, or wherever they might now be Hiding, Out of Sight, behind Curtains and Closed Doors in Abandoned Houses, lest some Young Inexperienced Red-necked Policemen might be trying to Evict them, or just Harass them — as if they were the Criminals on their "Most Wanted List," or just Unwashed Vagrants, who should be Tormented even more than their Homelessness has already Disgraced them!

00-08 [_] Brother John, it will not do me any Good to Cry on your Shoulder, even though I know that your Arms of Love and Mercy are Extended toward all of us Veterans: beCause you too have a Big Heart full of Tears, no doubt, being a Whistleblower, yourself. However, if it will Help you to Relate with those Millions of Victims of Capitalism and Communism, I Plead with you to spend just a Night or 2 under some Freeway Bridge on the Interstate Highway, or down in the Sewage System of New Yuck City, or in the Subway of some Train Station in Calcutta, India; or in some Cold Dimly-lit Back Alley in the Slums of Sao Paulo, Brazil, after spending the whole Miserable Day in those Back Alleys, searching around in Dumpsters for something to Eat. Otherwise, you could go to the Salvation Army on Lonesome Street and Suicide Avenue, in some large City of Confusion, and get yourself a Cot in a large Room with 40 other Bean-eating Farting Homeless Victims of Capitalism, some of whom are bound to be Veterans of some Hateful Capitalist War.

00-09 [_] Yes, you have probably noticed that I have been Over-emphasizing "Capitalism," which is Hailed in **"The Divided States of United Lies"** as "the Financial Salvation of Mankind," even while Producing more than 60 Million Unemployed Americans, and another 100 Million Underpaid Americans, who are just a few Steps away from being in some Long Boring Lines at the Salvation Army, or at some Rescue Mission in Chicago, Lost Angels, Californicate; or even in Lungdung, England, which used to put such People in Insane Asylums, if you can Believe it.

00-10 [_] Yes, it would be quite a Sacrifice for you to Try that little Experiment with Homelessness, even as it would be for at least 90% of Americans; but, a whole Month of that Kind of Self-inflicted "Penitence" would be Good for your Soul, and for theirs, and especially if you could persuade some Voluntary Friends to Shoot at you with Blank Cartridges and Fake Rocket Launchers, which make LOUD Harmless Noises in your Ears for at least half of the Night, beginning at Midnight, whereby you might not get much Sleep for the next 6 Months, whereby it would somewhat Simulate a Wartime Situation in Vietnam, Iraq, Afghanistan, Syria, or wherever, whereby you might at least get a Feel for the Realities of Death, which you could Greatly Enhance by your own Wonderful Imagination, while lying on Hard Sandbags, using one for a Pillow — except that in a Real War, there is TERROR, Spilled Blood and Stinking Guts, and a Constant Fear that you might be the next Victim of some Aggressive "Serviceman," who Glories in Wars, who takes Great PRIDE in Slaughtering as many Souls as Possible for "the kingdom of heaven's sake," as one Professing "Christian" put it, who was Dead Sure that he was going to Heaven when he Died, in spite of what Jesus said in the Gay King James Version (KJV) of *John 3:13:* beCause he was Working for "the greatest nation on the earth, which God loves more than all other nations: because he has blest us with atomic bombs, chemical and biological warfare, countless drugs, and all such *good* things, which is proof that we are his Blest Children — even the Chosen Sons of Israel, himself!" †§‡

00-11 [_] Yes, according to their Firm Belief, Almighty God is on OUR Side of every International Issue, or Dispute; and therefore, we cannot do any WRong, which False Belief has also been Adopted by those Warmongering Muslims, who even Sincerely Believe that it is their Allah-given DUTY to their Imaginary God to get Rid of as many of those "Satanic Americans" as Possible, who have a Proven Record of War Crimes on their own Bloody Streets, who Murder upwards of 100 Innocent Souls each Day, while some 800- to 900-thousand People are Killed each Year by Medical Malpractice, by wRong administrations of Drugs, and WRong Combinations of Drugs, which the Snooze Media simply overlooks — that is, those Lying Edomites, who Control the News Media, simply Ignore any of their Red Jew Sins. ‡

00-12 [_] Moreover, they Sincerely Believe that the Federal Government of **"The Divided States of United Lies"** cooked up the Witches Brew known as the Evil Events of September 11th, 2001, which they say was a False Flag Operation, which Americans Blamed on Osama bin Laden and Saddam Hussein of Iraq, who had nothing whatsoever to do with those Evil Events: because those Acts were far too Complicated for 19 Ignorant Saudi Arabian and Egyptian Hijackers to Perform, none of whom had ever Flown any HUGE Passenger Airplanes, which have well over a hundred Switches, Lights, Gages, and Levers in the Cockpits to keep their Eyes on, while being under the Great STRESS of Hijacking such Airplanes with only Box Cutters for Protection! ‡

00-13 [_] Yes, even Professional Pilots freely Confess that they could not do what was supposedly done during that Day of Woes by Inexperienced Pilots, who had never even Practiced Flying such Planes by Means of Simulators: beCause they were only PATSIES! Yes, they were Falsely Accused for a Military Industrial Congressional Bankers' Complex Terrorist Attack, which has been Proven on www.AE911TRUTH.org and Related Websites, for whomever has the Spiritual Fortitude to Study all such Important Things.

00-14 [_] Nevertheless, Brother John, that is not the Primary Reason WHY that I am sending this E-mail Letter to you: beCause there is a much more Important Issue at hand, which you seem to be Ignoring, as if that will make it all go Away! Yes, you are somewhat like the Proverbial Ostrich with your Head Stuck in the Sand, Wishing that you could somehow Escape your Journalistic

Duties! Indeed, as a Journalist — even as my Favorite, Innocent, Honest, Open-minded, most Lovable Journalist — you Carry a certain Burden of Responsibility to the General Public: beCause of your Position of Authority, which you could say is the Responsibility of Brian Lamb or Susan Swain, who are the "Decision Makers" at C-SPAN.

00-15 [_] However, as a Celebrated Host of the *Washington Journal,* you could "Twist their Arms a bit," and perhaps Persuade them that the entire Memorial Day should be Devoted Wholly to the *Washington Journal* and Memorial Day "Celebrations" for that Holiday / Holy Day, and for 24 whole Hours of Open Phone Lines for Veterans, between a few Parades and other Nonsense that is Conducted by the White House Super Snooper-intendents, who surely must be Bored by 60+ Years of Laying Wreaths at the Tomb of Unknown Victims of Capitalism.

00-16 [_] In other words, after the President lays his "Cover-up" Flowery Perfumed Wreaths on the Tombs of no less than 100 Million Victims of American Aggressions, Worldwide, ever since 1776, you and your Companions at C-SPAN should continue on with an Open Phone Lines Celebration of all such Glorious Wars, beginning with the Slaughter of no less than 20 Million American Indians, and 60 Million Bisons by Subtle Means, and 10,000,000+ Displaced Poor People in the Middle East, plus 2 Million Killed or Wounded Iraqis, plus Multitudes of Homeless Refugees, and ending with the present Conflicts in those Back Alleys, Sewage Systems, Subways, Highway Culvert Rest Homes for Used Veterans, and Freeway Bridge Encampments for Homeless Jobless Penniless PROUD Americans — all of whom would have been a thousand Times better off, if they had Joined one of our Selected King's **"Seven Great Armies of Working Soldiers!"** **(HOW to Provide a Way for Everyone to WORK: so as to Eliminate Poverty, Crimes, Drug Abuses, Prisons and Unnecessary Taxes!) By The Worldwide People's Revolution!® Book 015.**

00-17 [_] Yes, there is a Happy Ending to this Sad Legacy of American Insanity, and all other Insanities; but, only IF you, my Friend, Exercise a little Faith, and ask your Viewers and Listeners a few simple Questions. For Example, "Have you read any of the Inspired Books by the Selected King of **The Worldwide People's Revolution!®?**" Or, "Have you ever heard of a book, called: **'Does a Good Soldier have to be a MURDERER?' (Seven Great Swanky Armies of Voluntary Working Soldiers!)?**" Or, "Have you seen a book, called: **'GLORIOUS Swanky Hotels Castles and Fortresses!' (Beautiful Planned City States for WISE Intelligent Well-Educated People with Common Sense and Good Understanding!)?**" {See www.Amazon.com for all of the Available Books by Googling: **The Worldwide People's Revolution!®**}

00-18 [_] Yes, it would require some GUTS to ask such Serious Questions, and to Remind them that the Descriptions and Book Previews are FREE of Charges! But, you might Argue that C-SPAN cannot PROMOTE any Books that are for Sale: beCause it is against your Policies at the *Washington Journal.* However, it can easily be Proven in a Courtroom that C-SPAN Promotes the Sales of many books, which is WHY you have "BookTV," "Q&A," etc., etc.: beCause you would like to EDUCATE Americans, who are some of the most Ignorant People on the Good Earth, who do not even Capitalize "DUMBmocracy," let alone Liberty, Freedom, nor Justice for ALL! But, in your Minds, all of you at C-SPAN Capitalize Dumbmocracy, whereby the Voices of 99.999,999,999% of the People in this World of Woes do not get to Speak on the *Washington Journal,* which makes it a FARCE, just as our Selected King has Revealed in his Exceptionally

Good Book, called: "The Washington Journal is a FARCE!" (C-SPAN Managers are not very WISE!) By The Worldwide People's Revolution!® Book 006.

00-19 [_] Yes, you may Think that it is rather Funny, or that the *Washington Journal* is a Spiritual Pacifier for Political Babies to Vent their Frustrations and Indignations; but, I Assure you that it is a most Serious "Institution," "Propagandist Tool," or whatever you would like to call it, which can be used for either Good or Evil, just like most other Things in this World of Wonders. Therefore, as the "Caretakers" of the *Washington Journal,* it is your God-given DUTY to Publish as much Truth as you can Discover: beCause, as Jesus Christ Revealed in *John 8:32,* ONLY the Sword of Truths has the Power to Liberate us Earthlings from our Massive Problems, as well as our Minor Problems, including what to Do about this Epistle of the Apostle of Truths, himself, who would be Happy to Assist you to Overthrow Babylon, or Confusion, if you were at all Interested in putting Poor Old Debt-ridden Uncle Sam to REST in his Graveyard at Arlington Slimmetery, which is full of the Bones of the Radiated and Agent Orange Victims of Capitalism, who may easily enough have done some "Heroic Deeds" — such as Murdering other Victims of Fascism, Communism, and Islamism; but, behold, the Real Heroes are those Honest People with Strong Hearts and Educated Minds, who have taken up their Swords of Truths, and are Willing to DIE for all such Truths — such as Abraham Lincoln, Martin Luther King, Jr., Muhammad Ali, the Apostle Paul, Saint Peter, and Jesus Christ, himself, who would have Certainly NOT Approved of going to War in Iraq, nor even in Afghanistan, until a Thorough Unbiased Investigation was made of the EVIDENCES at the Scenes of the Crimes, in New York City, Washington, and the Field near Shanksville, Pennsylvania, which had NO Bodies, no Blood, no Luggage, no Airplane Parts, no Black Boxes, and ZERO Proof that any Airplane Crashed at such a Site, which you are Welcome to Study for yourself on the Internet, which has an Ax to Grind, you might say; but, their Axes are Justified: beCause there is MUCH Evidence that someone is Lying to us Tax Slaves, which C-SPAN and the entire CONgress just Ignores! ‡

00-20 [_] Yes, the Present President also just Ignores the Realities of Life, which are Orchestrated by the Puppet Masters of the Military Industrial Congressional Drug Cartel Bankers' Complex: beCause the Whole Truth is not very PROFITABLE! Indeed, almost everything in the World is now done for PROFITS, and not for the Peace, Happiness nor True Prosperity of the Masses of People, who are otherwise known as Work Slaves, Tax Slaves, Debt Slaves, Interest Slaves, Insurance Slaves, Drug Slaves, Sex Slaves, and Endless Bills Slaves!

00-21 [_] In Fact, you People at C-SPAN are a Part of the "Conspiracy" against all such SLAVES: beCause you Promote those Election Deceptions with Endless Broadcasts on the C-SPAN Network, when it is Possible and much more Practical for each Potential Politician to Post his or her Complete SURVEYS of Religious Spiritual Political Governmental Sexual Social Moral Business Economic Labor Habitual and Miscellaneous VALUES on the Internet for everyone to Study at their own Pace, whereby they would Know WHO might be the most Qualified to be Elected into any given Office of a Good Government, which would naturally have **"The Swanky Sword of Divine Truths"** on its Side of every Issue: beCause of being Perfectly HONEST about all Subjects. {NOTE: You can Discover **"The Complete SURVEYS of our VALUES!" (SURVEYS of Religious Spiritual Political Governmental Sexual Social Moral Economic Business Labor Habitual and Miscellaneous VALUES) By The Worldwide People's Revolution!®**, Book 059, on www.Amazon.com, which every Potential Political Leader and Elector in the World should have to Study and Check the Appropriate Boxes [_], and then Post their Surveys on the Internet for other Wise People to Study, before being Qualified to VOTE, as Plato, Aristotle, Socrates, Shakingspears, Steinbeck, Hymningway and Mark Twain might say, who Believed in Meritocracy, who would at least Confess that Wasting hundreds of Billions of Dollars on Election Deceptions is NOT the Riit Waa to go, while Billions of People are Living in Extreme Poverty, and Millions are Starving to Death for the Lack of **"Beautiful Swanky PALACES!" (A New Concept in Living Habits — Swanky Palaces for Poor People!) By The Worldwide People's Revolution!® Book 066!}**

00-22 [_] Yes, even the Taliban and ISIS (Israeli Secret Instigation Services) would have to Submit to their Sword of Truths: beCause the Truth cannot be Defeated by any Means, even as you cannot Defeat the Truths within this one little Epistle of mine, which you should Read Aloud on the *Washington Journal,* Word for Word, and Line by Line from the Beginning to the End: beCause it is Inspired by GOD — that is, by the same God who said: *"Love your Naaberz as much as you Love yourselves,"* and *"Do unto others as you would have others Do unto you."*

00-23 [_] For Example, how would you Feel if Russians and Chinese had made a Preemptive Attack on the United States of America for having "Weapons of Mass Destruction" during the 1960's? Awe, "We are Justified by Reason of our Holiness of Mind, Spirit, and Body, whereby all other Peoples are Inferior to us," says the Mockingbird to the Squirrelly Bankers, who go Out on Unreliable Limbs of Financial Scams to Loan Money to Ignorant Fools for Building Wooden / Plastic Firetrap Mouse-infested Cockroach Dens, which are Guaranteed to come to Ruin by one Means or another. But, in Reality, we are not one Degree Better than any other Nation of People on this Good Earth, including Cuba, Iran, Iraq, and North Korea, except by the Grace of GOD, who Blest this Land of America with an Abundance of Water, Rivers, Lakes, Forests, Fertile Topsoil, Fruit Trees, and thousands of Mountains of Rocks — not to Mention all of the Innovative Artistic Inventors, like Thomas Edison, Nikola Tesla, Alexander Graham Bell, Henry Ford, Bill Computer Software Gates, Steve Jobs, etc., etc., who just Happened to be Born here, instead of over there: beCause God Wanted to Bless America, just to Test the Spirits of Men and Wombmen, in Order to Discover their Goodness or Evilness, which they are Free to Choose! ‡

00-24 [_] Yes, if it were not for the Blessings of the Great Creator God, we too might be Equally as Poor as those Ignorant Africans, who have been Exploited for Centuries by Capitalist HOGS, who Used them as Slaves: beCause of taking Advantage of their Ignorance, Unemployment, Poverty, Muscles, and so on, who are easily Depressed by the Great False Economy, who are Prone to Consume and Sell Drugs, just to Try to Escape from the Realities of their Lives, which Realities were "Created" by the Military Industrial Congressional Drug Cartel Bankers' Complex, which does not Want to LIFT THEM OUT of their Bottomless Pit of Poverty and Confusion: beCause the Capitalist Hogs NEED X-amount of Slaves for doing their Dirty Work, including those Poor Persecuted Mexicans and other Immigrants from around the World, who could now be Living Healthy Happy Lives in **"Beautiful Swanky PALACES,"** if we had used the same Amount of Money and Energy to Build them, which has already been Wasted in our Airplanes, Lawnmowers, Cars, Trucks, Vans, and Buses, running around on Polluted Highways like Spiritual Babies in a Candy Store, who are not Aware of the Dangers of Rotting Out their Precious Teeth, much less the Dangers of Radical Climate Changes, whereby all such Cities might be DROWNED by the Rising Tides! Yes, we have already Wasted enough Energy to have Built those **"GLORIOUS Swanky Hotels Castles and Fortresses"** for everyone in the World! †§‡

00-25 [_] Yes, those Mechanical Slaves — such as Bulldozers, Track-hoes, Backhoes, Front-end Loaders, Dump Trucks, and Electric Trains — would have been Happy to have Helped us in a BIG Way to get those Beautiful Planned City States Constructed, Properly, for PEACE and True Prosperity, in Answer to the Pleading Prayers of BILLIONS of Poor People.

00-26 [_] However, you People in Washington, District of Corruption, even Refuse to Study all such Information: beCause of some Mysterious Reason, which I would call Chronic Constipation of the Mind. {See www.Amazon.com for: **"The Right Design for Living!" (A List of Great Advantages for Building Beautiful Planned City States!)**, Book 012, plus: **"Poverty Hunger Riots Strikes Brutalities Election Deceptions and Civil Wars!" (The High Price that we Earthlings have Paid for Leaving the Good Land!)**, Book 014, plus: **"The Swanky Associations of Working Soldiers!" (A Fascinating Collection of Various Kinds of Voluntary Working Soldiers!)**, Book 018, plus: **"Are Americans the Most STUPID People who ever Lived?" (HOW Working People can PROSPER and Live in PEACE Under the Rulership of a RIGHTEOUS KING!)**, Book 047, which will Enlighten your Minds — that is, IF you still have Riit Miindz to Think with, O Hypocrites, who say that you Believe in God; but, you Refuse to Do anything that he Commands you — such as Loving your Naaberz as much as yourselves!}

00-27 [_] Yes, I have my Doubts about you People at C-SPAN being in your Right Minds, seeing that I have yet to Receive even ONE Response from any of you, as if I were the Lowest Scumbag who ever Lived? What ever Happened to RESPECT? Have any of you ever Received such a GOOD Letter as this from anyone else? If so, WHY did you not read it on the *Washington Journal?* How come you Persist in reading the Newspaper Articles, after Knowing for a FACT that this Letter contains Real Substance to Work with, and Think about, and Discuss on the *Washington Journal,* which Subjects you have never Addressed?

00-28 [_] Yes, I Challenge you to find Better Solutions for our Massive Problems, than those that have already been Presented by **The Worldwide People's Revolution!®**, whose Selected King is a HOLY Man, who Speaks for Almighty God. Indeed, if you Doubt it, just read: **"God Speaks and the Whole World Listens!" (Fire on the Mountain from the Burning Bush by the Spirit of Truth!)** Book 026.

00-29 [_] Yes, you would have to Humble yourselves to Confess that someone in this World of Confusion might KNOW something that is Good for us Tax Slaves to Learn, in spite of any Religious Overtones, which seem to Spook you away, O Timid Political Rabbits! Yes, come Out of your Stinking Holes, O you Wicked Politicians, and Hold Up your Twitching Ears, and Listen to me: beCause I have Bad News for you!

00-30 [_] Yes, the Rejection of Truths is the Greatest of Sins, says the Master Farmer and Chief Architect. Therefore, do not Reject any Truth about any Subject, including the Great Truths about those **"GLORIOUS Swanky Hotels Castles and Fortresses,"** which just Happen to have more than 5,000 Good Reasons and Great Advantages over present-day Cities of Confusion, with ZERO Great Disadvantages!

00-31 [_] For Example, Swanky Fortresses have no need for Automobiles, Trucks, Buses, Lawnmowers, Motorcycles, nor any such Dangerous Stinking Noisy Abominations: because they use Elevators, Escalators, and Underground Electric Subway Trains, some of which Travel Slowly and some Rapidly over long Distances. That alone will Save Trillions of Dollars, which is Explained in: **"The Right Design for Living!" (A List of Great Advantages for Building Beautiful Planned City States!)**, Book 012, which is a Companion Book of: **"The Low Court of Supreme Injustices is Brought to Trial!" (Our Elected King Butts Heads with the United States Supreme Court, with or without their Black Robes of Hypocrisies and Lies!) By The Worldwide People's Revolution!®** Book 011.

00-32 [_] Yes, our Selected King offers a ONE-MILLION-DOLLAR REWARD to anyone who can Present so much as ONE Great Disadvantage for Building or Living within those **"Beautiful Swanky PALACES,"** which are Rot-proof Paint-proof Fireproof Mouse-proof Termite-proof Hail-proof Tornado-proof Insurance-proof and Self-air-conditioned, having Polished Marble-faced SOLID Stone Walls in Beautiful Stone Dome Home Complexes, which have Home-craft Workshops, Sales Shops, HUGE Cisterns for Water Storage, and Luscious All-Mineral Organic Gardens, Vineyards, and Orchards to Play in, Catching FRUITS and Vegetables, instead of Bullets, Grenades and Bombs! Yes, those Palaces also have Churches, Cathedrals, Temples, Mosques, Synagogues, Museums, Theaters, Auditoriums, Concert Halls, Art Galleries, Tennis Courts, Gymnasiums, Indoor Swimming Pools, Ice-skating Rinks, Bowling Alleys, Game Rooms and many Fragrant Flowery Gardens.

00-33 [_] Therefore, come now, and let us Reason Together, says the Supreme Ruler of **"Seven Great Armies of Working Soldiers,"** have any of you Presented Better Master Plans than that of my Selected King? Truly, Truly, I say to you: CEASE from your Childish Foolishness, and put on the Armor of Faith, Hope, Trust, Love, Patience, Persistence, and OBEDIENCE, which are **"The Seven Basic Spiritual Building Blocks of LIFE!"** (Book 036): beCause the Right Way to have National Security for all Nations is to Construct those **"GLORIOUS Swanky Hotels Castles and Fortresses!" (Beautiful Planned City States for WISE Intelligent Well-Educated People with Common Sense and Good Understanding!)**, Book 019.

00-34 [_] Yes, it will Require a LOT of HARD WORK, O Lady Doubtfulness; but, Work is Good for the Mind, Body, and Spirit, most of which can be done by Young Voluntary Working Soldiers, who can have and must have and will have the Correct Tools and Heavy Equipment to Work with, being Better Equipped than Military Armies, whereby some of those Mountains of Ugly Rocks will be Transformed into: **"The Environmentalists' Paradise!" (HOW almost Everyone could be Living in a Beautiful Manmade Paradise!)**, Book 035. Therefore, **"Terrorists Beware that your Days are Numbered!" (HOW to Bring those Terrorist Attacks to a Screeching HALT!)**, Book 043. Yes, **"SWANGKEENOMIKS Rules the Roost!" (HOW all People can Prosper in a RIIT WAA, and STOP Polluting the Earth with Capitalist TRASH!)**, Book 039. Yes, those Swanky Fortresses are **"A Sure Cure for GUN VIOLENCE!" (HOW TO STOP GANG WARS and CRIMINAL SHOOTINGS!)**, Book 031, while providing Cities of Refuge for: **"Aliens, Illegal Immigrants, Refugees, Migrant Workers and other Victims of Capitalism!" (AIIRMWVC and Reasonable Solutions!)**, Book 032.

00-35 [_] Yes, you might say that it will Cost too much! But, a RIICHUS One-World GovernMINT has an Unlimited Supply of New Money, which must be Earned by Honest Labor, without any Loans, without any Interest, without any Usury, without any Slave Labor, and without any Taxes: beCause all such Working Soldiers will Cheerfully and Voluntarily Contribute whatever Money is Necessary for Operating their Good Government, even as the Israelites did for Moses, whose

Headquarters will be Located in: **"The Great World TEMPLE of PEACE!" (The Glory of Jerusalem Arises Again!) By The Worldwide People's Revolution!® Book 017.**

00-36 [_] Yes, I know, you "FEAR such a Monstrous Government," you say: beCause you have never Studied: **"The CONSTITUTION for the New RIGHTEOUS One-World GovernMINT!" (HOW all Peoples can get True Justice, and Celebrate the Great Year of JUBILEE!),** Book 016, which is a Companion Book of: **"Mark Twain Races for the PRESIDENCY!" (The 2020 Presidential Candidates Desperately Need Some STRONG Undefeatable COMPETITION!),** Book 033. Indeed, you FEAR the Great Unknown, and Presume that no such Good Government can be Established: beCause, beCause, beCause ... beCAUSE you are IGNORANT!

00-37 [_] Yes, it is now Time to EDUCATE yourselves with a Capital E, and STOP Playing your Childish Political Games, says the Supreme Ruler of Great Armies of Working Soldiers, lest you Suffer with a Great Atomic NIGHTMARE: beCause, if you do not Yield to this Sharp Sword of Divine Truths, I will Inspire your Enemies to make New Yuck City and Washington, District of Criminals, into an Atomic Disposal Waste Dump! Therefore, FEAR and TREMBLE, O Bloodhounds and Wily Foxes: beCause your Judgment Day is Coming, O you Wretched Miserable Comforters, who Console yourselves with Flattering Lies and False Promises, even while your Stinking Polluted Highways are Crumbling, and your Bridges are Falling, and your Veterans are Mistreated, and your Children are Deprived of the True Riches, who do not even have Fresh Clean Air to Breathe, Pure Living Water to Drink, Wholesome Natural Foods to Eat, Natural Clothing to Wear, nor Secure Houses to Live in, which may Burn Up within 20 Minutes, or Blow Away within 10 Seconds, while those Smiling Political Rabbits in the District of Criminals Promise Federal Assistance at the Expenses of TAX SLAVES!

00-38 [_] Yes, Shame on you People, and Double Shame on the *Washington Journal,* which could Invite my Selected King to Present his most Reasonable Solutions to the United States Congress at a Joint Session of both Houses of Dimwitcrats and Reprobates, if they had the Intestinal Fortitude of a Piss Ant!

00-39 [_] Yes, you could have an All-Day Session with ALL Elected Officials in Attendance, including the President of Timid Rabbits, and the Low Court of Supreme Injustices, after the Wax of Unbelief has been Thoroughly Removed from their Inner Ears by Means of Fasting and Praying, says the Supreme Ruler of TERRIFYING ARMIES of Murderous Soldiers! {See www.Amazon.com for: **"HOW to Become a HOLY Man!" (40 Good Reasons WHY People Should FAST and PRAY!),** Book 045, which is a Companion Book of: **"The Proper RULES for FASTING!" (The Complete Instruction Manual for True Repentance!),** Book 046.}

00-40 [_] Yes, I will Raise Up an Enemy against you Lying HYPOCRITES, and Fry your Asses with your own Hateful Abominations, if you do not Surrender to **"The Swanky Sword of Divine TRUTHS!"** Therefore, SHAKE and TREMBLE, O you Squeaking Church Mice and Stinking Painted Highly-Perfumed SKUNKS, who Profess to be Christians, while Acting like the Synagogue of Satan! (See *Revelation 2:9 and 3:9.*)

00-41 [_] Yes, if you had the Guts of a Speckled Black and White Chicken, an Ostrich, a Zebra, or even a 2-Humped Camel, you would DEMAND: **"The Great Worldwide TELEVISED Court**

HEARING!" (That Great Meeting of the Most Intelligent Well-Educated Minds!), Book 041, whereby you might Discover the Whole Truth about all Important Subjects; but, behold, you have little or no Interest in the WHOLE Truth: beCause you are in Love with your Hateful Military Industrial Congressional Drug Cartel Fake News Media Bankers' Complex, which you have made Extremely Complicated, whereby the Normal Work Slave, Tax Slave, Debt Slave, Interest Slave, Insurance Slave, Drug Slave, and Endless Bills Slave cannot Understand it: beCause it is an Invention of the Synagogue of SATAN, as Honest Iranians and Palestinians might say!

00-42 [_] Yes, it can be, must be, and will be Proven at **that Great Meeting of the Most Intelligent and Well-Educated Minds,** by the Grace of God, who is now Watching over you People for EVIL Purposes, if you do not REPENT, and Change your Ways of Thinking and Living, and thus make up your Weak Minds to Do what is RIIT for yourselves and others, and to do your Best to Establish **"The New RIGHTEOUS One-World Government!" (HOW to Establish a Righteous One-World Government without Going to WAR!)**, Book 056, before you Exterminate your Ignorant selves! Yes, it is now Time to Think like GLOBALISTS: beCause there is only ONE World for you to Live on. Therefore Stop Ruining it for yourselves.

00-43 [_] And thus the Master Farmer has Spoken, Brother John McArdle; and therefore, I Trust that you will Forward this Epistle to whomever might be Interested in Surviving the Coming Atomic Nightmare, if I do not get some Cooperation!

00-44 [_] Sincerely, the Chief Agitator — even the Man with the Spirit of Elijah!

00-45 [_] PS — I will give to you 2 Weeks to Respond before I go Public with this Letter of Correction. PLEASE Kindly Respond with a Positive Peaceful Dialog. After all, I am a Man of Peace; but, I also know HOW to make WAR, and with Divine Powers!

00-46 [_] PPS — My Friends will be Happy to send a Copy of this Epistle to each Nation, Worldwide, including those Russians and Chinese, who may Interpret it Differently, and Decide to take Action into their own Hands, which could Prove to be Hazardous to your Good Health, since you are Located rather Close to: **"The BIG White OUTHOUSE on the Not-so-Biblical Capitol DUNGHILL!" (The Chief Sins of the Divided States of United Lies!)**, Book 023.

00-47-[_] Indeed, Brian Lamb might Live to Regret having Established the *Washington Journal,* and you might Regret having Partaken of his Neglectful Sins, as a Journalist, whereby you Sin by NEGLECTING to Inform the Ignorant Children about the Best Solutions for their Massive Problems. Moreover, I will also Forward a Copy to our Selected King, who will likely MAGNIFY it, and Publish it in one of his Inspired Books, which could Prove to be very Em-bare-assing for all of you at C-SPAN, and in Washington, D.C., at large — at least during the Day of God's Judgment, when ALL of the Good Books are Opened up for Righteous Judgment, including his own, which are Ranked among God's Best Inspired Books, being of a Higher Rank than most Books in the *Bible.*

00-48 [_] PPPS — This may be my Last Letter to you, if I do not Hear from you, which will Cause me to Cry even more. After all, I Love you for your Goodness. Can you not Understand that, John? Therefore, PLEASE Respond! Thank you in Advance.

00-49 [_] This Inspired Book is now DEDICATED to John McArdle at the *Washington Journal*.

00-50 [_] Please Check the previous Box, if you Appreciated the Letter. Please Grade it below:

    A-[_] Extremely Good,

    B-[_] Exceptionally Good,

    C-[_] Good,

    D-[_] Fair,

    E-[_] Poor,

    F-[_] Bad,

    G-[_] Very Bad, or:

    H-[_] Extremely Bad.

The Menu for a Feast of Truths

The Enticement can be found on the Inside of the Back Cover, or somewhere near there. {NOTE: There is no Practical Way to Determine the Exact Number of Pages within a Book: because the Formatting cannot be Embedded on an Apple Computer that is using Microsoft Word for Windows, which is just another Weakness of Capitalism, which Invents Confusion: because no one is in Charge of the Overall Systems of Communications, including the Publishing of Books.}

Explanations for the Symbols that are used within this Book, and within all other Literature by The Worldwide People's Revolution!®:

† This Dagger is called "the Sword of Controversy," which Means that someone Disagrees with the Statement, and especially the Author, himself, who Presents all Kinds of Opinions, even if he Disagrees with them: beCause he is a Firm Believer in *Freedom of Speech and of the Press,* according to the *First Amendment* of the Constitution of the United States of North America.

‡ This Double Dagger is called "the Double-edged Sword of Controversies," which Means that the Subject is so Controversial that it must be Settled at: **"The Great Worldwide TELEVISED Court HEARING!" (That Great Meeting of the Most Intelligent and Well-Educated Minds!) By The Worldwide People's Revolution!®** Book 041. In other Words, when we Conduct that Great Meeting, everyone in the whole World will be Able to Contribute their Honest Opinions by

Way of the Chain of Command of **"Seven Great Armies of Working Soldiers!"** **(HOW to Provide a Way for Everyone to WORK: so as to Eliminate Poverty, Crimes, Drug Abuses, Prisons and Unnecessary Taxes!) By The Worldwide People's Revolution!®** Book 015. For Example, let us say that you are the Captain of a certain Company of Working Soldiers, and one of your Workers has Discovered a Great Idea: beCause of being a Thinking Person, who might Want to be Promoted within the System, which Great Idea everyone in the Whole World Needs to Learn — that Person will simply Inform you, the Captain of the Company, what that Great Idea is, and if you Agree that it is a Great Idea, you will E-mail the Idea to your Commanding Officer, who will Pass On that Information to his Commanding Officer, and so on, until it is Delivered to the Ambassador of your Nation, who will Kindly Present that Information at **"The Worldwide TELEVISED Court HEARING!"** Indeed, it will Require TIME to Accomplish that; but, that Great Idea will not be Lost among Millions of Worthless Opinions, which might be Discovered on *Facebook, Tweeter,* or by some other Social Media Means of Communicating: beCause, at the very least, your Great Idea will be Published in: **"FREEDUM uv SPEECH!" (U Speshoul Maguzeen uv Onist Upinyunz!) By The Worldwide People's Revolution!®** Book 030-0002: beCause it was Approved by all of the Elected Commanding Officers of those Working Soldiers, who Passed On the Information to: **"The New RIGHTEOUS One-World Government!" (HOW to Establish a Righteous One-World Government without Going to WAR!) By The Worldwide People's Revolution!®** Book 056. And then that Working Soldier, who Contributed that Great Idea, will be Promoted within the Swanky Fortress System, which will Encourage other Working Soldiers to Think and Record their own Great Ideas. Therefore, if you now have a Great Idea, you should Write it within a Notebook; and, if you come up with a Great Idea while Reading this Inspired Book, you may Record it on one of the Blank Pages in the Rear End of this Book, or in some other Book by **The Worldwide People's Revolution!®**, whereby you cannot Lose it.

§ This Section Symbol is used to Identify Sarcastic Statements. 2 such Symbols (§§) Together, Means that the Statement contains a Double Sarcasm, which Means that the Statement is so Sarcastic that it Proves itself to be WRong. For Example, there are no Criminals in the District of Chief Criminals in Washington, District of Corruption, which is otherwise known as the Primary American Swamp, which President Donald Swamp-drainer Trumpeter was going to Drain and Clean Up with the Help of other Chief Criminals, like himself — none of whom have any Idea HOW to go about Draining such Swamps, which get Messier and Messier as one goes down Deeper and Deeper into them. In Fact, that Particular Swamp reaches all of the Way into the Edomite Sewage System on Wall Street, in New Yuck City, which not even a Hungry Alligator would Want to Wade into: because it is Full of Deadly Snakes, Chemical Abominations, Countless Drugs, and Hordes of Rats! Indeed, the STINK, alone, would Drive a Person Crazy; but, there is a Rational Way to Clean it all up, along with all other Hateful Political / Religious Swamps in this World of Woes, which is Revealed within this Inspired Book for our Enlightenment. †§‡§§

This Book contains about 75,000+ Words, and can easily be "red" in just one Day. Moreover, it should be read in some Quiet Peaceful Place, where the Reader can Devote his or her Full Attention to it, and not be Distracted by anyone nor anything. In other Words, SHUT OFF the Telephones, Radios, Televisions, Computers, and other Distractions, and Lock the Door on your Reading Room. Otherwise, take your Lawn Chair into the Woods, where you can be all alone with Nature, and Enjoy one of the Best Books in the Whole World.

— Chapter 01 —

General George Washington Set the Standard

01-01 [_] Unlike Canadians, the Founding Fathers of the United States of North America got the Good Idea that they should not be Taxed without Representation in London, England, which was under the Administration of King George, who had Control over them, and Taxed them about 20$ per Year, per Male Person, which certain Americans did not like, who Visualized themselves as being their own Masters, who mustered up an Army of Revolutionaries, who went to War against those British Masters, which Proved to be a very Bloody Miserable Gory War, which George Washington barely Won, and only Thanks to a FOG, which Unexpectedly moved into Place at just the Right Time, whereby George and his Rebels Escaped from being Captured by the British. {See *Wikipedia* for the Details about the American Revolutionary War from 1775—1783, which eventually became a World War! Notice that without the Assistance of France and Spain, George Washington would have Failed for a Lack of Weapons, Ammunition, and other Supplies. So, not much can be said for so-called "Independence," which does not Exist in the Real World, even as George Proved to all of the World, which has been Reconfirmed many Times, even until this very Day, whereby Americans are Dependent on China for most of its Products! Indeed, given enough Time, and Globalism will Win, and America will be Defeated by its own Stupidity! †§‡ {See www.Amazon.com for: **"Are Americans the Most STUPID People who ever Lived?" (HOW Working People can PROSPER and Live in PEACE Under the Rulership of a RIGHTEOUS KING!) By The Worldwide People's Revolution!® Book 047.}**

01-02 [_] O Selected King, I find it Hypocritical that American Tax Slaves would presently Uphold their own Wicked Tax Master Federal Government, which presently collects a much greater percentage of Tax Money than King George of Great Britain collected; and yet Americans do not Rebel, and call for another Revolutionary War: because at least 90% of Americans have Lost their Love for the Cover-up Lying Federal Government of **"The Divided States of United Lies!" (The so-called "United States of North America" in Disguise!)** Book 058. Yes, I find it Difficult to Believe that this is the Best Democracy that Money can Buy! †§‡

01-03 [_] Well, the Masses of People in America have not yet come to their Right Senses: beCause their Stomachs are too Full. Indeed, many of them are Pacified by Food Stamps (SNAP, which I cannot Discover in the Dictionary) and Welfare Checks, which Prevents them from Burning Down their Cities of Confusion, which they could hardly Afford to do, even as they cannot Afford to Eat Well on their Low Wages, whereby most of them are Unable to THINK, much less Remember what is found in Howard Zinn's book, called: **"A People's History of the United States,"** which Lists the EVILS of that Wicked Government from the Time of the Landing of Christopher Columbus (Cristoforo Colombo), who was Hungering for GOLD, who Murdered more than 8,000,000 Arawak Indians, just to get more Gold, which also Inspired the Forefathers of America to cross the Great Sea, in Search of more Gold, Silver, and whatever they could Exploit: beCause they were Driven by GREED, being Chief Capitalists at Heart, who had Visions of getting RICH! However, they had no Idea what True Riches are, much less True Prosperity, which only comes by United Effort, by Means of: **"Seven Great Armies of Working Soldiers!" (HOW to Provide**

a Way for Everyone to WORK: so as to Eliminate Poverty, Crimes, Drug Abuses, Prisons and Unnecessary Taxes!) By The Worldwide People's Revolution!®, Book 015.

A-[_] I am Surprised that you, being such a Well-Educated Person, would give any References to Howard Zinn, who was a Confirmed Marxist and Anti-American. †‡

B-[_] I Believe that Provable Truths should be Accepted, even if they come from the Mouth of Balaam's Ass. {See *Numbers 22, King James Version (KJV),* which is the only Authorized Version, which gives Opposing Translations in the Column References.}

C-[_] I Confess that I am Ignorant concerning the hundreds of Evidences that were Presented by Howard Zinn in: **"A People's History of the United States,"** which might Cause me to Doubt the Purity of the Puritans; but, I Promise to Read that Book, just in Case that there might be a Great Day of Righteous Judgments, when all such Things will be Proven unto my own Great Shame.

D-[_] I do not give a Damn what Howard Zinn might have Believed: because he was a JEW; but, Jesus Christ was NOT a Jew. †§‡

E-[_] Educated People Know that Howard Zinn was an Honest Person, who was only giving the FACTS in his Book, which can all be Proven in a Courtroom. Therefore, no Intelligent Person would Reject any of those Facts for any Reason; but, he or she would Accept them, and Meditate on them, and Ask what the Best Solutions might be for Preventing any more Similar Evils during the Future, lest we Repeat those Evils.

F-[_] I Fail to Understand what is so Shameful about Murdering 8,000,000 Arawak Indians to get their Gold. Did Father Abraham not do the same Thing in the Land of Canaan? Indeed, he did not get his Silver nor Gold by Digging in the Ground for it, like some Slave; but, he used his Head, and Sharpened up his Sword, and went to WAR! †§‡ (See *Genesis 13—19,* which Proves that Modern-day Jews are the Children of Father Abraham.)

G-[_] God knows that you are a Presumptuous Person, who Knows little or nothing about Father Abraham, who Earned his Riches by Exercising his Muscles and Brains, who Raised all Kinds of Livestock, which he Traded for Silver and Gold and whatever else he Owned.

H-[_] Heaven Knows that Howard Zinn was a Good Soul, even if he was not Perfect: because he was an Honest White Jew, and not a Betrayer of Trust like Judas Iscariot, nor Bernie Madoff. Therefore, Howard will likely be in the Kingdom of Heaven, while his Enemies will likely be found in Hell with Satan, the Devil. †‡

I-[_] I am an Innocent Person, who has no Interest in Learning any Fake News: because it seems that all such Fake News is Perverting the Minds of Americans, who must Learn to Accept only Provable Truths, which can only be Rightly Proven at: **"The Great Worldwide TELEVISED Court HEARING!" (That Great Meeting of the Most Intelligent and Well-Educated Minds!) By The Worldwide People's Revolution!®** Book 041. Therefore, we should all be DEMANDING that Meeting, rather than Prolonging this Capitalist Madness by having Endless Arguments and Vain Talk Shows. ‡

J-[_] Justice DEMANDS that Great Meeting of the Most Intelligent and Well-Educated Minds, just to Prove WHO is Correct about all Important Subjects, including False Religious Beliefs — such as that False Doctrine about People going to Heaven when they Die, when Jesus Christ Clearly said: *"NO MAN HAS ASCENDED UP TO HEAVEN ..."* — *John 3:13 RKJV,* which is just 3 Verses before *John 3:16,* which most Americans simply Ignore: because they are "Cherry Pickers," when it comes to their False Religions, who Pick Out the Verses of Scriptures that they Like, and just Ignore all of the other Verses that Relate with those Subjects. †§‡

K-[_] King Jesus will get the Household in Order when he Returns with Power and Great Glory in the Awesome Dark Rolling Clouds of a FEARSOME Sky, along with his Great Hosts of Holy Angels, who will be Flying like Flocks of Birds in the Sky, in Unison, who will be some 40 feet Tall with Great Blond Wings and Long Blond Hairs, which will put the FEAR of GOD into your Bones, O you Lying Hypocrites! ‡

L-[_] Lots of Laughs! King Jesus is nothing more than a Jewish MYTH, which can be Proven at **"The Great Worldwide TELEVISED Court HEARING!"** Book 041. †§‡

M-[_] MONEY is the KEY WORD in almost all Cases, including the Production of that so-called "Holy Bible," which was Originally a Collection of Jewish Fables, which was Designed for Selling more and more Copies of itself: beCause it was Big Business during the Time of Christ, even as it still is Big Business: beCause it is the most Sold Book in the Whole World, which comes in more than 200 Translations for us to Choose from — none of which could be 100% True, or else all of the others would have to be Untrue! †§‡

N-[_] Howard Zinn was just a Negative Person, whose so-called History of the United States did not point out even ONE Positive Thing about the United States! †‡

O-[_] I have an Opposite Opinion. I say that by Pointing Out the Negative Things about **"The Divided States of United Lies!" (The so-called "United States of North America" in Disguise!) By The Worldwide People's Revolution!®,** Book 058, Howard Zinn made it Possible for all of us to Learn all of those Truths, whereby we might all Confess them and Forsake our Evil Ways, and thus Straighten Out ourselves, rather than Hide our Heads in the Sand with the Republican Ostriches, who Deny most Provable Truths, unto their own Great Shame during God's Day of Judgment, when none of them will be Able to Run Out of the Courtroom, and Slam the Door in our Faces. Indeed, they will have to Sit there and Answer the Questions of the Supreme Judge and his Lawyers, who will have the Records of the Holy Angels, who Know the Facts about all Things — at least we Hope so. †§‡

P-[_] People like you are Living in a Religious Dreamworld: because there is no Way that any such Judgment Day can be Conducted for each Soul on this Earth, much less for all of the Souls in Multitudes of other Worlds, which are without Number: because there are Millions of Billions of them! Therefore, Try to Humble yourself, and Confess it, before you are Punished for it. †§‡

Q-[_] The Great Question is this: **"Are the Facts within Howard Zinn's Book Worthy of our Time to Study them, whereby we might Learn the Truth about the Divided**

States of United Lies, which Holds World Records — such as the Record Number of Prisoners, most of which are Black: beCause Black People are more Evil than White People, which is HOW they got themselves into those Prisons?" Indeed, they are the Primary Rapists, Murderers, Drug Pushers, and Dishonest Business People. However, if you Doubt it, just Visit the Black Swamp in Washington, District of Criminals. †§‡§§

R-[_] There is a Way for Righteousness to Overcome Wickedness, and this Inspired Book Reveals HOW. Therefore, the Great Question is, **"Will you have Faith to Finish Reading all of it?"**

S-[_] Satan has Deceived all of you Silly Ignorant People: because he Seeks to Save your Souls by Means of Capitalism, which is the Love of Money in Action, which has Produced X-amount of Criminals: beCause of Lusting after Wealth, which is **"The Root Cause for almost all Evils!" (The Strange Things that People Say and Do to Get more Money!) By The Worldwide People's Revolution!® Book 078.**

T-[_] Time will Prove that Jesus Christ was the Best of Men, which has already been Proven many Times. Therefore, Wise People will Seek his Wisdom and Provable Truths, whereby they might be Saved from their Troubles: beCause Jesus said, *"You shall Learn the Truths that I Teach, and those Truths will set you Free when you Practice them: because only the Whole Truth has the Power to Liberate People from their Prisons of Lies, which they were Born into, which have only One Way Out, which is to Pass through the Doorway of Confession. However, the Door of Confession is Locked, and the Key of the Nolij of All that is Good and Evil is Hidden in the Darkness of Ignorance, which can only be Discovered when a Humble Honest Person Discovers the Window of Faith, which is Up Above you, which is Covered with those Dark Curtains of Doubt and Unbelief, which the Wise Person will Draw Back, whereby the Light of Truths might Shine into his or her Prison of Lies, whereby he or she might Discover the Key of the Nolij of All that is Good and Evil, whereby he or she might Unlock the Door of Confession, and thus Open the Door, and Escape into the Paradise of Peace and Happiness on the other Side of the Mountain of the Knowledge of All that is Good and Evil, which is Extremely Difficult to Climb Over: because God only Wants the Best of Souls within his Good Government, which is otherwise known as the Kingdom of God, which is in Fact, a KINGDOM with a Great King in Charge of it, who must be the most Qualified Person among us, who has the Best Solutions for our Massive Problems, which must be Proven in a Courtroom, whereby all of the People can be the Judges of it, and thus Decide for themselves which Person they Want to Govern them."* — The Gospel According to Saint Bartholomew, Chapter 10:16. †§‡

U-[_] I Understood the above Words when I read them; but, I did not Believe that Jesus said them, nor will I ever Believe that he said them: because I am an Unbeliever, even though I Claim to Believe in Jesus Christ; but, I am a Spiritual Coward, you might say, who is Afraid to Prove any such Words to be Good or Evil. In Fact, I will now have to Confess that I am just another Lying Hypocrite, who only Pretends to Believe in All that is Good! After all, Verse T makes Perfect Sense. ‡

V-[_] The Victory will be to those Wise People who have FAITH in Provable Truths; and there is nothing within Verse T that cannot be Proven to be True. †§‡

W-[_] I am Wondering just HOW we will go about Proving whether or not there is a Kingdom of God, seeing that no Government on this Earth is anything Like the Government of All that is GOOD? In Fact, they can all be Proven to be Satanic in Nature. Indeed, each Nation could have a Howard Zinn's Book, which Records its Chief Sins. †§‡

X-[_] X-amount of Nations are more Righteous than **The Divided States of United Lies,"** which has the Appearance of an Innocent Lamb, while it Speaks like a Double-Tongued Snake, which will be Proven within this Inspired Book. ‡

Y-[_] I Yearn for the Whole Truth — whatever it might be, and I will Gladly Accept whatever is Proven at: **"The Great Worldwide TELEVISED Court HEARING!"**

Z-[_] The Zeal of **The Worldwide People's Revolution!®** will make it Possible to bring Satan into the Courtroom, and Prove him to be the Cause for all of this Corruption. See: **"The END of CONFUSION!" (The Great CELEBRATION of the Magnificent Wedding of the Most Humble Honest Nations, and the Grand Year of JUBILEE!) By The Worldwide People's Revolution!®** Book 050.

01-04 [_] So, O Selected King, after the Founding Fathers Failed to Discover any Mountains of Gold in America, what did they Do for an Income?

01-05 [_] Well, most of them took up Farming, and most of them Died in Poverty, including most of the Presidents and Vice Presidents; but, not President George Washington, who Acted "wisely," and became a Land Speculator and Surveyor, who Bought Cheap Land, and Doubled his Money on it when he Sold it. Moreover, he soon Discovered that there was a Market in England for Tobacco Products; and therefore, he Grew Tobacco by the Assistance of his 100+ Slaves, who also Attended to his Gardens, Cooking, House Cleaning, Washing Clothes, Fishing, and making Whiskey from Grains, which he also Discovered was very Profitable: beCause Tobacco and Whiskey are ADDICTIVE, which Means that there would Naturally be a Greater and Greater DEMAND for his Products, whereby his Capitalist Businesses Grew and GREW, which set a Pattern for Future Capitalists to Follow, which Explains WHY the Biggest most Profitable Business in **"The Divided States of United Lies"** has been the Sales of DRUGS, both Legal and Illegal: beCause they are Addictive! In Fact, George Washington became the Richest American before he Died — Thanks to the Addictions of the British and American Drug Slaves! Yes, what Great Honors should be Bestowed upon him for his All-American Achievements? ‡

01-06 [_] O Selected King, I will freely Confess that our Greatest Federal Government EXPENSE is Social Security Payments, followed by False Health Care, which includes those Unnecessary DRUGS, which People could Live without, if they were as Healthy and Happy as the Wild Animals, who have never used any Kind of Drugs, much less Sell any Drugs to their Naaberz. ‡

01-07 [_] Well, a few Animals might Eat some Weeds or Mushrooms that contain Natural Drugs; but, those Wild Animals certainly do not Capitalize on them, even as People have done for thousands of Years: beCause of not having a RIGHTEOUS One-World Government, which Teaches Truths to Children, and makes them Understand WHY they were Born here: so that they have something Good to Live for, and are not Depressed by Living Miserable Lives. {FOOTNOTE: It has been Reported that more than half of Americans have Experienced Various

Degrees of Depression, whereby Millions have Attempted Suicide, while many of them have Succeeded: beCause of a Multitude of Reasons; but, Primarily beCAUSE of having BAD Diets! See www.Amazon.com for: **"DIETS!" (A Reasonable Solution for the "Eternal Controversy"!)** Book 037. Trust me, there is a Sure Cure for Depression. However, like all Problems, one must be Willing to Search for the CAUSE of it. Indeed, there cannot be an Effect without a Cause. Remember that I never Suffer with Depression, nor even with Pains!}

01-08 [_] O Selected King, I am 40+ Years Old, and I have no Idea WHY that I was Born here, do you?

01-09 [_] Well, King Solomon said that there is a Purpose for everything that is done under the Sunstar. Therefore, we must have been Born here for a Purpose of some Kind. {See: **"ECCLESIASTES UNCOVERED!" (The New MAGNIFIED Version of Ecclesiastes and the Song of Solomon in Plain English!) By The Worldwide People's Revolution!® Book 034.}**

01-10 [_] I would say that we just Evolved from Lower Species of Humanoid Creatures, much like Elephants Evolved from Long-snouted Mice; and Kangaroos Evolved from Rabbits: because it is Obvious that nothing was Designed by some Big Boss up in the Sky, or else People would not be so Stupid, if they were Created in his Image, as the *Bible* Teaches. After all, such a Creator God would have to be Extremely Intelligent to be Able to figure out HOW to Create Eyeballs, for Example, which are Marvelous Creations, if you Think about the Entire Head of any Creature, and especially the Head of a Man, whereby the Basic Senses are Located in the Head — such as Sight, Hearing, Smelling, Tasting, Feeling, Speaking, and so on. But, those Eyes can Convey the Thoughts within the Mind of a Person, which can cover an entire Range of Feelings and Expressions that cannot be Found in the Eyes of a Chicken, Fish, Frog, nor Hog, Horse, Cow, Cat, nor Dog. Therefore, Evolution is the Greatest God of all, who Created us from some Primordial Slime in some Swamp in Africa. Moreover, there are no less than 10,000 Missing Links between us and that first Humanoid Creature, which probably looked much like an Ape of some Kind, without a Tail. However, I am just being Sarcastic: beCause it is most Obvious that it Required some Great Creator GOD to Design and Create all of the Millions of Species of Creatures that have Lived on this Good Earth. †§‡§§

— Chapter 02 —

WHY were we BORN?

02-01 [_] Now, I said to myself, "If anyone would Know Exactly WHY we were Born into this World of Wonders, it would have to be the Great Creator God, who made all of these Marvelous Bodies of People, Animals, Plants, and Multitudes of Stars, Nebulas, Galaxies, and perhaps Billions of Universes, even larger than our own Visible Universe! Indeed, who would Know the Extent of it, except some GOD?" Therefore, I went to my Spiritual Knees to that Great God in Prayer, and this is what he Answered to me:

02-02 [_] O Selected King, you and all others on this Good Earth are nothing but Ignorant Fools without the Assistance of my Holy Spirit. Therefore, Listen Carefully to all that I have to say: because I will now Reveal a few Mysteries to you, whereby Life will no longer be a Mystery to you; but, it will still be a Great Mystery to other People: beCause they will not get to Learn such Wonderful Enlightening Things. Indeed, many of them will Presume that the *Holy Bible* contains all of the Truths that they Need to Learn, whereby they will Greatly Limit themselves, and Cut Off themselves from what they could have been, if they had Presented themselves to me as Worthy Creatures, and not Acted Worse than Animals of the Lower Orders. Yes, they will Close their Spiritual Ears, and Refuse to Listen, Remember and THINK!

02-03 [_] Yes, suppose that Moses had Obtained such a Bad Attitude as many of those Professing "Christians" have now Obtained, by Misinterpreting what the *Scriptures* Teach? Yes, suppose he had said, "I will not go up on Mount Sinai, much less Fast and Pray for 40 Days and 40 Consecutive Nights: because I want to enjoy Eating and Drinking" — what would have become of Moses? Who would even know that Moses Lived? Where would the Books of Moses be? Who would have Led the Children of Israel Out of Egypt? Who would have Caused the Fresh Living Water to Flow Out of the Living Rock? Who would have Obtained Manna for those Hordes of People and their Millions of Livestocks to Eat for 40 Years? Yes, I Know that it is Pure Jewish Mythology, which has nothing to do with the Realities of Life, except for Moses, who was a Real Person with a Different Name, who was Actually just a Story Teller, and a Good Story Teller, whose Inspired Writings were later on Exaggerated by Lying Edomites, who Sought to Capitalize on his Words, and thus they Constructed what is now known as the *Holy Bible,* which is not Exactly very Holy in the Sense of Purity: beCause it has been Mutilated, Castrated, and made of little Effect on Societies, nowadays, who Desperately Need to Learn the Great Truths that were once Contained in the *Scriptures.*

02-04 [_] Truly, Truly, I say to you, if it had not been for the Faith of Moses, and other Holy Prophets like him, there would have been no Spiritual Foundation for People to Build their Lives on during all of those thousands of Years. However, it is Possible for me to now Provide a Better Spiritual Foundation for you People to Build your Lives on, and to do so within just 2 or 3 Chapters of a Book: beCause the entire *Bible* can be Greatly Simplified. In Fact, Yoshua Messiah summed it up in just 2 short Commandments, if you Recall, saying: *"You shall Love the Creator your God with all of your Mind, Spirit, and Body; and you shall Love your Naaberz as much as you Love yourselves,"* which would Naturally do away with the *Ten Commandments,* you might Imagine; but, it is not True: beCause it is still Wrong to Steal, Lie, Murder, Rob, Rape, and Covet or Lust after Things that do not Belong to you. Indeed, it is still Wrong to Defile the Sabbath Day, which is the Seventh Day, which none of the Gods ever Changed: beCause, if they Changed their Laws, they could not be Trusted? Therefore, the Sabbath Day is NOT the First Day of the Week, which you call Sunday; but, it is the Seventh Day, which Begins at Sunset on Venusday, and Ends at Sunset on Saturnday. Therefore, the First Day of the Week is NOT Moonday; but, it is Sunday.

02-05 [_] Moreover, there is nothing WRong with Honoring your Father and Mother when they get Old, by Supporting them: because that is a Good Tradition. Indeed, if your Houses were Built Correctly within Beautiful Planned City States, your Parents would not be far away, much less thousands of Miles away; but, they would be nearby, within your own City State, whereby you could look after them, as well as any other Old People without Children to look after them. Indeed, it would not be a Difficult Thing to do, if you were Set Up Correctly on the Land, which was Designed to Feed and Clothe you, even as it Feeds and Shelters all of the Wild Animals, whom you should Assist in a Proper Way: beCause you are the Stewards of the Earth. Therefore, you should Treat the Earth as your own Father and Mother, with Love and Tender Care: because the Ecological System is very Delicate, and can easily be Disrupted. {See www.Amazon.com for: **"Poverty Hunger Riots Strikes Brutalities Election Deceptions and Civil Wars!" (The High Price that we Earthlings have Paid for Leaving the Good Land!) By The Worldwide People's Revolution!® Book 014.**}

02-06 [_] However, it is often the Case that Children Learn certain "Truths" that their Parents do not Accept, whereby they are Divided and Separated. Indeed, such Children often run away from Home, just to get Away from such "Unbelief," which you could say is Good or Evil — Depending on HOW one Looks at it. Nevertheless, if you had a Righteous Government, all such Religious and Political Issues could be brought to Court, and Proven to be True or False, whereby all such Families could be United: beCause of coming to a Rational Agreement about all such Subjects, including those very Controversial Religious, Spiritual, Scientific, Ecological, and Political Subjects. Yes, you must have Faith in: **"The Great Worldwide TELEVISED Court HEARING!"**: beCause it is the Best Solution for many Massive Problems.

02-07 [_] For Example, some People might Claim that they are going to Heaven when they Die, while others do not even Believe in any such Heaven: beCause they have never Seen it, much less Tasted of the Good Fruits that might be over there. However, the Misunderstanding arises from Ignorance: because this Earth is your Eternal Home, unless you are Found to not be Worthy to Live here, in which Case your Spirit will be Cast Down to a Lower Order of Worlds, which will be Seven Times more Vile than this World: beCause, if you had been Found Worthy, you would have been Born in a more Heavenly World than this World. Yes, all of the Worlds come in Degrees of Goodness and Evilness, until the Righteous People Learn their Lessons, and then the Evil Spirits are Cast Down to Lower Orders of Worlds: so that those Worlds of a Higher Order might be more Blest, even as this World will Eventually be Blest with nothing but Righteous People: beCause Satan and his Followers will be Cast Out of this World, unto a Lower Order of Worlds, along with whomever Rejects this Great Truth that I am now Teaching to you — not because you are more Worthy to Learn it than any other Person on this Earth; but, because I have Chosen you to Convey the Message to the Masses of People — some of whom will Accept it, while others will Reject it.

02-08 [_] However, not to Worry — as some People say — because it does not matter whether or not they Accept it or Reject it, if it is not True. Indeed, if it is not the Truth, who Cares who Accepts it or Rejects it? The Great Question is this: **"Were People Born here to be Tested for their Goodness, or not?"** And I am telling you that they were Born here to be Tested: beCause there are Positions to be Filled in the Kingdom or Government of God, which will be Established during the Future, after all of the Good Spirits have been Discovered. Yes, the Person whom you call Jesus Christ, or the Anointed Savior, will be the KING of Kings and the RULER of Rulers in that Holy Kingdom, which will be Established right here on this Good Earth, and NOT anywhere in Heaven — as Up there somewhere in the Sky, perhaps beyond Orion and the Pleiades, which is Pure Mythical Nonsense: beCause this Earth was Created Especially for People like YOU.

02-09 [_] Yes, it is also Superstitious Nonsense, to Imagine that anyone is going to Heaven when he or she Dies, which comes from Pagan or Heathen Nations, which is not Supported by the *Scriptures,* and especially not by the Anointed Savior, who frankly said to Nicodemus that *"No Man has Ascended up to Heaven, except the Son of a Holy Man who came Down from a Heavenly Place,"* which was Referring to Mount Zion, which is the Holy City of the Great King, which is Inside of the Hollow Earth, which was left Hollow when the Moon was Born from it, even as many of the Planets are Hollow and Inhabited with many Kinds of Peoples and Animals: beCause they are Ideal Places to Live, being Protected from Meteors, Comets, Asteroids, and whatever. Yes, you could call the Outsides of all such Planets Mighty Fortress Walls, which also keep out the Heat and Cold.

02-10 [_] However, I am Sure that many False Scientists will Deny what I just now told you, rather than Prove it for themselves. Indeed, they Refuse to Study: **"The Secret City of the Great King!" (HOW the True Church will Escape from the Great Tribulation!) By The Worldwide People's Revolution!®**, Book 042, which is just one of many Inspired Books by my Selected King, who is my Chosen Servant, who has Revealed more Great Truths than any Man Alive, Today, which can be Proven in a Courtroom, even at: **"The Great Worldwide TELEVISED Court HEARING!" (That Great Meeting of the Most Intelligent and Well-Educated Minds!)**, Book 041, which should be Studied by all Open-minded Honest People, Worldwide: beCause it contains the Secret to Solving all of your Massive Problems!

— Chapter 03 —

HOW to Live Properly in this World of Wonders

03-01 [_] Now, as I was saying, just a few Verses of *Scriptures* could Save you People from Utter Destruction, which someone Carefully Edited OUT of the *Unholy Mutilated Bible,* which is Missing several Books — some of which are even Mentioned in the *Bible,* such as *the Book of Jasher, the Book of Jehu, the Book of Shemaiah, the Book of Nathan the Prophet, the Book of Iddo the Seer, the Acts of King Solomon,* and so on: beCause those *Scriptures* contained Important Information that was a Great Threat to the Edomites, which Revealed too much about them, which they did not Like. Therefore, they got themselves into Control in Jerusalem, and made themselves Chief Scribes and Pharisees, whereby they found the Opportunity to Edit the *Bible* as they Wanted it, who also Exaggerated certain Biblical Stories — such as the Noah's Ark Exaggeration, and King Nebuchadnezzar's Gold Statue in the Plain of Dura, which was nothing but a Dream.

03-02 [_] Nevertheless, in Order to be Saved for a Position in the Kingdom or Government of the Gods, one must be Purified in Mind, Spirit, and Body, which Purification Begins in one's Mind by a Confession of all Sins, which are Transgressions of the Laws of Yohoovu God, who is the God of the Hebrews, and Specifically the God of Abraham, Isaac, and Jacob, whose Name was later Changed to Israel, who was the Father of 12 Sons, while Esau was the Father of just 2 Sons, which Offended the Edomites, who Changed it into 12 Sons of Esau: beCause they Envied Jacob, who was the more Righteous Person, who was White with Blond Hairs and Blue Eyes, much like the Tribe of Dan, which Settled in Danmark, which you call Denmark. Yes, Jacob was a Holy Man to some Degree, even as Abraham and Isaac were Holy to some Degree; but, none of them were as Holy as Enoch, Melchizedek, Moses, nor Elijah, who were Special Souls, who will have Higher Positions in the Kingdom of God, which is made up of many Kings and Queens, who must also be Holy, even as I am Holy.

03-03 [_] Therefore, your Objective during this Life is to Live in such a Way as to Obtain a Position in the Kingdom of God; but, only IF — only on the CONDITION that you Want to be a Future Ruler in the Kingdom: beCause no one is Forced to be a King nor Queen; but, it is your Privilege to Choose it, if you Want it, and are Willing to Strive for it.

03-04 [_] However, only a very Few Wise People will Qualify for any such Positions: beCause the Kingdom of God does not Require a HORDE of Leaders, and certainly NOT any Elected Representatives by the Masses of Ignorant People: because all such Kings and Queens will be Appointed by the Gods, who are the Supreme Rulers. Yes, Jesus Christ will be the Supreme Ruler of this World, who will Appoint whomever he Chooses to Govern it. Therefore, you must Live in such a Way as to Please him, if you Want to be a Part of his Holy Kingdom.

03-05 [_] Therefore, Stop Thinking all Evil Thoughts, and Set your Mind on All that is GOOD: beCause that will Begin the Process of Purification that is Needed for Qualifying for his Holy Kingdom. Indeed, no Unclean Thing, nor Unclean Person, will Enter into his Holy Kingdom, which Means that you must also Humble yourself by Means of Fasting and Praying, until you become like an Innocent Child with a Pure Mind and a Clean Body, which will Require Time, Faith, Hope, Trust, Love, Patience, Persistence, and Obedience, which are: **"The Seven Basic Spiritual Building Blocks of LIFE!"** Book 036. Yes, you must Study that Good Book: beCause it Contains Important Information that is not Found in this Inspired Book, which is True of all of the Inspired Books of my Chosen Servant, who is Obedient to my Voice, who has been Blest with many Good Books, and not without Good Reasons.

03-06 [_] Therefore, when you begin to Purify your Mind, you will just Naturally Lose your Appetite to Eat with the Dogs and Hogs. In Fact, you will Develop a Craving for Sweet Juicy Fruits, Dried Fruits, Raw Nuts, and Fresh Green Leaves, including the Tops of Onions and Garlic, in spite of their Stink, which will not be Stinking to the People who Eat them; but, they will be Stinking to the People who do not Eat them, which might even Offend them. However, it is for your Good Health that you will Eat such Things, which will also make you Stronger. After all, Gorillas are much Stronger than any Man, and they Live on those Green Leaves. Therefore, the *Genesis* Account can be Trusted concerning your Diet, if it is Translated Correctly, like this:

03-07 [_] *Behold, I have Given to you every Tree that Bears Good Sweet Fruits — such as Mangos, Cherimoyas, Soft Dates, Figs, Yellow Sapotes, Sweetsops, Soursops, and certain Varieties of Avocados, as well as certain Nuts, which you should Eat in Moderation — and every Clean Green Herb — such as Kale, Collards, Lettuces, Fennel, Celery, and Cabbages, which are your Primary Foods. However, if you are still Hungry for something to Eat, you may Eat a Limited Amount of Cooked Foods, including Beans, Peas, Rice, Corn, Wheat, Rye, Barley, Oats, and other Seeds and Grains; but, Good Flavorful Squashes and Melons are Better for you to Eat, which are Survival Foods, if you do not have Good Sweet Fruits from those Trees to Eat.* Yes, it Requires Time for Growing all such Fruit and Nut Trees, now that you have been Cast Out of the Garden of Eden, who was the Holy Angel in Charge of Planting it.

03-08 [_] Therefore, seeing that you do not have Access to the Garden of Eden, which has other Kinds of Sweet Fruits, you must be Contented with whatever is Available, or whatever you can Grow, yourself: beCause you are still being Tested for your Faith, Hope, Trust, Love, Patience, Persistence, and Obedience. Indeed, you will be Constantly Tested, until the Day you Die; and then your Spirit will be Judged for its Goodness, and be Assigned to a New Body in this World, whereby you will be Tested again, and again, until your Spirit is brought to Perfection for either Good or Evil. And that is just the Way it is. Period.

03-09 [_] Therefore, do not Listen to the Temptations of the Devil and his Demon-possessed Servants: beCause they will say, "It does not matter what you Eat nor Drink: beCause, whatever goes into your Mouth, also goes into the Toilet, and is therefore nothing to Worry about." However, many of those False Foods contain Various Kinds of Harmful Poisons: beCause they are not Natural Foods. Therefore, you cannot Trust them to be Good for you to Eat, even if you Imagine that you can Trust the Cooks, who may be the most Deceived of all People, just as Mother Eve was Deceived, who was Symbolical of all of her Spiritual Daughters, among whom is Hillary Clinton, herself, who would do Well to Attend to her Granddaughter, and leave Politics in the Loving Care of my Selected King and his Associates, who has a Far Superior Master Plan. {See www.Amazon.com for: **"Mark Twain Races for the PRESIDENCY!" (The 2020 Presidential Candidates Desperately Need Some STRONG Undefeatable COMPETITION!)**, Book 033.}

03-10 [_] Yes, the Forbidden Fruit in the Garden of Eden was Symbolical of all Forbidden Foods in this World of Woes, which you must Learn to Resist, if they are Unnatural Foods and Drinks, and not made of Wholesome Natural Foods, as they should be, and as they would be, if my Selected King were in Charge of the Whole World for no less than 6 Years, whereby his **"Seven Great Armies of Working Soldiers"** would Transform this World into a Living Paradise for almost everyone! Nevertheless, if you do Transgress, you can always Fast and Pray, until your Body Eliminates any Unwanted Poisons and Accumulated Filth, which is a Good Thing to do for at least 30 Days per Year, even if you Eat Moderately between all such Fasts: beCause it gives your Bowels a Break, or Rest, and will also Assure you of a Longer Life: beCause each Body was Designed to Regenerate itself, which is another Great Truth that those Lying Edomites Removed from the *Scriptures:* because they did not want People to Discover any Way to get around Consuming all of the Vast Array of Addictive Foods and Drugs that Lying Edomites have for Sale, which all of the Wild Animals have always Avoided; and every last one of those Wild Animals is Healthier and Happier than any of those Lying Edomites, Guaranteed! — that is, IF they have not been Poisoned by Ignorant People, in which Cases they may also Contract Cancers and other Diseases, which are common among Domesticated Animals: beCause of Feeding them Contaminated Waters, Chemically-grown Devitalized Foods, and whatever Satan and Sons, Incorporated can come up with for Sale: beCause that is **"The Nature of CAPITALISM,"** which is the Love of Money in Action, which I HATE! Yes, it is an Invention of Lying Edomites, who must be brought to COURT for Judgment, and Proven to be Guilty as Charged: beCause they ARE Guilty as Charged, even as I have now Charged them: beCause I am the Supreme JUJ!

— Chapter 04 —

New Discoveries

04-01 [_] So, O God, if the Primary Objective during this Life is to become HOLY — even as you are Holy in Mind, Spirit, and Body — what will Happen to all of the Billions of Deceived People in this World of Woes, who are not even Working on Overcoming their Sins, much less becoming HOLY?

04-02 [_] Well, Depending on how Bad their Sins are, they may be Born into this World, once again, whereby they might Discover the Truth about WHY they were Born here. Otherwise, they will have to be Recycled, over and over, until they Discover the Truth about it, which is in the Care of my Disciples, who are Good News Reporters, whose Responsibility is to Inform all such People about these Truths and many other Truths: because no People will be Qualified to Govern in the Kingdom of God, until they have Learned ALL of their Lessons. Therefore, it is Wise of them to be Working on their own Salvation, whereby they might be Saved for such Positions in the Future Kingdom of God.

04-03 [_] But, as for the Unbelievers, if they Sincerely Repent of their Sins, and Seek All that is Good, Holy Angels will Visit with them, and Direct them in the Right Direction — that is, IF they Live According to their Nolij, and do not put on a Mask of Pretense, like the Hypocrites do, who Pretend to be Worshiping God in their Churches, while Acting like Satan in the Dark, in Secret; or, while Mistreating other People for Gain, as those Lying Edomites have done for thousands of Years: because they are Possessed by Evil Spirits. Yes, you shall know them by their Fruits, who like to take Advantage of other People's Ignorance, rather than be Honest with them, like True Christians would be, who have no Desire to take Advantage of anyone. Selah.

04-04 [_] So, O God, if the Israelis are Beating Up on the Poor Palestinians, it is unto their own Shame, huh? So, what should they be doing for them?

04-05 [_] Well, you have a Perfect Example in the Land of Israel, which Land could be Shared with all of the People, who should Build those **"GLORIOUS Swanky Hotels Castles and Fortresses"** for ALL of the People who Want to Live there: beCause all such Fortresses could Contain millions of People, who could also Spread Out into Arabia, Egypt, Iraq, Iran, and wherever there is Space for them to Build such Beautiful Planned City States. After all, each Person only needs about one-quarter of an Acre for Feeding himself. Therefore, if each Family has one whole Acre on their own Roof, for the Gardens of their Naaberz in the Terrace above them, 20,000 People would only need 5,000 Acres, or about 8 square Miles. Therefore, if there are 8,000 square Miles of Land in Israel, you could Theoretically Build 1,000 Small Swanky Fortresses, which would contain about 20 Million People. Therefore, if there are 10 Million People Living in Israel, it might be Possible for them to have a Mile or so of Space around each Fortress, which could be about 3 Miles square, which would be easy to Walk across during one Hour, or cross during a few Minutes on a Bicycle. I Prefer the FOURTH Swanky Fortresses, which are about 4 Miles in Diameter, and 4 Terraces High around all Hotels, Castles, and Fortresses. However, I do not Object if you Want

Cities that are 60 Terraces High around all Hotels, Castles and Fortresses: beCause you will have to Deal with whatever Problems you Invent, while I will simply Enjoy my own Private Paradise with the Holy Angels, Inside of Jupiter! Yes, you have my Permission to Mock what I have said: beCause I will have the Last Laugh when your Destruction comes on you for Rejecting Truths without a Justified Cause!

04-06 [_] However, not all Land is Good for Building such Fortresses, without Greatly Modifying the Land, which would Naturally Destroy the Beauty of it, if it had any Special Beauty. Personally, I cannot Think of any Place in the Land of Israel that has any Special Beauty that could not be Improved on by Building Swanky Hotels, Castles, and Fortresses, or at least Swanky Palaces with Fortress Walls around them, which would Require a LOT of Energy for Moving all such Terrain around, in Order to make it Conform to some Complicated Plan. Therefore, I Recommend that most of the Land of Israel is just left alone: beCause there is Plenty of Ideal Land to Build Fortresses on, which Land is FLAT, like much of Iraq, which is not Good for anything except those Swanky Fortresses, which could be a hundred Miles in Diameter, and a Mile High, in Order to Moderate the Temperatures. After all, that is WHY that I have Provided hundreds of thousands of Mountains of Rocks for you People to Work with. Therefore, get your Lazy Asses UP, and go to WORK, O Workhorses: beCause you have no more Good Excuses for Living in your Hateful States of Extreme Poverty!

04-07 [_] So, O God, if a City is Built Up on a Flat Plain, how many Large Terraces should it have? What is an Ideal City to Build?

04-08 [_] Well, that all Depends on what People Want, who must Judge that for themselves: because they are Free to do that. After all, it is Possible to Build Up any City, almost any Size, by using Large Cisterns as Foundation Stones in Terraces, which have Barrel-vault Tunnels between the Cisterns for Subway Trains and Tombs, which Line the Tunnels, where you may Bury the Dead Bodies in Family Tombs. In other Words, one Tomb might hold the Bones of a hundred People or more. Therefore, such Cities could reach up to a Mile High, in Great Terraces, if they were Needed. However, I would say that 7 Terraces would be Good in most Cases. In other Words, if a Terrace were 40 to 50 feet Tall, 7 of them would be 280 to 350 feet Tall. However, if the Temperature is very High in a Low Valley, you can Obtain Cooler Temperatures by Building Upwards, which is an Advantage. After all, you Want Comfortable Houses, Workshop, and Sales Shops.

04-09 [_] So, O God, do you not Care if we Tear Down all of the Mountains of Rocks, just to Build all such **"GLORIOUS Swanky Hotels Castles and Fortresses,"** which would Require MILLIONS of Large Cisterns, which would never be Filled with Fresh Water: because there is not enough Fresh Water in Israel to Fill any such Cisterns, much less 7 Billion of them, whereby every Person in the World might have a One-million-gallon Cistern for Water Storage?

04-10 [_] Well, if the Fortresses are Designed Correctly, the Rainwater can be Caught by them, and Stored in the Cisterns. Otherwise, they can be Filled with the Water that is now Running Away into the Atlantic Ocean from the Amazon River, and many other Rivers, which is just going to Waste, which could be Saved and Used Wisely, and also Recycled within those Fortresses. After all, most of the People will be Drinking Fresh Immature Coconut Water from Samoan Coconuts, as well as Natural Fruit Juices from Various Kinds of Sweet Juicy Fruits: beCause they are Better for your Good Health, having no Artificial Flavorings nor Sugars added, much less any Preservatives: beCause of the Abundance of Fresh Fruits, which can be Shipped by Solar Power around the World; and therefore, not much Fresh Pure Water will be Required for those People to Drink, and certainly no Chlorinated Recycled Sewage Water. However, there are Clothes and Dishes to Wash, as well as Houses to Clean, and Gardens to Water, which will Require a LOT of Clean Water, which must not be Contaminated with any Kind of Harmful Chemicals nor Poisons, including Chlorine: because it is no Good for Gardens. Therefore, you will have to Discover HOW to Use your Fresh Water Properly: so as to Preserve Holy Cities, which will be Inherited by many Generations of Wise People: beCause they will be Designed to Endure the Test of Time, even as they should be: beCause you People will Inherit them when you are Born here again, and again, O Lady Doubtfulness. Therefore, do not Listen to that Lying Devil, nor to any of those Lying Edomites, who might Teach otherwise: beCause this Good Earth is your Eternal Home, which you must make into a Living Paradise for everyone who Chooses to Live a Righteous Life, no matter what their False Religions might otherwise Teach: beCause they have been Deceived by Satan, the Devil, and thus they cannot Help themselves to Understand the Realities of Life, until they do much Fasting and Praying and Eating those Garden of Eden Foods and Drinks.

— Chapter 05 —

Uncle Sam gets a Facelift

05-01 [_] Recent News Reports on TV showed Vast Territories in Texas that were Swamped with Contaminated Muddy Water, mixed with Sewage, Chemicals, Spilled Oils, Gases, and whatever got in the way of FLOODS: beCause of Heavy Rains, which raised the Water Table in some Places by as much as 50 feet above Normal!

05-02 [_] O Selected King, no one was Forced to Live in such Places. Indeed, they CHOSE to move in there. Therefore, it is their own Problem, not mine, nor yours. †

05-03 [_] Well, the Truth is that most of them were Born and Raised in those Places, and just Inherited most of the Farms that got Swamped. Moreover, most of those People had no Idea that the Water could Rise that much, which would be like the Water Rising 50 feet above the Hudson River, in New York City, or 50 feet above the Potomac River in Washington, D.C., or 50 feet above Lake Superior. Indeed, everyone in Washington would be in SHOCK to see the Water Table above the White House! But, as we already Learned in Texas, all such Things are Possible! Yes, the Missouri and Mississippi Rivers could also RISE UP by 50 feet, or even 100 feet: beCause of Torrential Rains on the Great Plains, and in the Rocky Mountains and Foothills. Therefore, Denver, Colorado, would be one of the few Safe Places on the Great Plains — except that it is also Subject to being Flooded by Torrential Rains pouring in from the Mountains!

05-04 [_] Yes, Floods, Fires, Tornadoes, and Erupting Volcanoes can Transform those Shanties into Uninhabitable Trash Dumps, if not Ashes! Indeed, some People call it "the Wrath of God":

because of Great Destructions that follow in the Wake of Winds, Fires and Floods — all of which can be and should be Totally Prevented for Wise Human Beings! ‡

05-05 [_] Yes, that is the Good News — that there is in Fact a Way to AVOID all such Horrible Disasters, just by having the Correct DESIGN for a PLANNED CITY STATE, which is made Possible by the hundreds of thousands of Mountains of ROCKS, and the Modern Heavy Equipment for us Voluntary Working Soldiers to Work with! Indeed, if there were no Mountains of Rocks, no Trains, no Trucks, no Bulldozers, nor any Computers, we might have Justified Excuses for Living in Constant FEARS of "the Wrath of God." However, we can now Thank God that there is a Way to Use those Rocks WISELY for Constructing those **"GLORIOUS Swanky Hotels Castles and Fortresses,"** which will Solve no less than 5,000 Problems, including those Flooded Homes Problems: because the Fortress Walls can be 200 feet Tall, if need be, and 40 feet THICK! In Fact, I Recommend such Good Strong Walls around very LARGE Planned City States: beCause they need to be SECURE in all Ways. After all, Heavy Equipment — such as Bulldozers and Rock-Cutting Machines — will make it Possible to "Harvest" those Rocks by the Use of Railroads, whereby Trainloads of Rocks can be Moved from the Mountains to the Fortresses, which could be Built on the Taller Hills, whereby they are just Naturally far above the Flood Plains.

05-06 [_] O Selected King, are you not Educated enough to know that Tidal Waves from the Oceans can Overwhelm all such Fortresses? For Example, if a large Chunk of some Island in the Atlantic Ocean should BREAK OFF, and Crash into the Sea, the Ocean Waves could be as much as a MILE HIGH, and thus Sweep across the Great Plains, taking away every House and Car and Truck in Sight, whereby everything would be TRASHED! Indeed, such a Tsunami would make Hurricane Katrina look like a Sunday Picnic, in Comparison: beCause most of New Orleans would end up at the Foothills of the Mountains in Colorado: and Billings, Montana, for Example, would be Covered with MUD, up to the Top of the Rim Rocks on both Sides! Yes, the entire Valley would be Filled with MUD! Therefore, without Fortress Walls, and at least a thousand feet Tall, such Fortresses would be DOOMED! †§‡

05-07 [_] Well, even if a Swanky Fortress is Overflowed with Water, it will not Ruin the Stone Dome Home Complexes, if all of the Doors and Skylight Windows are Closed and Locked, if they are Designed Correctly. Indeed, the Fortress would only have to be Cleaned up, and Life would carry on as Usual: beCause of the Tall Stone Walls in Great Terraces, 50 feet or more Tall, each. In other Words, the Wall of Flood Water would be Broken Up by Hitting the Outermost Stone Wall, which could be 100 feet Tall and 50 feet Thick, which would Turn the Tide Back to some Degree, even as it Naturally does along Costs with Mountains of Rocks. Therefore, it is not as if the Wave had no Resistance at all against it: because it would have some Resistance, and a LOT of Resistance, if there were hundreds of such Fortresses on the Great Plains, all of the Way from Louisiana to Montana. Indeed, the Ozark Mountains, alone, would Greatly Resist such Flood Waters. Therefore, in spite of the Devastation of Lowland Cities and Farms, those Swanky Fortresses would most likely Survive in Good Shape, and could certainly be Cleaned up, and made Habitable, once again. After all, the Higher Terraces in the Fortresses would not likely be Greatly Effected by such a Tsunami, which would be Refuges for all of the People within such Fortresses, which is WHY it is a Good Idea to make SPACIOUS Stone Dome Home Complexes: so that 40 or more People could Live within just one of them, in an Emergency, if they took their Bedding and Clothing with them when they Fled from Lower Terraces. †‡

05-08 [_] O Selected King, if God is out to Destroy People, there is no Way to Prevent it. Indeed, they could be Struck by Asteroids! ‡

05-09 [_] Well, that is True. However, there is no Connection between the Actual "Wrath of God," and a Tsunami, which could Happen at any Time to any Coastal Nation: beCause none of them are Exempt from Natural Disasters — such as Earthquakes. Therefore, it is Wise to be Prepared for the Worst Conditions, while Hoping and Praying to God that we get **"The Right Design for Living!"** Book 012. Yes, the Architects and Engineers must have their Acts Together, as the saying goes, or else we will still have Major Natural Disasters. However, like General Hadrian's Pantheon, in Rome, those Beautiful Stone Dome Homes will likely Endure all Natural Disasters, and especially if we Build those **"GLORIOUS Swanky Hotels Castles and Fortresses"** all around the World, and make those Terrace Walls at 33° Angling Slopes, like the Great Pyramid in Egypt: so that they will be Earthquake Resistant, which should be Faced with Polished Granite no less than 3 inches thick in large Slabs, even though 6 inches to one foot thick would be Better: because that would make them Resistant to Hydrogen Bombs, just in case another George Warmonger Bush, Incorporated, should get into Power in **"The Divided States of United Lies!"** Yes, the Russians and Chinese might Decide that a Preemptive Attack on us is Necessary to Save themselves from the MADNESS of some Lunatic like George Warmonger Bush, who might Decide to STRIKE FIRST: beCause, the Nation that Strikes First, will be the Winner of the War: beCause their People can be Secured Underground before the War Begins, while Americans will be getting Drunk on Christmas Eve, and their Soldiers will be on Leave. Yes, it is the Perfect Opportunity to Strike First when you have Intercontinental Guided Missiles in Submarines, whereby it only Requires 5 to 10 Minutes to LEVEL all large American Cities, and make them into Parking Lots for the Planet of the Apes! †§‡§§

05-10 [_] O Elected King, I am now Unemployed, and Ready to go to WORK on the Construction of those **"GLORIOUS Swanky Hotels Castles and Fortresses,"** which will not be Gravely Affected by any Hydrogen Bombs! Indeed, a THICK Solid Stone Wall is as Good as a Mountain of Rocks at a 33° Angle, whereby such Bombs would only Bounce Off! Therefore, where do us Used Veterans Sign Up?

— Chapter 06 —

The Used Veterans go to WORK for Swanky Wages!

06-01 [_] O Selected King, when a Young Veteran comes back Home from some Foreign War, he often Suffers with PTSD (Post-Traumatic Stress Disorder), whereby Employers might say that he does not have a "Right Mind," which is an Under-exaggeration of the Reality of it: beCause some of those Veterans are near to Totally INSANE, who should be placed in Special Veteran Refugee Camps, where they might do something like Hoeing Weeds in a Garden, or Picking Fruits from Trees, if they can Distinguish the Ripe Fruits from the Green Fruits. Otherwise, they might Peel Carrots for making Carrot Juice, whereby they would have some Self-worth for Accomplishing something that is Needed by the Society, rather than be Fed Countless Drugs, which only make them more Victimized by the Hateful EVIL Empire, which Mistreats all such Veterans, over and over: beCause it is Truly an Act of *"the Synagogue of Satan,"* as the *Bible* puts it. ‡

06-02 [_] Well, I Suggest that all such Veterans should be Employed by **"Seven Great Armies of Working Soldiers!" (HOW to Provide a Way for Everyone to WORK: so as to Eliminate Poverty, Crimes, Drug Abuses, Prisons and Unnecessary Taxes!)**, Book 015, whereby they can TRANSITION from "Murderous Soldiers" to "Working Soldiers," whereby they would still Feel like Valuable Wanted People, whereby they would not have Suicidal Thoughts: beCause of Setting their Minds on Constructive Projects — such as Building those **"GLORIOUS Swanky Hotels Castles and Fortresses,"** Book 019 — which would Naturally become their Future Homes, which they would Build and Move into, Free of Charges, Loan-free, Interest-free, Insurance-free, and Tax-free: beCause of Establishing **"The CONSTITUTION for the New RIGHTEOUS One-World GovernMINT,"** Book 016, which would have an Unlimited Amount of CREDITS to be Earned by Honest Labor, which Credits could be Exchanged for Foods, Drinks, and Clothing: beCause it would not be Necessary that any such Working Soldier should have to OWN his or her own Multi-million-dollar Swanky Stone Dome Home Complex with the half-million-gallon Swanky Cisterns with Ceramic Linings: beCause that would only put more STRESS on his or her Mind, which would only make him or her more Traumatized! Indeed, it must be made Clear to them that they can Live in all such Houses within all such Fortresses, until they Die, if they simply Help to do the Work to Build them, and Live by their own Elected Laws and Flexible Rules: beCause, if such Stone Dome Homes are Built Correctly, they will Endure for as Long or Longer than the Pantheon in Rome, which has been there for more than 1,800 Years, and is still in Good Condition with Polished Marble Walls! Therefore, having such a GOOD Government, with an Unlimited Supply of New Money, in the Form of CREDITS, no People on the Earth will have to OWN their Multi-million-dollar Swanky Stone Dome Home Complexes, each of which would include several half-million-gallon Cisterns for Water Storage, a Spacious Home-craft Workshop with Well-made Tools for each Family, a Spacious Sales Shop Dome, a Living Room Dome that is at least 24 feet wide, and preferably 30 to 40 feet wide; a Kitchen Dome that is at least 16 feet wide, and preferably 20 to 24 feet wide; a similar Dining Room Dome, a Walk-in Cooler / Freezer / Pantry Dome that is at least 30 feet in diameter, and preferably 40 to 50 feet; and several Bedroom and Bathroom Domes that are connected with the other Domes by Barrel-vault Tunnels that are at least 4 feet wide and 10 feet tall, but preferably 6 feet wide and 15 feet tall, having Skylights in all

Domes, which Vent the Domes while letting in Light, having Luscious All-Mineral Organic Gardens on the Roofs of all Domes, which are the Gardens for the Families that Live in the Above Terraces: so that all Gardens are directly in Front of each House: so that no one must Climb up Steps, just to get to his or her Garden, which Gardens will be Cared for by **"The Swanky Associations of Working Soldiers!" (A Fascinating Collection of Various Kinds of Voluntary Working Soldiers!)**, Book 018. Yes, all such Gardens will be Cared for by Professional Organic Gardeners: so that all of them are Beautiful and Productive. Moreover, all of the Excess Fruits and Vegetables will be Preserved by **"The Swanky Association of Cooks and Preservation Artists!"** — who will have all of the Correct Tools for doing it Properly, which none of them will have to Own, even as no Soldier presently Owns his own Rifle, Rocket Launcher, Army Tank, or whatever; but, he gets to Use it, even as the President gets to Use the White House in the District of Criminals, in Washington. Likewise, all of those **"GLORIOUS Swanky Hotels Castles and Fortresses"** will Belong to ALL of the People, Collectively; but, NOT Individually: beCause no Individual could ever Afford to Buy any such Fortresses, even if they were as Rich as Bill Computer Software Gates! Therefore, whomever Objects to this Plan, is Suspect of being a Greedy Selfish Capitalist Son or Daughter of SATAN! ‡

06-03 [_] O Elected King, I must Confess that you have Won my Heart and Head — yes, my Whole Body, Mind, Spirit and Soul now Belong to YOU: beCause I would Bow Down and Kiss your Feet for all such Comforting Words! After all, WHY would anyone Object to Living in one of those **"Beautiful Swanky PALACES!" (A New Concept in Living Habits — Swanky Palaces for Poor People!) By The Worldwide People's Revolution!®**, Book 066, when millions of them are presently living in Wooden / Plastic Firetrap Mouse-infested Cockroach Dens, which are Subject to Fires, Floods, Tornadoes, Hurricanes, Earthquakes, Tsunamis, Volcanoes, and whatever? Meanwhile, Billions of People are living in Mud Huts, Slums, Ghettos, Shanty Towns, and other Trash Dumps, while millions are sleeping in Cars, used Vans, Buses, and Old Musty Moldy Motor Homes. Indeed, IF some Swanky Fortress does get Destroyed, we can simply Build another one, Bigger and Better, and Move into it, Tax-free! Yes, all Young People should LOVE your Master Plan, O Elected King: because they can now Forget about going to College, and going into Debt, just to Earn a Good Living: beCause they will Inherit Swanky PALACES, if they Cooperate with you! {See www.Amazon.com for: **"The Luscious All-Mineral Organic Method of Gardening!" (HOW to Grow DELICIOUS Satisfying Foods for Potential Kingz and Kweenz in Swanky PALACES!)**, Book 021, which is a Companion Book of: **"Orgimmick Gardening at its Best!" (HOW to Grow Delicious Satisfying Foods without a 10-Milion-Dollar Investment!)**, Book 079, plus: **"Are you a Jobless Graduate of the SKQL uv FQLZ?" (HOW to get a GOUD EJUKAASHUN without Robbing the Bank!)**, Book 020.}

06-04 [_] Well, my Friend, I do Hope to God that no one is Bowing Down and Kissing my Feet, when I would much rather have a Good, "I-Love-you" HUG, which is Free and Comforting and Satisfying to the Soul. Yes, LOVE and AFFECTION is what the World Needs MOST, which can begin by Hugging some Used Veteran, and Offering to him a Copy of this Inspired Book, whereby he might have some Hope. After all, until now, there has been very little Hope for all such People, which is WHY many of them Commit Suicide, while many more Contemplate it.

06-05 [_] O Selected King, most of those Veterans do not like to read books: because the School of Fools Discouraged them from it, just by presenting them with Trash Literature in **"The Public School of IGNERUNT FQLZ,"** which Turned them Off from Reading. Indeed, have you ever "red" that Nonsense in school books, which have no Spirituality in them, at all? No wonder so many Young People do not like to read anything! Moreover, I would say that your own Books LACK the Necessary Spirituality to Satisfy any given Soul. †‡

06-06 [_] Well, the Bible has a LOT of Spirituality in it, and very few People actually Read that Bible: beCause it Pricks their Consciences, which are Guilty of Sins. Therefore, why would I want to Follow the *Biblical Plan,* which might Turn Off my Readers?

06-07 [_] Are you saying that you do not Recognize the Fact that each Person has Spiritual Needs, which Materialistic Things cannot Satisfy?

06-08 [_] To the Contrary — I Agree with you, which is WHY that I Recommend that everyone should read: **"The New MAGNIFIED Version of The Book of MORMON!" (The Story of the White and Dark Indians in the Americas!)**, Book 040, which is one of the Best Books in the World, which is Rich with Spiritual Subjects, which will Satisfy your Soul, while also Entertaining you with lots of Sarcastic Humor: beCause that Exceptionally Good Book was an Invention of some Lying Edomites. †§‡

06-09 [_] O Selected King, I could never Afford to Buy such a Book, which Costs no less than 50$!

06-10 [_] Well, the DESCRIPTION for the Book, which can be found for Volume 1, tells HOW you can Obtain that Inspired Book for FREE! Therefore, just read the Free Description and the Free Book Preview on the American Version of www.Amazon.com.

— Chapter 07 —

WHY did People not Think of this Plan, Centuries Ago?

07-01 [_] Well, first of all, they did not have Trains, Bulldozers, Rock-cutting Machines, Rock-polishing Machines, nor any of the Good Tools that we presently have to Work with, whereby we can easily Move those thousands of Mountains of Rocks, and Transform them into something like HEAVEN on Earth! Therefore, it was Impractical for them to Build those **"GLORIOUS Swanky Hotels Castles and Fortresses!" (Beautiful Planned City States for WISE Intelligent Well-Educated People with Common Sense and Good Understanding!) By The Worldwide People's Revolution!®**, Book 019; but, now it is most Practical, Reasonable, Logical, Conservative, Pollution-Eliminating, Money-Saving, Economical, and just plain GLORIOUS! Indeed, we can now take Advantage of all such Mechanical SLAVES, who will be Happy to Work for us, and for all Wise People, Worldwide, including those Silly Muslims, who have been Greatly Deceived by a MADMAN!

07-02 [_] O Selected King, are you Sure that the People of Vienna, Austria, for Example, are going to be Interested in Building Swanky PALACES for all of the Poor People over there, whereby no one would bother to Visit that Tourist Trap, just to See their Old Palaces? (See *Wikipedia* for Photos of Austria and Vienna, which is one of the most Beautiful Places on the whole Earth, except for the Stinking Polluting Vehicles, Foreign Thieves, Highway Robbers, etc., etc.)

07-03 [_] Well, it is Possible to Surround Vienna with a Swanky Fortress, whereby all of those Old Palaces will be Well Preserved, Protected, and Visited by millions of Tourists, just as usual: beCause they are Worth Preserving, which is also True of all such Similar Places, including Venice, Italy, which is about to Disappear under the Ocean! Yes, it could have a Tall Stone Wall Built around it, just to Protect the Tourist Sites, which would be quite a Project: beCause we are talking about going around several Islands of Territory! But, with the Assistance of **"Seven Great Armies of Working Soldiers,"** and **"The Swanky Associations of Working Soldiers,"** all such Things are Possible and Practical: beCause a lot of Young Italians are now Unemployed. ‡

07-04 [_] O Selected King, will you also Recommend Surrounding the Old City of Rome with a Swanky FORTRESS, whereby most of the Old Houses would have to be Removed!? And what about New Yuck City, and Washington, D.C. — will you MOVE the Monuments to Higher Ground, or what?

07-05 [_] Well, since the District of Criminals was Built in a SWAMP, it is probably Best to just leave it be — at least until all People in the World are Living in those **"GLORIOUS Swanky Hotels Castles and Fortresses,"** whereby they might not Object to Wasting any Time nor Energy on Protecting: **"The BIG White OUTHOUSE on the Not-so-Biblical Capitol DUNGHILL!" (The Chief Sins of the Divided States of United Lies!)**, Book 023. Indeed, Washington, itself, is a Monument to the Insanities of Capitalists, which is already Surrounded by a Horde of Tax Slaves, Interest Slaves, Insurance Slaves, Drug Slaves, Debt Slaves, Sex Slaves, and Work Slaves, who are very likely to Abandon it, and leave Uncle Sam rather Em-bare-assed, you might say. After all, there is no Law against MOVING, even if they have to Move to some Friendly Place like Venezuela, Colombia, Brazil, Argentina, or even to Mexico, which Countries have Vast Territories that need to be "Developed" Properly, with Beautiful Planned City States — that is, IF the United States Federal Government becomes Uncooperative, and Rebels against **"The Swanky Sword of Divine Truths,"** which is Wielded by your Elected King. Yes, it will be most Difficult to Defeat him with any Weak Capitalist Un-capitalized Rubber sword. However, those Edomite Banksters might Try to Prevent such a Revolution, which might call for other Actions. Yes, the God of Justice might have to Intervene in that Case, and Wipe Out Washington with a FLOOD of Protests. †§‡

07-06 [_] O Selected King, you would not be Suggesting that we might have to get into another World War, just to Wipe the Slate Clean, and Forgive all Debts, and begin all over again with NEW Money, which you call CREDITS, would you?

07-07 [_] Well, whatever is Necessary to get the Job Done will have to be Employed: beCause the Sufferings of Mankind have now gone on Long Enough. Yes, the Inequalities of Incomes and Wages between the Rich Hogs and the Work Slaves have become EXTREME! Therefore, it Calls for Extreme Measures, beginning with: **"The Great Worldwide TELEVISED Court HEARING!" (That Great Meeting of the Most Intelligent and Well-Educated Minds!)**, Book 041, which will Solve those Problems in a Peaceful Manner, without any Hateful Gory Wars. Moreover, whomever Disagrees with that Statement is Suspect of being Anti-American. Yes, they must be Related with those Lying Edomites, who should be brought to COURT, Found Guilty as Charged, and Sentenced to 40 Years of Hard Labor in Rock Quarries, if they do not Freely FORGIVE us of all Debts, and Distribute the Land among ALL of the People, whereby they can Build those **"GLORIOUS Swanky Hotels Castles and Fortresses,"** Book 019, and thus Solve their Massive Problems, without Borrowing any more Money from those Sneaky Conniving Lying EDOMITES, whose Forefathers Crucified the Most Righteous Person who ever Lived, according to the *Bible,* which seems to be Reasonable enough concerning that Subject: beCause it was a Typical Act of Lying Edomites, who have not Ceased to Carry on with Similar Acts ever since then, who were the Chief Slave Masters, themselves, who also Rounded up those Poor African Victims of Capitalism, and Loaded them onto their Edomite Slave Ships, which the History Channel Agrees with: beCause it was a Centuries-old Edomite TRADE, or Occupation, which can be, should be, and must be Proven in a Courtroom, if any Arm-twisting is Necessary to get their Cooperation at that Great Meeting of the Most Intelligent Minds, which will only be Calling for JUSTICE for ALL Peoples, Worldwide, including those Poor Chinese Slaves, who now get 50 Cents per Hour for their Slave Labor Wages, when they should be getting at least 20 Dollars per Hour, and Double the Pay for Overtime! After all, a single Woman at a Sewing Machine can Sew the Parts Together of as many as 100 Shirts per Day, which Sell for 10$ or more, each, which would Equal at least 1,000 Dollars. Therefore, could those Slaves not be Paid more than 10US$ per Day for their Slave Labor? Why not 100$ per Day, Tax-free, and for only 4 Hours of Boring Sewing? After all, a Good Government is LOVED by all of the Righteous People, who are like Workhorses, Bovines, Sheeps, Goats, Camels, Asses, Deers, Antelopes, Yaks, Caribous, Reindeers, Musk Oxens, Bisons, Water Buffaloes, Wildebeests, Mooses, Elks, Giraffes, Elephants, Rhinos, Hippopotamuses, and all other Honest Hardworking Creatures, who only Want to Live in PEACE, without being Tormented by those Lions, Wolves, Tigers, Laughing Hyenas, Jackals, Wild Dogs, Coyotes, Foxes, and Poisonous Snakes, much less be Sprayed by Stinking Highly-perfumed Painted SKUNKS, who Divorce them and leave them BROKE! †§‡

07-08 [_] O Elected King, I swear to God that I have never Heard anyone Talk like you do. Are you Sure that you are not an Alien?

07-09 [_] Well, it is True that a UFO Visited my Parents just before I was Conceived in the Womb of my Mother, which was a Heavenly Sign, you might say, Stating Clearly that I would be a Special Child, which, of course, I turned out to be, which is an Undeniable FACT of Life. After all, very few People since Adam have come up with such Fascinating Books as mine and those of **The Worldwide People's Revolution!®**: beCause we are one and the same Person with Different Pen Names, or Pseudonyms: because it is Necessary to HIDE in this Jungle, lest some Wild Beast should Murder me! Yes, I am Sure that you can Understand that.

07-10 [_] Yes, I can Understand it; and therefore, I have Checked the Box [_] with an X: beCause I am not Ashamed to Admit that you have the Best Master Plan for True Prosperity. However, if all that you Propose were Implemented, it seems like the Great False Economy would CRASH, and perhaps without the Construction of even ONE of those **"GLORIOUS Swanky Hotels Castles and Fortresses!"** Book 019. Indeed, I can Visualize the Destruction of Babylon (Confusion), without any Savior to Guide us, if you should Die from Old Age, or otherwise be Assassinated. {See www.Amazon.com for: **"The Great False Economy is now DEBUNKED!" (Adolf Hitler had a Much Better Economic Plan!)**, Book 053.}

— Chapter 08 —

Will our Selected King be Assassinated?

08-01 [_] O Selected King, what you Teach is far more Radical than anything that was Taught by your Spiritual "Father," Adolf Hitler, who Suffered with no less than 5 Assassination Attempts, which must have been Depressing and Exhilarating at the same Time: beCause, if someone is out to Murder you, it is Worrisome, Stressful, and Depressing — and especially when you have not Said nor Done anything that is Worthy of being Assassinated! However, it is Exhilarating to Survive any such Assassination Attempts: beCause it is the Equivalent of saying, "God must be Protecting me," which was Certainly the Case with Adolf Hitler, who, in one of those Assassination Attempts, just Happened to be Standing on the other Side of a large Solid Oak Table Leg, when the Suitcase Bomb EXPLODED on the other Side of it! Yes, that was a very Close Call, you might say: beCause he would have only had to Move just one Step in either Direction to have been Blown to Pieces! Therefore, I would say that God was on his Side: beCause he never got a Scratch from it! ‡

08-02 [_] Well, I have also Barely Escaped from Death, and many Times, ever since I was 10 Years Old, when a Bunch of Students in the Public School of Ignorant Fools yelled: "DOG PILE," at which Time about 10 of them Jumped on Top of me, after Tripping me, whereby I fell down with my Head under my Body, which they Piled on Top of, which almost Broke my Neck! However, being used to Hard Work, carrying no less than four 5-gallon Buckets of Coal to 2 Furnaces, Daily, during the Winter in Montana, and also Carrying similar Buckets of Water from a Tank to 200+ Hogs, and similar Buckets of Grains to 40+ Cattle 100 Yards from the Grain Bin, I was able to hold those Children Up; but, not enough to keep my Neck from getting Badly Hurt. Moreover, 2 of those Children weighted more than 200 Pounds, being in Higher Grades, and Fat as Hogs. However, to Multiply that Near-death Experience, during that same Summer I was Riding a Young Horse without a Saddle, going about 30 Miles per Hour (MpH), when he Suddenly STOPPED, and sent me Flying over his Head! However, I made the Mistake of Hanging onto the Reins, which Caused me to Land on my Head, which nearly Broke my Neck, once again, and left me in Bed for 2 Weeks to Recover from it, after Riding another Horse Home, for about one Mile, which was Painful at every Step of the Journey, which gave to me Time to THINK! Yes, it Provided Time for me to Think about GOD, whom I had Heard about on the Radio from such Famous Preachers as Theodore Epp from *Back to the Bible* Broadcasts (1939—1985), Charles E. Fuller from *The Old Fashioned Revival Hour* (1937—1968), and Oral Roberts from Tulsa, Oklahoma, with his *Seeds of Faith* Ministry, who, at that Time, had Impressed me to Believe in Miracles, one of which Happened to me during that same Summer, when I Contracted Tonsillitis, and was Sick in Bed for 14 Days, and felt like I might Vomit, if I tried to get up. Therefore, I did not Eat for several Day: because I had a Sore Throat and no Appetite. However, my Dad got himself Worried about me: beCause he had nearly Died with Diphtheria when he was 8 Years Old. However, there was a Wise Doctor in Canada, at that Time, in 1917, who told my Grandmother that the only Sure Cure that he knew of was FASTING. Therefore, he told her to give my Daddy 2 Tablespoons of Welches Concord Grape Juice mixed with one Cup of Water, twice per Day, until he Recovered, with nothing more, which she did, whereby he Totally Recovered 21 Days later! Therefore, beCause of Feeling so Badly when he was Sick as a Child, he was Worried that I might not Recover. Therefore, he came into the House after Working all Day, and said: "There is a Beautiful Sunset outside this Evening, and I want you to get up and go out there and look at it. I have set a Chair on the White House Porch for you to Sit on." Therefore, being Extremely Sick Feeling, and Wanting to Die, I did not Want to get Up: beCause of Fearing that I would be Vomiting Up BILE, again, which I had already done several Times. Therefore, I looked out of the Window into the Sky, and I Prayed to God in the Name of Jesus Christ, asking him to give to me the Strength to Obey my Daddy, who had used his Leather Belt to Persuade my Older Brothers to Obey him during previous Times of Rebellion. Therefore, God Helped me to get my Shoes on, and then, just as I Stepped through the Outside Doorway, I was Instantly Healed, and Felt as Good as I had ever Felt! Yes, it was an Instant Cure, you might say, without Consuming any MediSINZ, which was a Wonderful Feeling, which Dumbfounded me, whereby I was Speechless and Amazed. Therefore, I sat in the Chair on the White House Porch, and Looked Up at the Beautiful Sky, which was like the Healing Balm of Gilead, as King David might say! Yes, up to that Point, I had never Seen such a Beautiful Sunset!

08-03 [_] O Selected King, are you Sure that you are telling a True Story? Are you Sure that some Doctor Pill Popper did not Sneak something into one of your Drinks? Moreover, why did your Daddy not take you to a Naturopathy Doctor?

08-04 [_] Well, he had already Experienced a Total Recovery from his own Illness, without taking any Medicines; and therefore, he did not have any Faith in Doctors, and had never Heard of a Naturopathic Cure for anything; and neither did his Mother, who Fasted every Time that she Lost her Appetite: beCause she was more Connected with Nature's God than most People, who Wore one of those Long Modest Dresses, who never used any Make-up, Paint, Perfume, nor Fingernail Polish, who Believed in Reading her *Bible,* which was not a Bad Idea: beCause she Lived to be

121, if you Recall, and simply gathered up her Feet into her Bed, like Jacob did in *The Book of Genesis,* who also Believed in FASTING! Yes, he took a 40-day Fast when Joseph was Sold into Egypt, which you can read about in: **"The New MAGNIFIED Version of The Book of MORMON,"** Book 040, which contains the New MAGNIFIED Version of the Story of Joseph, which is very Enlightening to the Mind of Greater Faith! †§‡

08-05 [_] O Selected King, what did you Eat after your Tonsillitis was Cured?

08-06 [_] Well, they just Happened to have a Bunch of Red Garden Beets for Supper, which I helped myself to, and Ate all that I Wanted, along with the Cooked Green Leaves, which Naturally Caused a Radical Bowel Movement the next Morning, which made me Feel even Better: beCause my Bowels FLUSHED OUT all of the Accumulated Poisons within them, which was like going to Heaven, you might say!

08-07 [_] So, O Selected King, if it was Good enough for Abraham, Isaac, Jacob, Joseph, Moses, Elijah, the entire City of Nineveh, and Jesus to Fast and Pray for 40 Nights and 40 Days, have you Undertaken any such Experiments, lately?

08-08 [_] Well, I am Seriously Thinking about it, even though I can hardly Expect any Positive Results: beCause of not having any Really GOOD Sweet Juicy Fruits to Eat, after Fasting, which is very Discouraging: beCause I Know for a Fact that all such Fruits are Necessary for True Success, which Moses and Elijah would Agree with: beCause the Holy Angels Administered such Sweet Tree-ripened Fruits to them, when they Broke their Fasts. Therefore, I Hesitate to take any Radical Horse Cures like Moses Undertook, who Refused to Eat nor Drink anything for 40 Days and 40 Nights, which you can read about in *Deuteronomy 9:9 and 18.*

08-09 [_] O Potential King, if the Holy Angels could Deliver such Sweet Fruits from Mount Zion for Moses to Eat, they could also Deliver such Fruits to YOU, if you had the Faith of a Mustard Seed! †‡

08-10 [_] Well, there is more to it, than that: beCause a Person has to be Worthy of such Visitations by Holy Angels. Indeed, I might have to Give Up Watching the Evening Snooze Reports, C-SPAN, and all such Things: beCause Holy Angels might be Offended by all such Things. In Fact, they might be Offended by the Radioactive Computer, itself, which I use for Writing Books. Therefore, People with Compassion will just have to take Care of my Foods, which I get at the Gambling Grocery Stores, if you know what I Mean. Indeed, it is a Big Gamble, just to go Shopping: beCause I have no Idea HOW such Foods have been Treated nor Mistreated; but, for Sure, you can Bet that they were NOT Grown in those Luscious All-Mineral Organic Gardens, Vineyards, nor Orchards! {See Verse 06-03 for the Book.}

— Chapter 09 —

Will the Abused Veterans come to the Rescue?

09-01 [_] O Selected King, I just Listened to a Political Pep Talk by Dr. Obama, who is a Big Proponent of ObamaScare Healthcare, which helped to Fill the Coffers of those Lying Edomites who Sell Insurance Policies; but, it seems to me that if Americans Returned to the early 1800's with Thomas Jefferson and George Washington, who were Professional Gardeners, most Americans would not Need ObamaScare Healthcare: beCause they would just Naturally be Healthy and Happy, even as you are. After all, you have not been to a Medical Doctor in more than 50 Years, and have not Consumed any Kind of Medicines during all of that Time, and can Honestly say that you do not Suffer with any Pains in your entire Body, which few Old People could say. Indeed, I have a Nephew, who is not yet 50 Years Old, who has Constant Back Pains, and he did not even Move the Millions of Pounds of Rocks that you have Moved, by Hand, some of which Weighed no less than a Ton! Yes, it can be Proven in a Courtroom. Therefore, Americans should Study your Book, called: **"The Great False Economy is now DEBUNKED!" (Adolf Hitler had a much Better Economic Plan!) By The Worldwide People's Revolution!®** Book 053.

09-02 [_] Well, most Americans and Europeans are Spooked Away by the NAME of Adolf: beCause of not being Aware of the Good Things about my so-called "Step-Father," Adolf Hitler, who has been Greatly Maligned by Lying Edomites, who are Welcome to Defend their "Stance" at: **"The Great Worldwide TELEVISED Court HEARING!" (That Great Meeting of the Most Intelligent and Well-Educated Minds!) By The Worldwide People's Revolution!®,** Book 041, which will Prove to be the Undoing of 70+ Years of Propagandist LIES, which those Lying Edomites have gotten by with: beCause they are NOT Israelites; but, they are Children of the EDOMITES, who are of the Tribe of ESAU, the very Hairy Brother of Jacob, whom God Hated from his Birth, according to the *Bible,* which is Understandable: beCause they are Impostors! Yes, they call themselves ZIONISTS, who are the Chief Bankers and Puppet Masters of almost all Politicians and Supreme Court Judges in the District of Criminals, in Washington, which can be Proven in that Courtroom. (See *Genesis 25:25; and 27:11.* Notice that Esau had Married the Daughters of Heth, who were Black, whom Rebekah Loathed: beCause she was White. See *Romans 9:13, KJV.*)

09-03 [_] O Selected King, if you get into a Legal Battle with those Lying Edomites, we will never get so much as ONE of those **"GLORIOUS Swanky Hotels Castles and Fortresses"** Built: because those Edomites know how to draw out Court Proceeding for Decades. Remember the President Kennedy Assassination, for an Example. Moreover, they Control Hollywood Movie Productions, as well as the News Media in general, plus Magazine and Book Publishing Companies; and therefore, they will be Defaming you and Demeaning everything that you Teach, saying that you are a Racist BIGOT, in spite of the Fact that you have Black Blood in you! Furthermore, they also Control the Medical and Drug Industries: beCause they have their Sticky Fingers and Long Hook-billed Noses Stuck into almost all Corners and Holes of the World! †§‡

09-04 [_] Well, I am not going to Worry about it too much: beCause the VETERANS of Vietnam and other Useless Wars, and the VICTIMS of Capitalism, will come to my Rescue! Yes, *Greenpeace, Earth First, Move-on.org, ActionTaker.org, EVERYTOWN for Gun Safety, Alliance for Gun Responsibility, Other98, CREDO Action, WALKFREE.ORG, DivestInvest, ENVIRONMENTAL ACTION, ColorOfChange.org, Americans for Tax Fairness, Common Cause, Alliance for Retired Americans, Pesticide Action Network (PAN), Union of Concerned Scientists, GodLovesSoldiers.com, DemandProgress.org, Fight for $15,* and many more Organizations are on MY SIDE, even as I am on their Sides. Therefore, how can I Lose? †§‡

09-05 [_] O Unelected King, your "Step-Father" Lost World War 2, and he had 98% of Germans on his Side, and Enthusiastically so: beCause he had a Justified Cause that was Worth Fighting for, which Required the Combined Forces of all Capitalist and Communist Nations to Defeat them, while your Cause is Pure Speculation that it will even Work! After all, not one of those Fortresses has ever been Built, much less Prove to be an Economic Success Story! Indeed, no one knows whether or not People will be Happy to Live in **"Beautiful Swanky PALACES,"** and Attend to their Gardens with Reincarnated Thomas Jefferson and George Washington in Charge: because they might only be Interested in Consuming Drugs, even if they have to Live in Used Rusty Vans down by Polluted Rivers, and in Trash Dumps on Long Island, New York, which Receives no less than 400 Boxcars full of Trash and Garbage every Working Day of the Year, which Presents an Everlasting Testimony against Capitalism, which has no Reasonable Solution for it. †§‡§§

09-06 [_] Well, it is not the Duty of **"The New RIGHTEOUS One-World Government"** to Babysit all of the Spoiled Children; but, it is their Duty to Provide a Way for everyone to Live a Healthy Happy Life, while being Secure Inside of the Borders of Strong Fortress Walls: beCause, as of now, no one is Secure. Indeed, there are some 200+ People Dying each Day from Overdosing on Drugs; and 100 or more People Murdered on Average per Day in **"The Divided States of United Lies,"** and many more Wounded: beCause the Streets of Chicago, for Example, are like War Zones! Moreover, some silly People are Recommending that everyone should Carry a Firearm for Self-defense, and be Suspicious of everyone on the Street: because it is like the Wild West of the 1800's. However, I Propose that all Righteous People should Move into those **"GLORIOUS Swanky Hotels Castles and Fortresses,"** and then they will not have to Worry about any such Criminals: beCause no one can get into any such Fortresses without Filling Out and Filing **"The Complete SURVEYS of our VALUES,"** Book 059, whereby they can Discover other People of Like-mindedness, whereby they can Live in PEACE: beCause of having Similar Beliefs. For Example, why would a Person who Hates the Stinking Smoke of Cigarettes and the Toxic Perfumes of Painted Skunks want to Live with People who Love such Hateful Things?

09-07 [_] O Selected King, most of the Veterans LOVE those Stinking Cigarettes! Therefore, HOW are you going to Discover enough Voluntary Working Soldiers to Build a Swanky Fortress?

09-08 [_] Well, I dare say that most of those Veterans will be Happy to Give Up their Smoking, in Exchange for the Privilege of Living within those **"GLORIOUS Swanky Hotels Castles and Fortresses"**: beCause of the 5,000+ Good Reasons and Great Advantages for doing that. However, not everyone will be Interested in Raising their Standard of Living by a hundred Times, who may continue to Live in Abandoned Warehouses, in Subways, in Sewage Systems, in Old Junk Cars, or wherever they Want to Live, and it will not Bother me the Slightest Bit! However, if some Young Person Wants to Join one of those **"Seven Great Armies of Working Soldiers,"** he or she can easily Retire after 6 Years of Common Skilled Labor — such as Setting Polished Marble Tiles on the Solid Stone Walls of their own Stone Dome Home Complexes, after being Trained to do so, at which Time they may get Married, Settle Down, and Live in Peace with other People of Like-mindedness, according to their Political, Religious, Spiritual, Social, and Moral Beliefs. And thus Goodness will Overcome Evilness, just by Building such Beautiful Planned City States.

09-09 [_] O Selected King, are you Sure that Drug Pushers will not be Trying to Sell Drugs to the Young Vulnerable Inhabitants of all such Planned City States, whereby they will be Corrupted?

09-10 [_] HOW could they Sell any Drugs to them, if they have NO Money?

— Chapter 10 —

Living without Drugs

10-01 [_] O Selected King, are you not Aware that WALLS have never been Effective for Protecting People? For Example, there was the Great Wall of China, the Berlin Wall, and the Walls of many Castles and Fortresses throughout Europe, which Failed to Accomplish whatever they were Built for. Therefore, your Chances of Keeping Out all of the Unwanted Drugs from any certain City State, even if the Walls are 1,000 feet Tall, and 2,000 feet Deep, and Surrounding the entire City, someone will figure out HOW to Sneak in with their Drugs: because of being Challenged by it, if nothing else. †§‡

10-02 [_] Well, the "Wall" that will Keep Out all of those Drug Pushers will be within the Minds of the People within each Swanky Fortress, who will have no Desire to Consume any such Drugs: beCause of being Naturally Healthy and Happy. Therefore, WHY would they be Buying Drugs? Moreover, HOW could they be Buying any Drugs, if they have NO Money? Indeed, their CREDITS would be of no Value to Drug Pushers, whose Bank Accounts could not be Credited for any Drugs: because the Credits would only Work within the Swanky Fortresses, for Products that are Needed — such as Natural Foods, Natural Drinks, Natural Clothing, and Well-made Tools.

10-03 [_] O Selected King, People could Trade Drugs for Sex, Diamonds, Furniture, TV's, Computers, or whatever, whereby they would not have to Use any Money, nor Credits in your Closed Society. Indeed, a Drug Dealer could come into a Swanky Fortress with Fake Bananas, which are Loaded with Drugs, which he could Trade for a Laptop Computer, or whatever; and thus walk out of the Fortress without getting Caught. But, first of all, such a Drug Dealer would have to make Contact with some Teenager who might Want such Drugs, who would then use his Credits to Buy a Laptop Computer, for Example, which he would Trade for the Drugs. †§‡

10-04 [_] Well, a RFID (Radio Frequency Identification Chip) in the Computer would Detect it at the Exit Gate, and that Person would be Investigated by the Elected Officials, who would no doubt Discover the Drugs, whereby that Teenager would be Banished from the City, which would be his Just Reward for Transgressing the Law. After all, if such a Teenager Wants to Use Drugs, he is

Welcome to Visit a City that has Legal Drugs, where he can make a Fool of himself, much like the *Prodigal Son of Luke 15.* Yes, he could Experiment with the Devil, and thus Discover the Glories of Sins when he Discovers himself digging around in some Dumpster for something to Eat, whereby he will Remember the Swanky Fortress, which had Royal Swanky Buffets, Beautiful Polished Marble Walls, Waterfalls, Streams of Living Water, Flowery Gardens, thousands of Fruit Trees, Healthy Happy Trustworthy People, and no Bills to Pay: beCause of being FREE with a Capital F.

10-05 [_] O Elected King, I cannot Imagine WHY any Young Person would Want to Rebel, unless his or her Parents were Hypocrites, which would Naturally Turn their Children Against them?

10-06 [_] Well, if Children are Born of Unholy Seeds, they will just Naturally Rebel against their Parents to some Degree, if those Parents try to Impose any Religious Beliefs onto them. However, if they are Born of Clean Seeds, they will just Naturally Accept most Religious Teachings that make Sense to them, which they will Discover as they Study Books; but, for Sure, they will not become Criminals, if they are given Good Instructions for Living. But, if they are not given Good Instructions, how can anyone Think that they will become Good Citizens?

10-07 [_] O Selected King, it is the Duty of the Church and School to give the Children Good Instructions. Otherwise, it would be left up to Ignorant Parents to Instruct them, who might not know their P's nor Q's, who might be Grade-school Dropouts. Therefore, the Children are at the Mercy of whomever Teaches them.

10-08 [_] Well, that is exactly WHY we should have a RIGHTEOUS One-World Government, which Teaches all of the People Important Truths, every Day, whereby they might become Good Citizens, rather than Ignorant Idiots like George Warmonger Bush, Incorporated, who got a Hateful and Needless War going in Iraq, whose Citizens had nothing whatsoever to do with the Evil Events of September 11th, 2001.

10-09 [_] O Selected King, without some Righteous Person Controlling the News Media, the Masses of People would never Learn much of anything.

10-10 [_] Well, I Propose that Jesus Christ should Return and take Charge of ALL Information on TV's and Radios, and even Manage the Songs that are Sung. Yes, some Silly People actually Believe that he will Do such Things, even though there are no *Scriptures* to Prove it: beCause he will not be a TYRANT! However, he will Defeat all of his Enemies with the Sword of Truth that comes out of his Mouth, as *the Book of Revelation* Reveals, which is most Reasonable, if you Think about it. After all, if it were not Possible to do so, how come someone of Superior Intelligence has not taken me to Court, and Proven my Inspired Words of Provable Truths to be WRong, whereby I might have to Step Down from my Lofty Throne in: **"The Great World TEMPLE of PEACE,"** in Jerusalem? Yes, I am the King of the Mountain, right NOW, whereby I Challenge anyone on this Earth to Prove my Master Plan to be Unworkable, Unreasonable, Insane, or otherwise Impossible to carry out! Indeed, the Masses of People only need to Learn what I Believe, and then OBEY what I Teach, and in a Logical Order, beginning with **that Great Meeting of the Most Intelligent and Well-Educated Minds,** and we will soon Discover WHO is RIIT: beCause each Beautiful Planned City State will be FREE to Elect whatever Laws and Rules that they Choose to Love and Obey, which will be Reported about in: **"FREEDUM uv**

SPEECH!" (U Speshould Maguzeen uv Onist Upinyunz!) By The Worldwide People's Revolution!® Book 030-0002. Therefore, it is just that Simple. However, it could be that Jesus Christ has other Plans! Who would Know?

10-11 [_] O Selected King, you should Watch YouTube Videos about the History of Abraham Lincoln, which are very Enlightening; but, also very Depressing, if you Think about it all. For Example, Honest Abe Lost his Mother when he was only 9 Years Old, and his Daddy was about as much Comfort as a Tyrant, who had little Use for Abe, as well as Books and Schooling: because he Prided himself with being Ignorant and Proud of it, who only wanted to Earn an Honest Living by Manual Labor: because he was one of those People who was Born to be a Servant, while Abe was Born to be a Master. However, Abe was Greatly Confused by his own Sexual Orientation, and Lived in Denial for his entire Life, who Desperately Wanted to be Normal, and a Real Man; but, like Alexander the Great, he was more Attracted to Men, than to Women. However, it was too Difficult for him to Confess it to himself, much less to anyone else, even though he did not keep it a Secret: because that was almost Impossible. For Example, his Best Friend, Joshua Speed left him Brokenhearted and so Depressed that other People thought that Abe might Commit Suicide, which would have never been the Case for a Man who was not Gay, or at least Bisexual. †‡

10-12 [_] Well, I have already Watched several of the YouTube Videos about Abe Lincoln, and must Agree with you — that Abe was most likely Bisexual; but, that was an Unacceptable Thing in the Society at that Time, which did not Want to Confess the Possibility of it, even though the Majority of Men would be so Classified by the Creator God, with whom are no Secrets: because he Created the Spirits of People both Male and Female, according to *Genesis 1.* Indeed, the Spirit of a Person can be put into any Body that God Chooses, whereby they can all be Tested for their Goodness. Therefore, do not Think that it is Strange if most Men Act a little Feminine, and thus Shave the Whiskers Off of their Faces, whereby they might Look more like Women than Men, and also Act more like Women, who have Seduced them, who Hate those Beards: beCause they are Signs of Authority over the Weaker Vessels, as the Apostles of Jesus Christ might say, who all Wore their Beards, and Spoke with Authority, saying that Wives should Submit to their Husbands, while Mary Ann Todd preferred it the other Way around: because she was a bit Crazy. ‡

10-13 [_] O Selected King, if Abraham Lincoln was GAY, why did he Marry Mary Ann Todd?

10-14 [_] Well, according to those Videos, he Loved several Women; but, he was Afraid of them, and did not Feel Comfortable around them, and neither did Joshua Speed; but, Abe and Joshua got along like Fresh Butter and Honey on Hot Whole Wheat Bread, which was the Perfect Match, you might say; but, that is not to say that they were Sodomites, nor even Distant Relatives of Sodomites: because they were NOT. However, there is Strong Evidence that they were Secret Lovers: beCause of the Letters that were Written, most of which have been Lost. Nevertheless, being a Man of his Words, Abe had already Committed himself to Mary Ann Todd, who came from a Wealthy Family, who was Determined to Mary him, even if she had to Seduce him: because she Loved Prestige and Fame, who Longed to be one of the Upper Class, while Abe ran for the Presidency to Right the Wrongs, and to Abolish Slavery: because he had already Experienced some of that Slavery when he was Boy, whom his Father Loaned Out for his own Gain, who took the Money that Abe Earned: because that was the Tradition at that Time, until the Boy turned 21, at which Time he could Save his own Money that he might Earn. Therefore, being a very Bright Boy, he Educated himself with Books, until he became a Lawyer, and took on the Task of

Defending Accused People, whom he Believed to be Innocent. (No such Opportunities would be Possible, nowadays: because all Lawyers must have Licenses, while Abe only needed a Good Reputation at that Time. Therefore, he did not have to Borrow Money to Attend Colleges, and thus get himself into Deep Debts, whereby he would have been Forced to Charge Extortionist Prices for his Services as a Lawyer. Indeed, he could Charge a Fair Price for his Services, and Earn an Honest Living with a Good Conscience, which was his Just Reward.)

10-15 [_] So, O Elected King, have you not also done something Similar, and without any College Degrees? Remember that I have "red" your Inspired Book, called: **"The Process of Making a RIGHTEOUS KING!" (A Fascinating Autobiography of our Selected King!) By The Worldwide People's Revolution!®** Book 082.

10-16 [_] Well, it has yet to be Proven whether or not anyone will VOTE for me to be the Elected King of **"The New RIGHTEOUS One-World Government!" (HOW to Establish a Righteous One-World Government without Going to WAR!) By The Worldwide People's Revolution!®** Book 056. Indeed, other than having **"Guaranteed Solutions!" (HOW to Solve our Local and Global Problems in the Most Rational Manner Possible!)**, Book 080, I have no Qualifications at all, according to the Political Puppet Masters, being "the least qualified of any person on this earth," if you can Believe it! Yes, only Jesus Christ was less Qualified, who had no Schooling at all, according to the *Scriptures,* which Word is Derived from *Script,* such as the *Script* for a Play in a Roman Theater: beCause the *Scriptures* were Actually Jewish FABLES for the most Part! But, that is not saying that there were no Truths in them: because there most Certainly was, and still is, which can easily be Proven in a Courtroom. Indeed, those *Scriptures* are otherwise known as *Sacred Writings, which were Inspired by God.* Therefore, if that can be Proven, we must Accept them as Sacred Writings. ‡

10-17 [_] O Elected King, there is no Doubt that you were Born to be our Righteous King: because no one on the Whole Earth is Willing to Challenge your **"Guaranteed Solutions!"** with Better Solutions. In Fact, you are the one and only Person who has Reasonable Solutions for ALL of our Massive Problems, which all Intelligent People Agree with when they get Backed Up in an Intellectual Corner! Therefore, you are the King of **"The New RIGHTEOUS One-World Government"** by Virtue of the Fact that you have no Challengers! Therefore, no Election Deceptions will have to be Held for your Election to that Highest Office in the World. ‡

10-18 [_] Well, now the Challenge is to Discover a Way to get those Facts into the Minds of the Electors, who could Save themselves a Bundle of Money on those Election Deceptions — as in Trillions of Dollars over the next 100 Years, seeing that I could easily Live for another 100 Years! Yes, all I Need is the Correct Living Conditions, and then I could Do that, beginning with Fresh Clean Air to Breathe, Pure Living Water to Drink, Wholesome Natural Foods to Eat, Natural Clothing to Wear, and a SECURE Swanky Stone Dome Home Complex to Live within Inside of a Beautiful Planned City State, which is Designed for Proper Living. ‡

10-19 [_] O Elected King, you are likely to be Assassinated by some Republican Hypocrite, who Falsely Claims to Love God, without Realizing that God is "All that is GOOD," while the Devil is "All that is EVIL," who is the Stepfather of almost all Republicans: because they cannot Tolerate Provable Truths — such as the Truths about the Evil Events of September 11th, 2001, which was a False Flag Operation, according to www.AE911TRUTH.org and hundreds of other Websites, which have Presented Irrefutable Evidences, which have never been Addressed in any Courtrooms with Righteous Judges in Charge of them. In Fact, just to get some Justice, you will have to Raise Up Abraham Lincoln from the Dead, along with Lee Harvey Oswald, Osama bin Laden, and other Victims of Capitalism, who will be Happy to Testify in Favor of those Provable Truths. †§‡

10-20 [_] Well, at least we will not have to Raise Up Timothy James McVeigh: because he is still Alive and Well, after they Faked his Death! Indeed, there is hardly any Institution on this Earth that is more Phony than **"The Divided States of United Lies!" (The so-called "United States of North America" in Disguise!)** Book 058. †§‡

10-21 [_] O Elected King, I am Curious as to just Exactly HOW that you would Know that for a Fact?

10-22 [_] Well, just in case that you have not yet Heard, the Holy Spirit did not Die, and she Knows the Truths about all such Things, and can Reveal them to whomever she Pleases. Therefore, whomever Murders Timothy James McVeigh is in Double Trouble during the Judgment Day: because of Seeking to Destroy the Evidences that should be Presented at: **"The Great Worldwide TELEVISED Court HEARING!" (That Great Meeting of the Most Intelligent and Well-Educated Minds!) By The Worldwide People's Revolution!®** Book 041.

— Chapter 11 —

The Dictator, Jesus Christ!

11-01 [_] So, O Selected King, if you had your way, Jesus Christ would quickly Return, and Establish his Righteous One-World GovernMint, and thus put all of those Lying Edomite Banksters OUT of Business, huh?

11-02 [_] Well, that would be the most Practical Way to do it; but, since he has not Returned, we are left to Manage it, ourselves, which is also quite Practical if most of the People go along with us; but, you can be Sure that X-amount of Edomite Lovers in the District of Criminals, in Washington, will not go along with such a Plan: beCause they Love Lies more than Truths, even though most of them Claim to be "Christians," and even go to Churches and Sing Hymns to their Imaginary God of Justice, who Created Mosquitoes to Kill Innocent Babies with Malaria and other Horrible Diseases: because he is Supposedly "the creator of all things," they say.

11-03 [_] So, O Unelected King, are you saying that Jesus Christ did NOT Create Mosquitoes, Ticks, Chiggers, Fleas, Bedbugs, Lice, Mice, Rats, Scorpions, Poisonous Spiders, Snakes, Skunks, Raccoons, and all such Pests? Are you Suggesting that SATAN Created them, or what??

11-04 [_] Well, if Jesus did Create those Pests, he must have done it for the Devil's Sake: because he Certainly did not do it for the Sakes of the Millions of Babies who have Died with Malaria, Smallpox, nor other Lovable Diseases — that is, IF he is the Man of Compassion that we read about in the *Holy Bible,* which is a Book of Massive Confusion and Ridiculous Contradictions. After all, the least Worthy People to be Inflicted with such Diseases are the Innocent Children. Meanwhile, such Criminals as Judge Merrick B. Garland and Bill Adulterous Lying Clinton go Free! For Example, there is much Evidence that the Oklahoma City Bombing was a False Flag Operation: beCause there were Pillars / Columns in the Basement of the Murrah Federal Building, which were EXPLODED by Demolitions, which were farther away than the more nearby Columns to the Truck Bomb, which you can Learn about on YouTube Videos. Even *Wikipedia* admits that there are many "Conspiracy Theories" about it, which has an Article concerning it. The Primary Reason WHY there are so many "Conspiracy Theorists" in this Country, and around the World, is beCAUSE those Federal Cover-up Criminals quickly Destroy any Physical Evidences, which might be Investigated, whereby they "Hang" themselves with their own Lies: beCause, if they were Perfectly Honest People, they would PROTECT the Remaining Evidences, to make Sure that a Thorough Investigation could be made by Unbiased Investigators, which might Require a Year or more of Investigating by Scientists and Professional People, including Good Journalists, like John McArdle, who could Ask Important Questions, and Report the Responses. For Example, it was said that Explosives were Discovered in the Basement, attached to those Columns of the Murrah Federal Building, which Timothy McVeigh could not have Set Up: beCause he did not have Access to the Building; but, the FBI did, as well as other Top Secret Societies of Satan, Incorporated. Whatever the Case, like the Kennedy Assassination Cover-up, and the Evil Events of September 11th, 2001, much of the Investigated Information is kept a Top Secret for "National Securities' Sake," which is "Pure 100% Fruit Juice," you might say, which "is made from Reconstructed Concentrated Fruit Juices with Recycled Chlorinated Sewage Water, Imitation Flavors, and a long List of Chemical Preservatives," as an Honest Grocery Shopper might Observe, who is not Fooled by the Good Drugs nor Bad Foods Administration (FDA), which is about as Trustworthy as the Lying Politicians, themselves. After all, if it is Profitable, it is GOOD (at least to them), which Explains WHY Addictive Tobacco Products are still for Sale: beCause the Federal Government LOVES us; but, not as much as Jesus Christ Loves us, who would have all of them brought to Court and Punished Properly! †§‡ {See www.Amazon.com for: **"Those Ridiculous Contradictions within the Holy Bible!" (HOW to Read the "Holy Bible" with an Open Mind!) By The Worldwide People's Revolution!® Book 057.**}

11-05 [_] O Elected King, if all of the Criminals in Washington were put in Jail, the City would be mostly Emptied of Officials! Indeed, as President Richard Nixon said, "I am not a crook." But, then it was Proven that he was a Crook, whom President Gerald Ford PARDONED: beCause High-ranking Crooks are Excusable in **"The Divided States of United Lies!"** Meanwhile, Wrongly Convicted Men have Wasted 10, 20, 30 or more Years in American Prisons: because of being in the Wrong Places at the Wrong Times. Moreover, if some Peon makes the slightest Mistake — such as Failing to come to a Dead STOP at a Stop Sign on a Deserted Street, he can get a 100$ Traffic Ticket for it, or even be Cast into Prison, if some Copperhead Discovers some Planted Marijuana in the Trunk of his Car: beCause of not Liking the "Attitude" of the Black Driver, who could not see any Reason for coming to a Dead Stop at a Deserted Avenue. Indeed, whatever Happened to Common Sense and Good Understanding? Why would the Law Support some Copperhead who is Living by the Letter of the Law; but, not by the Spirit of the Law, which Requires LOVE and MERCY above all else, lest another Rebellious Criminal should be Produced by a Heartless Mindless Cop, who runs through Red Light Stop Signs, who Breaks Speed Limits every Day, and who Disregards most of the Laws of God, routinely — such as Loving their Naaberz as much as they Love themselves! ‡

11-06 [_] Well, when Jesus Christ Governs this World, there will be no more Copperheads, nor even any Stop Lights: beCause those **"GLORIOUS Swanky Hotels Castles and Fortresses"** have no Need for any such Lights: beCause they use Electric Elevators and Subway Trains, which run One Way on one Track, which makes it Impossible for them to Crash into other Trains on other Tracks.

11-07 [_] O Selected King, suppose some Depressed Person, who just Experienced the Bad Effects of a Divorce, decides to Commit Suicide by Jumping in front of one of those Trains — HOW will you Prevent that?

11-08 [_] Well, if there is a Solid Thick Stone Wall between the Train and the Passengers, with Locked Doors, here and there, it will be Impossible for anyone to Jump in front of any Train: because the Doors will not Open, until after the Train has Stopped and Opened its Doors.

11-09 [_] So, O Elected King, how come the Capitalists did not Think of that Plan?

11-10 [_] Well, they would have the same Sorry Excuse that they almost always have, which is "a Lack of Money," they say; but, with the New Government that I Propose, there would be no Lack of Money for Doing any Good Thing: beCause that Good GovernMint, alone, would be in Charge of the Printing Presses — that is, IF any Money were even Used! I say that it is Best to do Away with all Money, and only Deal with Credits for Exchanging Goods and Services, which will do Away with the Multitudes of Problems that arise for having Money to Deal with — such as Trading Drugs for Money. For Example, if you Work for one Hour of Common Labor, you could Trade it for a Large Sweet Watermelon, or you could simply go into your Private Garden and Gather all of the Watermelons that are ready to put into your Private Walk-in Cooler, whereby you might Move 100 Watermelons within that Hour, by using a Garden Cart, and thus have a 2-Month Supply of them for the whole Family, and Plenty to Share with your Friends and Naaberz, as well as make Watermelon Juice for Wholesome Natural Drinks. Otherwise, you could go Eat at a Royal Swanky Buffet, if you put in 4 Hours of Common Skilled Labor per Day, 6 Days per Week, or the Equivalent thereof, which would Cover all of your Costs for Living. Indeed, each Swanky Fortress will Adopt its own Economic System, whereby it can be Happy with itself; and some of them will no doubt Adopt the System that uses Money of some Kind and Color: beCause of being Addicted to Using it. However, in the System that I Propose, Money will not be Needed for a very High Standard of Living with an Abundance of all Kinds of Natural Foods and Drinks, whereby Sicknesses and Diseases will be Minimized, while Good Health will be Maximized. ‡ {For a Good Example of that Perfect System, you should Study: **"The New MAGNIFIED Version of the Book of ACTS!" (The Understandable Version of the ACTS of the Apostles in Plain English!) By The Worldwide People's Revolution!®** Book 063.}

11-11 [_] O Selected King, what will you Do with the Lazy People, who have no Heart in your Economic System, which Shares all Material Things in Common among the Believers, who Collectively Pick only one Quart of half-ripe Blackberries in one whole Hour, for Example, as Opposed to Harvesting 2 Gallons per Person of Fully Ripe Blackberries within one Hour, whereby we might make Extra-sweet Blackberry Juices to Drink? Indeed, if a Fruit Picker Works Rapidly, and Professionally, he can Harvest as many as 4 Gallons of Blackberries in just one Hour; but, a Lazy Person, who has no Heart in it, might only Discover a Pint of Blackberries within that Hour, and half of them might not even be Ripe nor Ready to Pick. †§‡

11-12 [_] Well, **"The Swanky Association of Professional Fruit Pickers"** will be Trained HOW to Harvest the Fruits Properly, and Separate the Ripe Fruits from the Unripe Fruits; but, the Secret to Producing the Best Fruit Juices is Dependent on Vine-ripened Fruits from Properly-grown Vines, which Means that they must be Grown by **"The LUSCIOUS All-Mineral Organic Method of Gardening!" (HOW to Grow DELICIOUS Satisfying Foods for Potential Kingz and Kweenz in Beautiful Swanky PALACES!)**, Book 021, which is a Companion Book of: **"Orgimmick Gardening at its Best!" (HOW to Grow Delicious Satisfying Foods without a 10-Million-Dollar Investment!) By The Worldwide People's Revolution!®** Book 079. Therefore, none of that Gardening should be Done by any Lazy nor Crazy People, who should Commit themselves to **Swanky Fasting Sanitariums**, whereby they might get the Laziness Removed from themselves without any Great Sufferings. After all, when did anyone ever See a Lazy Mountain Goat, or Crazy Deer? {See: **"Did God or Satan Ordain Medical Doctors?" (Ask Huck Finn and/or Nigger Jim: because neither Tom Sawyer nor Judge Thatcher would Know!) By The Worldwide People's Revolution!®** Book 022.}

11-13 [_] O Elected King, we would not Want to put any Voluntary Working Soldiers under any Kind of Pressure to get their Work Done Correctly: beCause STRESS is the Number 1 Killer of Mankind, which Causes Various Kinds of Sicknesses and Diseases, which gets the whole Body and Mind Out of the Right Order, which Requires Peace and Happiness. Therefore, if we Expect those Working Soldiers to Harvest 4 Gallons of Blackberries every Hour, when they are only Able and Willing to Harvest 2 Gallons per Hour, we are Sinning against them by putting Unnecessary PRESSURE on them to Meet some Imaginary Deadline. Indeed, if there is an Abundance of Blackberries to be Harvested, more Voluntary Working Soldiers should be Called on for Harvesting them, rather than Force a few People to do more Work than they can Rightly Handle. Therefore, the Proper Way to Manage it, without any Stress, is to allow those Working Soldiers to Harvest as many Blackberries as they can Comfortably Manage to Harvest within 4 Hours, even if they can only Harvest 4 Gallons within 4 Hours: beCause that is enough Blackberries to make no less than one Gallon of Blackberry Juice, or 4 Quarts, which is enough for a Working Soldier to Drink a Quart of Juice for 4 Days, in Exchange for only 4 Hours of Labor. Moreover, it is not Wise for any Swanky Fortress to Plant more Blackberries than it can Reasonably Handle, even if that is the one Fruit that does Extremely Well in that Particular Swanky Fortress — that is, unless they can Persuade some other Swanky Fortress to Send Working Soldiers to Help them to do the Harvesting with them in Charge of the Project: because those are their Blackberries. Indeed, that could Prove to be a Proper Time for Romance among Young Working Soldiers, who could also Work for 8 Hours per Day this Week, and take Off next Week for some Romance, if the Berries got Harvested before Falling on the Ground, or Spoiling on their Vines. †§‡

11-14 [_] Well, my Friend, when we Calculate everything that is Required for Producing a Quart of Fresh Fruit Juice for each Person, each Day, for 2 Million Swanky Fortresses around the World, and no less than enough for 7 Billion People, it is not Difficult to Understand WHY a Working Soldier must Harvest no less than 2 Gallons of Blackberries per Hour, just to make that Possible: because other Working Soldiers must Wash Canning Jars, Sterilize them, Dry them, and make the Juices that go into them; while other Working Soldiers must Pack them into Boxes and Move them to Cool Trains for Transporting them to Fortresses that do not have such Juices, which they can Trade for other Kinds of Juices, whereby each Swanky Fortress can have an Abundance of Juices to Drink, as well as Top Quality Products, which are not now Available to anyone, Worldwide: beCause of not doing Professional All-Mineral Organic Gardening, Scientifically and with

Enthusiasm for it: beCause the Workers are only Looking for their Paychecks, and could care less about Drinking any Fruit Juices: beCause those Juices are not very Tasty, as they should be and will be if we do our Best to make them Delicious, and also Produce a certain Amount of Natural Wine for Special Holy Days and Holidays. In other Words, it is a very Complicated Operation, which Requires the Management of Professional People. For Example, all Educated People know that Blackberries, for Example, are Seasonal, and come in a hundred Different Varieties, along with Raspberries, Blueberries, Gooseberries, Strawberries, and a thousand other Kinds of Berries and Grapes, which must all be Kept Sanitary, and Preserved Properly in Various Ways, Scientifically and Professionally: because of Following Scientific RULES — one of which is to have Clean Workers, who are not Coughing nor Sneezing on the Fruits, much less Spitting into the Juices, as might Presently Happen in Unsanitary Fruit Juice Factories: beCause of Underpaid Workers, who are Unhappy with their Work, who do it for Revenge, who might even Piss in those Juices: beCause of being Pissed Off with the Management, or even with the Government. †§‡

11-15 [_] O Elected King, that is the very Reason that I Want to Grow and Harvest my own Fruits from my own Vineyard and Orchard: because I cannot Trust other People to be Sanitary, even as I would be with my own Fruits. (Please Check the above Box with an X, if you Agree.)

11-16 [_] Well, I Hear what you are Saying. However, with your Private Independent Plan for Gardening, most of the People in the World would never get to Drink any of your Home-made Blackberry Juice, whereby they might be Inspired to Live within a Beautiful Swanky Fortress, and Grow their own Blackberries. In Fact, they might Live in some Country that has no Blackberries at all; and therefore, they would be Deprived for their entire Lives of something so Good, unless they Visited a Swanky Fortress that Grew the Berries, and thus got to Taste of the Juices. Likewise, the People who Live in the North might Live for their entire Lives without Tasting of Good Tree-ripened Mangos of the Heavenly Varieties: because there are no less than 5,000 Varieties of Mangos in this World of Wonders to Choose from, and some are Extremely GOOD! Therefore, **"The Swanky Associations of Professional Gardeners"** would be going out of their Way to Reproduce those Extremely Good Mangos, which Capitalism has utterly Failed to Do: beCause those Best Mangos are "Temperamental," you might say, which Require Special Care, which might not even Like to be Shipped anywhere; but, they can be made into Fresh Sweet Juices, or be made into 100% Pure Mango Iced-cream, and be Shipped all over the World in Reusable Glass Containers. And that is where **"The New RIGHTEOUS One-World Government"** comes in very Handy: beCause of having Professional Architects, Engineers, Designers, Planners, Organizers, Professional Gardeners, and Well-Trained Workers, who do their Best to make it all Workable and Proficient. However, the Weather cannot be Controlled by anyone, and therefore it can make Unexpected Changes, which might Ruin the Best of Plans, some Years. However, the Main Objective is to have an Abundance of Good Sweet Juicy Fresh Raw Fruits to Eat: beCause the Life of People is found in those Fruits, which can be Proven in a Courtroom! ‡

11-17 [_] O Elected King, it would Require the Cooperation of hundreds of millions of Sincere People, just to make it all Work Correctly, which is an Unlikely Thing to Happen, seeing that most People are now Drug Addicts and Junk Food Addicts, who would have to REPENT, just to get their Taste Buds Working Correctly. {See: **"HOW to Become a HOLY Man!"** **(40 Good Reasons WHY People Should FAST and PRAY!)**, Book 045, which is a Companion Book of: **"The Proper RULES for FASTING!" (The Complete Instruction Manual for True Repentance!) By The Worldwide People's Revolution!®** Book 046.}

11-18 [_] Well, my Friend, I Hear what you are Saying, and I Agree; but, it only Requires just ONE of those **"GLORIOUS Swanky Hotels Castles and Fortresses!" (Beautiful Planned City States for WISE Intelligent Well-Educated People with Common Sense and Good Understanding!) By The Worldwide People's Revolution!®**, Book 019, in Order to get most of the People in this World of Woes CONVERTED to the Truths that I Teach: because of being such a Good Example of Holy People, who Shine with the Glory of God, who can Do Miracles, who can Preach Marvelous Sermons, and who Actually Practice what they Teach! Therefore, Goodness can Overcome Evilness by that Method. Therefore, it is now in the Hands of Professing "Christians," who need to put their Hypocritical Masks in their Trash Cans, and take up Fasting and Praying with Jesus Christ, Moses, Elijah, Daniel, David, Samuel, Isaiah, and the Apostles — all of whom would Agree with me, that the Best Solution is to Build those Swanky Fortresses, whereby they can put Aside their Hypocrisies, and be Done with them. For Example, if we Want to Stop Polluting God's Air, Water, Land, Animals, and our own Bodies, we will have to STOP Using those Stinking Noisy Greasy Vehicles that are the Primary Causes for our Pollutions. For Example, those Gasoline-powered and Diesel-powered Vehicles Contribute about a Trillion Tons of Carbon Dioxide to the Atmosphere each Year, which comes back down in the Form of Acid Rains, which Ruin the Oceans, Seas, Lakes, Rivers, and Lands. But, if you Doubt it, just Ask the Scientists who Study it. Indeed, the Evidences Overwhelmingly Testify in Favor of Swanky Fortresses with Billions of Organic Gardens. ‡

11-19 [_] O Elected King, that Acid Rain is just ONE of a Multitude of Good Reasons for Building those Beautiful Planned City States, which are of no Interest to the Capitalists, who Fear that their Unnecessary Businesses might be put into the Dumpsters of the Devil, who Inspired them — such as the Cosmetics Industries, Paint and Solvent Conspiracies, Stinking Perfumes, Pesticides, Herbicides, Chemical Fertilizers, and all such Abominations. Therefore, your Master Plan is likely to get another World War going, if X-amount of People Believe you: beCause, whichever Nation takes up your Good Doctrines will be Branded as the "Enemy," while you will be Branded as "The ANTI-CHRIST," himself! †§‡

11-20 [_] Well, my Friend, all of their Arguments will easily be Defeated by **"The Swanky Sword of Divine Truths!" (The Most Powerful Weapon in the Whole Universe!) By The Worldwide People's Revolution!®**, Book 067, at: **"The Great Worldwide TELEVISED Court HEARING!"** Therefore, the Edomites do not stand a Chance of Survival, unless they Cooperate with us. {See: **"The END of CONFUSION!" (The Great CELEBRATION of the Magnificent Wedding of the Most Humble Honest Nations, and the Grand Year of JUBILEE!) By The Worldwide People's Revolution!®** Book 050.}

— Chapter 12 —

HOW to Live a Simple Life!

12-01 [_] O Selected King, you make things seem Simple, when they are Actually very Complicated. For Example, I now Live in a little Cramped Apartment House, on the Fourth Floor of a Condominium, which barely has enough Space for turning around, much less a large All-Mineral Organic Garden with Fruit Trees, Nut Trees, Berry Bushes, Grape Vines, Flower Gardens, and Vegetable Gardens of Various Kinds, which have nothing to do with the Spacious Community Gardens, Vineyards and Orchards, which are Grown for the Foods that are Served at Restaurants and Royal Swanky Buffets. Moreover, my Uncle in Mississippi has a Garden, which is Overrun by Grasses and Weeds: because he has not figured out HOW to get them Under his Control. †§‡

12-02 [_] Well, that is beCause he has no Swanky MULCHING ROCKS, which are Slabs of Granite, being Cut 2-feet square and 1-inch thick, having one inch Cut Off of each Corner, which leaves 2-inch spaces for Planting Cucumbers, Watermelons, Tomatoes, Grape Vines, Raspberries, Blackberries, Blueberries, Squashes, Melons, and whatever might Grow in those Holes. However, before the Mulching Rocks are Carefully laid down, the Ground must be Properly Prepared, according to: **"The LUSCIOUS All-Mineral Organic Method of Gardening!" (HOW to Grow DELICIOUS Satisfying Foods for Potential Kingz and Kweenz in Swanky PALACES!)**, Book 021, whereby the Topsoil will be full of those little Brown Earthworms, who Thrive under those Mulching Rocks, who are the LIFE of a Good Garden, who have Gizzards, which Grind Up Powdered Rocks, which Provide Minerals for the Roots of the Plants to Absorb, which makes those Roots BROWN. Therefore, if the Roots of your Plants are not Dark Brown, they are Lacking Minerals. Yes, they may also be Lacking Nitrogen, Phosphate, and Potash, which are the Basic Ingredients for Growing Good Healthy Fruits and Vegetables, which is a SCIENCE, which Requires Special Nolij, and Years of Practice, which is WHY all such Gardens will be Cared for by: **"The Swanky Associations of Working Soldiers,"** Book 018, and particularly by **"The Swanky Association of Professional Organic Gardeners,"** who will Specialize in All-Mineral Organic Gardening, who will Perform MILLIONS of Experiments on hundreds of thousands of Plantations. For Example, there are Variations of Carrot Seeds; but, there are also Variations of Climates, Different Kinds of Topsoils, and a thousand or more Varieties and Combinations of Powdered Rocks, which will Require Years of Experiments, just to Discover HOW the Grapes of Eshcol were Grown, which Required 2 Strong Men to Carry just one Cluster of Grapes on a 6-feet-long Staff, on their Shoulders! (See *Numbers 13:23—24.*) {FOOTNOTE: It is Interesting to Note that Spain grows about 3 Times more Grapes for making Wine, than the United States of America, and the People of Spain have less Heart Attacks and Strokes per capita. China produces about 3 million more metric Tons of Grapes than the U.S.A., which Brags that it "feeds the world," which is just another American Lie. Wine Grapes are about 24% Sugar by Weight, while Table Grapes are about 15% Sugar. 1 Wine Grape Vine can produce as much as 11 Tons of Grapes per Year; and the World Record is like 14 Tons, which makes them the most Productive of any "Fruit Tree," including Mangos, which might produce 5 Tons. The Trunk of a Grape Vine can be 8 inches or more in diameter, and the Vines 100+ feet long, reaching up into the Tops of Trees in Kentucky. Muscadine Wines are very Aromatic, and thus make the Finest of Wines, Juices, and Smoothies.}

12-03 [_] O Selected King, what makes you Vainly Imagine that Young People will be Interested in all such Gardening, seeing that most of them would rather be Murderous Soldiers, Sailors, Marines, and Airmen? Indeed, I would like to Drop Atomic Bombs on the Heads of Innocent Women and Children from 20,000 feet up in the Sky: so that I would not have to See any Dead Bodies, nor Radiated Flesh, which might be Peeling Off of their Bones. Yes, I could Fly over their Heads, and Smile at them, while Dropping Bombs on them; and I am NOT Insane! †§‡§§

12-04 [_] Well, before you get Enthusiastic about Terrorizing other People with your Hateful Bombs, you might want to Meditate on a little Verse from the *Bible,* which Jesus gave to us, saying: *"Do unto others as you would have others do unto you."* In other Words, would you Want other People Dropping Atomic Bombs, or any other Kinds of Bombs, on YOU? Of course not! So, why would you be Wanting to do such Hateful Things to them? Well, I will tell you why — it is beCause you are INSANE, or Demon Possessed! Otherwise, you could be Spoiled, in which Case you need your Ass Whipped with a Bull Whip in some Public Square or Ball Park. However, I know that you are only being Sarcastic, whereby you are making fun of all such Murderous Soldiers. †§‡

12-05 [_] O Selected King, would you have us to Close Down all of the Military Bases in the Whole World? Are you not Aware that our Great False Economy is Based on the Military Industrial Congressional Drug Cartel Bankers' Complex? Therefore, HOW could we ever give it up, just to Live in those **"Beautiful Swanky PALACES!" (A New Concept in Living Habits — Swanky Palaces for Poor People!) By The Worldwide People's Revolution!® Book 066?** †§‡

12-06 [_] Well, I would Think that you would find it rather easy to give up all such Foolishness, and take up some Musical Instrument to Play, after doing your Gardening, early in the Mornings, when the Weather is Cool, which will get your Blood Vessels and Muscles Pumped Up a bit, whereby you will Feel Better, all Day long. However, if you Doubt it, ask some Body Builder. ‡

12-07 [_] O Selected King, I much Prefer making Fine Hand-crafted Furniture, which I never get Tired of Looking at, nor Tired of Making. Therefore, will I have to do any Hateful Gardening?

12-08 [_] Well, a little Gardening for 15 to 20 Minutes per Day is not going to Hurt you. After all, you do like to Eat. Therefore, why not Learn to Enjoy the Gardening? After all, you have all Day to do your Furniture Making. Indeed, you will no longer be Under any Pressure to get more Money: beCause you will already be Moderately RICH, having your Stone Dome Home Complex to Live in, and your Well-made Tools to Work with, which will be Provided by **"The Swanky Association of Professional Tool Makers,"** who will Naturally Want to Produce the Best Tools in the World, which will Endure the Test of Time, whereby everyone will be Able to Accumulate much True Wealth, and only with an Average of 4 Hours of Common Skilled Labor per Day, 6 Days per Week, or the Equivalent therefore, according to whatever is Needed. For Example, if there is a Shortage of Hoes for Hoeing the Gardens, that Association can Concentrate on Producing more Hoes, until there is a Surplus Supply of them, which can be Found at all Tool Houses, for FREE: beCause no one is Sitting around Waiting for some Customer to Buy any such Tools, which is a Waste of that Person's Precious Time, which should be Spent Wisely, doing something Constructive and Useful for the Prosperity of the whole Community, if it is Needed. Otherwise, he could be in Bed with someone he Loves, who also Loves him, which might take the Meanness Out of him, if he has any. After all, a Lack of Love can be Blamed for an entire List of Evils, including Insanity! ‡

12-09 [_] O Selected King, with such an Easy Life, People are likely to become Fat and Lazy. Therefore, what is the Remedy for that Massive Problem, which now Plagues most of the Industrialized Nations? Moreover, when People have nothing Constructive to Do for at least 8 Hours per Day, their Minds Sink into the Sexual Sewage Systems of Babylon! Therefore, that does not seem to be very Good to me. †§‡

12-10 [_] Well, when a Person's Primary Food is a Sweet Juicy Fruit — such as a Fresh Tree-ripened Fig, Date, Peach, Pear, Mango, Banana, or Papaya — such a Person is not likely to get Fat, nor Lazy: because all such Fruits are Energizing, and Especially for Children, who get Full of Energy from Eating Fruits, who have to be Fed Greens of Various Kinds, just to Slow them down! Yes, I have done most of my Work, and even very Hard Work with Heavy Rocks, while Eating nothing but Sweet Fruits, or Fruit Juices, during the Mornings, followed by something more Substantial during the Evenings — such as a Good Swanky Potato Salad, made with Swanky Pickles, Avocadoes, Chopped Green Onions fresh from the Garden, Cucumbers, Lettuce, Olives, and a little Garlic. Raw Sweet Corn can also be added to such a Salad, if it is Ready in the Garden, as well as Sweet Bell Peppers, Mild Hot Peppers, Fennel, Cabbage, Celery, or whatever you like. After all, when you are Free, you can Grow and Eat whatever you like, just as long as it is Permissible within your Swanky Fortress. Therefore, be Sure to Check the Appropriate Boxes in **"The Complete SURVEYS of our VALUES!" (SURVEYS of Religious Spiritual Political Governmental Sexual Social Moral Economic Business Labor Habitual and Miscellaneous VALUES!) By The Worldwide People's Revolution!®** Book 059.

12-11 [_] O Elected King, there is a Multitude of Things that People can Entertain themselves with during their Spare Time — such as Swimming, Playing Tennis, Basketball, Baseball, Volleyball, Ice Skating, Roller Skating, Bowling, or Playing Chess; but, I Prefer to spend my Precious Time Wisely, reading Good Books, or Watching Educational Information on YouTube Videos. Indeed, no one must be Bored during their Time Off at a Swanky Fortress: because there are so many Things that a Person can Do — if only to Visit some Old People, who often have Interesting Stories to Tell, who also Need some Company, lest they should go Insane. For Example, you could Read an Inspired Book to them. Therefore, all such Children Need Encouragements, until they Discover whatever they might Like — such as Playing some Musical Instruments, or Writing their own Books. Indeed, let each Person Discover a Special Hobby — such as the Study of certain Wild Animals, since it is Possible to Work for 2 Months, Picking Fruits for 8 Hours per Day, and then take 2 Months Off to Study some Wild Animal on the Outside of their Swanky Fortress.

12-12 [_] Well, I Strongly Suggest that all Young People should Immerse themselves in a Serious Study of all of my Inspired Books, for at least 2 Years, whereby they might have something Good in their Heads to Think about for the Remainder of their Lives, which Information can be Refreshed in their Minds by a Daily Devotion of at least one Hour, early each Morning, after they are Well Rested, which will be the Routine at all Basic Training Camps for Voluntary and Involuntary Working Soldiers, just to get them into Good Habits and Good Moods. ‡

— Chapter 13 —

Will Medical Doctors be Happy with this Plan?

13-01 [_] O Elected King, if Medical Doctors get "Wind" of this Book, they will just Naturally become Chief Enemies: beCause, if People are Healthy and Happy, they will have no Use for their Drugs nor Lotions, Potions, Shots of Puss, and whatever they and their Coconspirators have for Sale at the Drug Stores. Indeed, it is just a Matter of Time when they will Discover such Truths as you Teach, and will Feel Threatened by all such Truths, even as it was for those Ancient Scribes and Pharisees at the Time of Christ. After all, no Wild Animals have any Use for their Drugs and MediSINZ, and have Lived in Good Health for thousands of Years without any such Drugs. Therefore, why would People Imagine that they would have to Consume hundreds of thousands of dollars-worth of Pills and Poisons, just to Maintain some semblance of "Health," which is never as Good as the Health of a Wild Mountain Sheep, for Example, who never Suffers with Indigestion, Colds, Flues, Diarrheas, Headaches, Legaches, Sore Throats, Whooping Cough, Gout, Arthritis, Heart Attacks, Strokes, nor Cancers — that is, unless they come into Contact with PEOPLE and their Cooked Foods, which are often Highly Processed, and Adulterated with Various Kinds of Chemicals, Preservatives, and Poisons — such as Nitrites and Nitrates in Processed Meats. Yes, just check out those Ingredient Labels on the Packages for Sale in a Gross Grocery Store, and you will See what I Mean. †§‡

13-02 [_] Well, I already Checked them Out of my own Life, several Decades Ago: beCause they are Capitalist Deceptions, which are Designed to get us Addicted, whereby the Capitalists can rake in a lot of Money from Ignorant Fools, who are not Aware of the Garden of Eden Story, where Satan Tempted Mother Eve with some Forbidden Food, which Symbolizes all Forbidden Foods, which are all of those Unnatural Food Stuffings, which never Satisfy the Soul. ‡

13-03 [_] O Selected King, I Propose that we bring all of those Capitalist Hogs to COURT, and make them Prove to us that their Products are Good for us to Eat and Drink, or else be put Out of Business. After all, if it were Necessary that we should Eat all such Things for Good Health, why would the Bald Eagles not be Eating them? Indeed, they Live for 120 Years or more without any such Abominations. Likewise, some Tortoises Live for as much as 400 Years on Grasses, Weeds, Fruits, and Seeds. Therefore, it is Possible that Adam Lived for 930 Years, just as the *Bible* states, even though it was probably only 93 Years. After all, Jews are well-known Exaggerators, who do not Object to Adding Zeros to Important Numbers — such as 600,000 Victims of the Holocaust, to which they Added a 0, and made it read 6,000,000, when there were never more than 600,000 Jews in all Nazi Concentration Camps, Combined. Yes, you can Discover that just by Looking at the Photographs of Auschwitz, Poland, which Shows the Barracks that they Stayed in, each of which contained a Maximum of 300 Bodies in the most Crowded Conditions. Therefore, 100 such Barracks would have had a Maximum of only 30,000 Bodies. †§‡

13-04 [_] Well, some very Well-Educated People say that the Jews just added a Zero to the 93 Years that Adam Actually Lived: beCause they like to Exaggerate almost everything, even as they added a Zero to the 600,000 Jews who Died during the so-called "Holocaust," which has now grown from 6 Million to 17 Million, even though there were only 19.5 Million Jews in the Whole World before the HoloHOAX; and, according to the World Almanac, there were 17.2 million Jews in 1949, 4 Years after the Second World War. Therefore, they must have Multiplied more Prolifically than Rabbits and Chickens, in order to Multiply that much during only 4 Years. In Fact, the Babies must have been having Babies. But, we Know for a Fact that such was not True, even as we also Know for a Fact that not even one Million Jews were Killed during the Holocaust: beCause the International Red Cross kept Accurate Records of every Death, being Stationed in each Concentration Camp, including Auschwitz, Poland. Indeed, they Reported some 189,000 Deaths, combined, in all of Europe. Therefore, the Holocaust Museum in Washington will have to be Updated, after we bring those Lying Red Jews to COURT! Yes, it is called: **"The Great Worldwide TELEVISED Court HEARING!"**, Book 041, which will Prove to be most Interesting: beCause the Federal Burden of Investigation (FBI), the Central Unintelligent Agencies (CIA), the Bureau of Alcoholic Tobacco and Firearms Fanatics (BATF), the Federal Emergency Mismanagement Agencies (FEMA), the Infernal Revenue Snakes (IRS), the Federal Communications Criminals (FCC), the Bad Foods and Good Drugs Administration (FDA), the DEPARTment of Agriculture, the DEPARTment of Homeland Insecurities (DHS), the DEPARTment of Trashy Houses and Bad Construction (DHC), the DEPARTment of Inhumane Services and Bad Healthcare (DHSH), and the DEPARTment of Immigration Scams (DoI) will be Relieved of their Duties: beCause no one will have any more Use for any of them after that Great Meeting of the Most Intelligent and Well-Educated Minds! †§‡§§

13-05 [_] O Selected King, if you had your Way, you would do Away with almost everyone in the Federal Government, except for the Departs of Communications and Transportations, which would be Totally Controlled by **"The New RIGHTEOUS One-World Government,"** which would Provide FREE Wide-screen Flat TV's, iPhones, iPads, and all other such Toys to whomever Joins: **"The Swanky Associations of Working Soldiers!" (A Fascinating Collection of Various Kinds of Voluntary Working Soldiers!)**, Book 018, who would also get to Live in those Extravagant and **"Beautiful Swanky PALACES,"** Book 066, which would have Churches, Cathedrals, Basilicas, Temples, Mosques, Synagogues, Sanctuaries, Theaters, Concert Halls, Gymnasiums, Auditoriums, Bowling Alleys, Tennis Courts, Indoor Heated Swimming Pools, Fish Ponds, all Kinds and Sizes of Aquariums, Waterfalls, Rivers of Living Water, Huge Cisterns for Water Storage, Half-dome Stone Wind Generators in Beautiful Arcades around the Tops of the Stone Terraced Walls around all Swanky Fortresses; plus Bat Houses, Honeybee Houses, hundreds of billions of Fruit Trees, Nut Trees, Berry Bushes, and Grape Vines; plus Countless All-Mineral Organic Vegetable Gardens, billions of Home-craft Workshop and Sales Shops; plus Museums, Ball Parks, and whatever People are Willing to Work for: beCause, you would have an Unlimited Amount of Credits to be Earned by Honest Labor, whereby each Person could Choose how much Work that he or she Wants to do, and thus Live a Better Life than King Solomon, himself! †§‡

13-06 [_] Well, I doubt that each Person could have as much Silver and Gold as King Solomon had; but, for Sure, we could Haul Out that Silver and Gold, which is now Stashed in the Bank Vaults of Rich Edomite Banksters, and use it Wisely for Decorating those Churches, Temples, Mosques, Synagogues, Cathedrals, Basilicas, Theaters, Auditoriums, Gymnasiums, Royal Swanky Buffets, Restaurants, and the Thrones for Elected Kings and Queens in their Swanky Palaces, which would have Zero Pollution from Stinking Lawnmowers, Weed-eaters, Noisy Motorcycles, Chainsaws, Snow Blowers, Leaf Blowers, Hedge Trimmers, Noisy Dusty Vacuum Cleaners, and other Abominations, including Toxic Paints: beCause Polished Marble Walls do not Require any

Painting. For Example, the Pantheon in Rome has never been Painted during the past 1,800+ Years, and it is still Looking Good! †§‡

13-07 [_] O Elected King, I must Confess that you do have a Sense of Humor: beCause the Chances of those Lying Edomites going along with your Master Plan is less than one in a Billion! In Fact, you will do well to Escape from being Assassinated by some Thug, who is short on Change. †§‡

13-08 [_] Well, all such Murderers will be Recycled through Africa, if not through Hell, itself. After all, if I were Guilty of any Great Crime, I should be brought to Court for it; but, having a Clean Record, my Enemies are left in a Perplexing Situation, whereby they must Rely on the Tactics of Satan, who was a Murderer from the Beginning, who Inspired Cain to Murder his Brother Abel, and for no Just Cause.

13-09 [_] So, O Selected King, could the Federal Government of **"The Divided States of United Lies"** not use some Secret Weapon to get Rid of you by Means of some Drone? Have they not already Murdered thousands of People in the Names of Freedom, Liberty, Democracy, and Justice for ALL? †§‡

13-10 [_] Well, it would be Difficult to say just how many millions of People that they have Murdered by one Means or another, ever since they began Murdering the American Indians. For Example, when they Dropped Cluster Bombs in Laos, Cambodia, and Vietnam, they did not take into Account the Fact that X-amount of Children would have their Eyes, Ears, Noses, Legs, and/or Arms BLOWN AWAY, whereby thousands of them are now Hobbling around without Legs, Feet, Hands, Eyes, or whatever: beCause those Cluster Bombs can lay around in the Ground for 60 Years or more, and finally EXPLODE when they get Moved — Thanks to Modern Technology. Moreover, they Dropped those Bombs without the Consent of any other Nations, and all in Secret, which the History Channel kept a Secret for some 40 Years, along with the Cruelties of the Communist Russians before and after World War 2, which should get them a Good Reward during God's Day of Judgment. They now Confess that Saint Joseph Stalin had more than 40 Million White Russian Christians Exterminated, which would Explain WHY **"The Divided States of United Lies,"** France, and Great Britain would Join him during World War 2: beCause he was the GOOD Guy, while Adolf Hitler was Supposedly the BAD Guy, even though they Struggled to Discover even ONE Bad Thing that he did before the War broke out. Otherwise, they could have Reported it in the American Snooze Papers. For Example, had Adolf Hitler made a Preemptive Attack on England: beCause of Suspicioning them of having Weapons of Mass Destruction, whereby more than a Million Innocent People were Killed, and more than 3 Million Displaced from their Homes — like George Warmonger Bush did in Iraq — they would have surely made it Headline News around the World. But, the Casualties of George Bush have never been Counted: beCause George was the "Good Guy," who did no Wrong, who kept Americans Safe for the next 7 Years, they say. Well, America was plenty Safe enough, until the Government False Flag Operation on September 11th, 2001, was carried out, which those Lying Edomite Bankers know all about: beCause their Headquarters was Located in World Trade Center Tower 7, which came Crashing Down in less than 7 Seconds at 5:20 p.m.; but, it Failed to make a Hole in the "Bathtub" that surrounded those World Trade Center Towers, which would have Caused the Hudson River to FLOOD the entire Area. Therefore, Towers 1, 2, and 7 were PULVERIZED and VAPORIZED by the Military Industrial Congressional Bankers' Complex, according to Dr. Judy Wood, who has YouTube Videos about it, which can easily be Proven to be True in a Courtroom, if anyone is

Interested enough to make a Big Issue over it, which every Honest American should be; but, most Americans are Spiritual COWARDS when it comes to Confessing the Sins of their False Federal Government. ‡

— Chapter 14 —

Justice Demands that
Uncle Sam should be Strip-Searched!

14-01 [_] When American Law-enforcement Officials Arrest some Suspected Criminal, they like to Strip-search him, and put their Fingers up his Rectum, and perhaps Kick him in his Testicles, behind Closed Doors: beCause they are the "Good Guys," much like George Warmonger Bush and Little Dick Chicanery, who did not Object to Water Boarding the Falsely Accused Victims of Capitalism in Guantanamo Bay, Cuba, who did not manage to come up with even ONE Conviction for any Crimes that they had Supposedly Committed, for which some of them Suffered for 14 Years, or more — Thanks to American "justice" without a Capital J, which is as Phony as the "Moon Landings" and the "Surprise Attack on Pearl Harbor," among many other Phony American False Flag Operations and Cover-ups, including the Kennedy Assassination Cover-up, whose Top Secret Files are still "a threat to our national security," they say. I wonder WHY? WHO was Behind the Assassination? WHO Orchestrated it? Was there a Jewish / Edomite Connection, since Jack Rubenstein was in on it? Was it the Holy Work of the Synagogue of Satan?

14-02 [_] O Selected King, it is for Sure that Lee Harvey Oswald did not Act Alone in the Kennedy Assassination, since he was just a PATSY, who was Falsely Accused of it, being the Perfect Person to Blame for it: beCause he had Lived in Russia at one Time, and had Married a Russian Woman, who still Claims that he was Innocent: beCause he WAS Innocent, which can be, should be, and must be Proven at: **"The Great Worldwide TELEVISED Court HEARING!"** Book 041. Yes, there is no Doubt about it: beCause Jack Ruby was NOT a Lover of President Kennedy by any Means: beCause he was a Cold-blooded Murderous Republican! Moreover, he supposedly Died with Cancer; but, I have Heard that he was taken from Prison to a Government Retirement Home, where he Lived for another 20+ Years! Moreover, I have also Heard that Timothy McVeigh is also Alive and Well in a Federal Government Secret Hideout: beCause he was Working for the Central Unintelligent Agency (CIA), which Orchestrated the Brokelahoma City Bombing, and then Pretended to Kill McVeigh by Lethal Injections, who got up and Walked Away, after being Removed from the Room: because he did not Die. Therefore, there is something really Strange going on in **"The Divided States of United Lies!"** †§‡ (See YouTube Videos for the Proof.)

14-03 [_] Well, it is for Sure that there are a LOT of Strange Things going on — such as Chemtrails or Chemical Trails in the Sky, which come out of Jet Airplanes, which leave long-lasting White Streaks in the Sky, which are NOT Contrails: beCause normal Contrails only last a few Minutes at most, while those Chemtrails hang around for Hours, if not all Day! Therefore, that is something that should be brought to Trial as soon as Possible: beCause it is said that they are Spraying Aluminum Oxide into our Atmosphere, which has Contaminated Rivers, Lakes, Forests, and Pasturelands all over the Country, up to 90,000 Times the Permissible Contamination Levels! Therefore, you might Ask yourself, WHO might be Behind all such Evil Actions? Well, of course, it would be the Synagogue of Satan at Work, who knows how BAD it is for People to Eat Aluminum, or to Drink it from Aluminum Cans, which is perfectly "Legal": beCause a Person does not Instantly DIE from Drinking a single *"Scant Measure that is Abominable,"* as the *Bible* puts it in *Micah 6:10.* Indeed, one might have to Drink the Contents of several thousand such Cans to Contract Alzheimer's Disease, whereby one cannot even Remember his or her own Children's Faces; but, you can be Sure that it is a Major SIN to Cook or Can anything in Aluminum, which has been Permissible for more than a hundred Years — Thanks to those Lying Edomites, who should be brought to COURT for it. †§‡

14-04 [_] O Selected King, it seems that almost everything for Sale is an Abomination, nowadays, including an Innocent Coke, which is mostly Sugar Water, as in 10 Teaspoons per Can, which Causes Headaches and other Health Problems among Sensitive People, whose Bowels are not full of FATS, which might Absorb some of all such Poisons, even as it is possible for Fat People to Drink more Alcohol than Skinny People, which Alcohol will Destroy their Livers. Therefore, it is Best to Eat and Drink at the same Time, beginning with just a Swallow or 2 of Booze, first, followed by Potato Chips or something Greasy, which will Help to Absorb the Alcohol, before it Immediately Floods the Liver with Toxic Poisons, which Causes Sclerosis of the Liver, whereby the Liver becomes HARD, or Pickled and cannot Perform its Normal Functions, which amount to more than 7,000 Different Processes. For Example, the Liver Produces Special Chemicals to Counteract the Poisons that we Eat by Combining Incompatible Foods — such as Flesh and Sweet Fruits, which Causes Putrefaction within the Bowels, which Produces those very Nasty-smelling Farts and Bowel Movements, which a Strict Fruit Eater does not Experience. Therefore, it is Best to Eat Fruits by themselves, alone, unless you Want to Suffer the Consequences of Dietary Sins. ‡

14-05 [_] Well, Life is a very Complicated Thing, and the Human Body is a Part of the Complications, which is so Complicated that no one has Totally Figured it Out: beCause just one Evil Thought can Totally Change a Person's Digestive System, and even Cause a Heart Attack, or Stroke! Therefore, it is Best to not Think Evil, nor Eat anything too late at Night, and especially any Heavy Difficult-to-Digest Foods — such as Meats, Eggs, Beans, and Nuts. However, those Things will Help you to Sleep Better, if you Want to be Drugged by them, which can be Enhanced by Eating some Raw Honey just before going to Bed, which is almost Guaranteed to "Knock you Out," as they say, and especially if the Honey was made from Plants / Trees that were Sprayed with Deadly Herbicides, Pesticides, and other Poisons, even as Capitalists might see Fitting for more Profits, being Free to do almost anything that they might Want to for the Sake of Ungodly Gain. Yes, it Reminds me of a so-called "Organic Avocado Orchard," which I Discovered in Mexico, which was so heavily Sprayed with Chemicals that the Ground was WHITE around the Trees, and the Leaves were Covered with it, which Naturally made me Want to Eat some of them. (They were being Shipped to German Health Food Stores.) Therefore, Buy such Foods at your own Risk, O Chancy Gambler. †§‡

14-06 [_] O Selected King, if you were in Charge of Things in this World of Woes, and some Swanky Fortress pulled off a Trick like that, and Sprayed all of the Organic Fruit Trees with something that came out of the Rectum of Capitalism, you would probably have those Evil People Boiled in HOT Used Motor Oil, huh?

14-07 [_] Well, I would Certainly have Government Inspectors going all about, just to Discover any such Lying Edomites: beCause, with a little Work, it is Possible to have Healthy Happy Fruit Trees by Means of: **"The LUSCIOUS All-Mineral Organic Method of Gardening!" (HOW to Grow DELICIOUS Satisfying Foods for Potential Kingz and Kweenz in Beautiful Swanky PALACES!)**, Book 021, which is a Companion Book of: **"Orgimmick Gardening at its Best!"** Book 079. See also: **"Did God or Satan Ordain Medical Doctors??" (Ask Huck Finn and/or Nigger Jim: because neither Tom Sawyer nor Judge Thatcher would Know!)**, Book 022. Moreover, I would Greatly Reward any Whistleblowers who might Report about the Snakes.

14-08 [_] O Selected King, if that is True, how come Organic Gardeners cannot Presently Produce all such Healthy Fruits?

14-09 [_] Well, that is beCAUSE of Acid Rains, which Weaken Trees of all Kinds, and make them Susceptible to Various Kinds of Diseases, which is another Sin of Capitalism, which those Lying Edomite Snooze Reporters do not Mention: beCause they are Capitalist Sons of Satan, who Live Inside of the Smelly Rectum of Capitalism, you might say! However, when we Build those **"GLORIOUS Swanky Hotels Castles and Fortresses,"** we will be able to Shut Off those Polluting Vehicles, and then most of the Acid Rains will STOP, and the Lands will be Blest, once again. Therefore, as Moses said, *"Be Sure that your Sins will be Found Out and Exposed."* — Numbers 32:23. Indeed, many books have been written about the Sins of Lying Edomites, and yet I have yet to Hear any Confessions: because the United States of American does no Wrongs, according to our Traditional Lies; and when we do any Wrongs, they are so Minor as to not be Worthy of more than Mentioning; and certainly not Worthy of tens of thousands of Hours of Confessions on the C-SPAN Network. {FOOTNOTE: C-SPAN Devoted no less than a Million Hours of its Time on 3 Channels to the Evil Events of September 11th, 2001, including Years of Radio Broadcasts concerning Terrorist Attacks, and Special Senatorial Hearings about Government Goof-ups and Remedies, which were often Repeated 24/7, with the Hope that Weak-minded Old Ladies might Worry themselves over those Terrorists, and thus Agree with Republican Warmongers, and not Feel at all Bad about Paying Taxes to Support the Military Industrial Congressional Drug Cartel Bankers' Complex, in spite of the Fact that more than 100,000,000 Times as many Americans have been Killed by Gang Wars, School Shootings, Drug Overdosing, Suicides, Government False Flag Operations, and Medical Mistreatments, which are seldom Mentioned on C-SPAN!} ‡

14-10 [_] O Selected King, I sure Hope to God that ALL of our Sins are Discovered and Exposed and Overcome: because I am getting Sick of being Sick! Yes, I have Suffered Long Enough for one Lifetime, and am now Ready and Willing to Move into one of those **"GLORIOUS Swanky Hotels Castles and Fortresses!" (Beautiful Planned City States for WISE Intelligent Well-Educated People with Common Sense and Good Understanding!)**, Book 019, which should be Mandatory Reading in all Public and Private Schools, Churches, Synagogues, Temples, Mosques, Cathedrals, Basilicas, Theaters, Auditoriums, Ball Parks, and wherever Crowds of People are Gathered for Rational Dialogs, including those TV Talk Shows, and Radio Talk Shows. However, I have no Power to Enforce any such Orders. ‡

— Chapter 15 —

HOW to get the Cooperation of the News Media

15-01 [_] Well, "there is more than one Way to Skin the Cat," as the old saying goes. In other words, if you could Transform Rocks into Pure Gold, and a whole Mountain of such Rocks, you would no doubt get the Attention of the News Media, as well as everyone else, which would be a very Unusual Way to "Skin the Cat," or even the Cow that Jumped Over the Moon; but, only the Great Creator God has the Power to Do such a Marvelous Thing, and he is not about to do it for People who are Totally Unworthy of it. †§‡

15-02 [_] O Selected King, if that Mountain of Gold were in **"The Divided States of United Lies,"** the Wicked Greedy Selfish Federal Government would CLAIM the Mountain, and put up a 100-feet-tall Solid Stone Wall around it, and Post Armed Guards every 20 feet around the Wall, and put up "No Trespassing" Signs every 10 feet, with a Warning that all Violators will be SHOT — even if Poor Old Ladies are Begging for just a Pinch of it at the Gate, whereby they might Pay their Medical Bills for one Week: beCause of not Studying our Selected King's Inspired Book, called: **"Did God or Satan Ordain Medical Doctors??" (Ask Hunk Finn and/or Nigger Jim: because neither Tom Sawyer nor Judge Thatcher would Know!)**, Book 022. †§‡

15-03 [_] Well, your Analysis of that Wicked Anti-Christ False Cover-up Federal Government is quite Accurate, except that if God did such a Miraculous Thing for our Selected King, that particular Mountain of Gold would not need any Wall nor Guards around it: beCause, whomever might be so Foolish as to Touch the Gold without Permission, would simply Die on the Spot! Moreover, whomever might Touch that Dead Person, within less than one Month, would also Die on the Spot. Therefore, given enough Time, and most People would Learn to OBEY the Man with the Spirit of Elijah! Indeed, if he said to JUMP, they would JUMP! Guaranteed. †§‡

15-04 [_] O Selected King, I would get myself a Backhoe, and Scoop into that Mountain of Gold, and get myself a large Bucket of it, and Drive Off with it, whereby I would be Obeying the Man with the Spirit of Elijah, according to the Letter of the Law: beCause I would not be Touching it with my Body. However, I would not be Obeying according to the Spirit of the Law: because, even though my Hands would not Touch it, the Backhoe would. †§‡§§

15-05 [_] And then, when you got to wherever you were going with it, WHO would Touch it? How could you make Use of it?

15-06 [_] Well, O Selected King, I would ask some Ignorant Person to Handle it, who was not Aware of the Dangers of it; and therefore, the Curse would not be on him: because of his Innocence, whereby God would have Mercy on him, even as he has had Mercy on all of the Innocent Children, ever since Adam, who have Died with Malaria. †‡§§

15-07 [_] Well, with that Kind of Benevolent Mercy, I would not Want to Experience his Wrath, would you?

15-08 [_] So, O Selected King, such a Fool would no doubt be Stricken Dead, sooner or later, for Touching that Gold, if it had a Curse on it. However, if no one can Touch that Mountain of Gold without Permission, WHO would be given Permission? After all, there is no Government on the Earth that could be Trusted with it: beCause they are all Corrupt. †‡

15-09 [_] Well, I say that they can all be Trusted, if the Curse Covers any Disobedience, Thievery, Robbery, or whatever. In other Words, each Country in the World could have a Mountain of Gold, if there were a lot of People to Earn it by Honest Labor — such as 60 Silver Dollars per Hour for Setting Polished Marble Tiles on a Solid Stone Wall within a Swanky Palace, which would Represent that New Money: beCause, if it is Possible to Transform a Mountain of Rocks into Pure Gold, it is also Possible to Transform 10 Mountains of Rocks into Pure Silver, whereby 10 Silver Dollars would Equal one Gold Dollar, which could be about as big as a normal Quarter of a Silver Dollar, whereby it would not be too Burdensome to Pack a hundred Gold Dollars around with you. After all, it is Heavy and Burdensome, if you have to Carry a lot of it.

15-10 [_] O Selected King, I Believe that you could get the Attention of the News Media with such a Magician's Act; but, I Seriously Doubt that you could get their Cooperation, whereby they might Publish whatever Truths can be Discovered in Good Books: beCause those Truths would put all of them Out of Business within a Day or 2: beCause most People would simply Join one of those **"Seven Great Armies of Working Soldiers,"** Book 015, and go to Work, Building those **"GLORIOUS Swanky Hotels Castles and Fortresses,"** Book 019: so as to Raise their Standard of Living by at least 100 Times! Therefore, the Snooze Media would mostly DIE OUT, and be taken over by Honest Journalists, who would only be Interested in Reporting TRUTHS and Important Information from there onward. Indeed, if it were Possible to Communicate the Truths within this one Inspired Book to the Masses of People, Worldwide, hardly anyone would pay any Attention to Politicians, Preachers, Propagandists, and Weekly Tabloids with Sensational Nonsense — such as "Elizabeth Taylor had Sex with a Bull Elephant," which is Pure Nonsense; or, "Little Green Men were Discovered on Mars," or, "Red Jew Bankers have Forgiven all Debts!" Otherwise, those Tabloids might read: "Uncle Sam has had a Change of Heart!" — followed by a Long Explanation about how Uncle Sam has Proposed an Amendment to the Constitution, stating that no more Edomites will have any Control over any Banks, including the Federal Non-reserve Bank (FRB), which is neither Federal nor a Reserve of any Kind: beCause it is a Private Edomite Bank, which Controls the Money Supply for **"The Divided States of United Lies,"** which is Supposed to be Regulated by the CONGRESS, according to our Constitution, which is also Supposed to Mint and Print and Regulate the Value of the Money, which Information has not been Deleted nor Overridden by any Means by other Amendments. After all, it is only Reasonable that our Money Supply should be under the Control of Elected Public Servants, who are Responsible to the Electors, which the Federal Reserve Bank is NOT; nor was it ever in the Control of Elected Officials! Nevertheless, on certain Occasions, the Chairman of the Federal Reserve Board gives a Special Speech about the Dealings of the Federal Reserve Bank to the Selected Members of Congress, who are always Edomites of the same Clan, which Speech is very similar to the Previous Speech, which is only slightly Modified: because it has been the same Carefully-Crafted Speech ever since 1913, which is Composed of Intellectual Non-comprehensible Financial Terms, which only those Edomites can Interpret: because no one else has any Idea what the Speech is all about. Indeed, you can Search for all such Speeches on the C-SPAN Network, and Listen Carefully to the Deceptive Words for yourself, and thus Understand what I am saying. †§‡

— Chapter 16 —

HOW to get the Whole Truth Published, for Free!

16-01 [_] Well, the First Line of Action is for us Work Slaves, Tax Slaves, Interest Slaves, Insurance Slaves, Drug Slaves, Debt Slaves, Sex Slaves, and Childcare Slaves to DEMAND: **"The Great Worldwide TELEVISED Court HEARING,"** Book 041, whereby we might Learn whatever the Whole Truth might be about any given Subjects — including what Happened on the Moon, if anything: beCause that is a Great Controversy among People who Study YouTube Videos about Moon Landings. {See *MoonHOAX* on the Internet, as well as *HoloHOAX* for the Truth about the Holocaust, which Links up with many Related Videos; plus www.AE911TRUTH.org which is Upheld by more than 3,000 Professional Architects and Engineers, who have a special Video, called: *Experts Speak Out,* which should be Mandatory Study by all CONgress People, who should be brought to Court for TREASON: beCause it is their Constitutional Duty to Investigate all such Terrorist Attacks by their own False-Flag-Waving Federal Government, which had much to do with the Evil Events of September 11th, 2001: beCause there was Military-grade THERMITE found at the World Trade Center Ruins in New Yuck City for all 3 Towers that Collapsed into DUST, which were mostly Vaporized! Indeed, a 110-story Building should leave no less than 20 Stories of RUBBLE in a Big Pile, rather than Pulverize a half-million Tons of Concrete and 90,000 Tons of Steel in each Building, leaving less than ONE Story of Rubble!}

16-02 [_] O Selected King, if what you say is True, it Means that the Federal Government was a Co-conspirator with Osama bin Laden! However, that is Unbelievable!

16-03 [_] Well, as Unbelievable as it might be, that does not Alter the Facts that we have been Presented with by the EVIDENCES at the Scenes of the "Crimes," which, in the Case of the so-called "Plane Crash" near Shanksville, Pennsylvania, did not even leave any Bodies, Blood, Guts, Teeth, Wedding Rings, Suitcases, Luggage, 6-ton Titanium Jet Engines, Cockpit, Fuselage, Tail Section, nor even ONE Seat for Evidence, which never Happened in any other Plane Crash in all of Aviation History, Worldwide! Therefore, if you Accept some False News Reports, you are an Extremely IGNORANT Credulous Person, who should Educate yourself! After all, I am NOT Lying to you; but, your Wicked Anti-Christ FALSE Cover-up Federal Government is most Certainly Lying to all of us, which can be, should be and must be Proven in a Courtroom, in Order to get JUSTICE for ALL! ‡ {See the Appendix in Chapter 22, which contains a Letter to Andrew Maloney, who is a Lawyer for the September 11th, 2001, Families who Survived it.}

16-04 [_] So, O Selected King, just Exactly WHO would Pay for Airing **"The Great Worldwide TELEVISED Court HEARING"**? After all, Television is one of the most Expensive Ways to Communicate, when Compared with Radios and Newspapers. A one-minute Ad = 1 million US$!

16-05 [_] Well, if you Good People Elect me to be your Leader, and put me in Charge of that Court as the Chief Judge, I will Negotiate with those Snooze Reporters, who will be given 2 Options to Choose from. 1) Publish the entire Court Hearing for FREE, Worldwide; or, 2) Be brought to Court yourselves for Advertising all Kinds of Drugs and Poisons and Junk that People never Needed, and should have never Consumed — such as those Cigarettes, Viagra, Whiskey, Cars, Peptoobizmuk, and a Host of Unnecessary Drugs. After all, the only Reason that such TV Networks ever Advertised any such Things was for Financial GAIN — NOT for the Good Health nor Happy Welfare of the Masses of Ignorant People. Therefore, they should be Sued for Advertising Addictive Things that Lowered the Standard of Living for Billions of People, who would have much rather been Moderately RICH, while Living in **"Beautiful Swanky PALACES,"** doing an Average of only 4 Hours of Common Skilled Labor per Day, or the Equivalent thereof for 6 Days per Week, for 300 Days per Year; or 8 Hours per Day every other Week, as in 1 On, 1 Off: beCause half or more of the Population is now sitting around doing nothing Constructive, who could be Working and Contributing to the Economic System, rather than being an Economic Burden on the Society, and a Drain on the Treasuries of all Nations. †§‡

16-06 [_] O Selected King, the Masses of People are like Herds of Bovines, such as the Wildebeests in Africa, who could all Decide to Turn Against those Lions and Laughing Hyenas, and Trample them under their Feets, if they could only make up their Minds to do so: beCause they Outnumber them a hundred to one! Likewise, the Masses of Working People could Unite themselves Against those Rich Hogs, and put them Out of Business, beginning with those False News Reporters, who can easily be Replaced with Honest Trustworthy People — such as yourself, who could be the Major News Anchor for all TV Networks — that is, unless People like Scott Pelley of CBS wants to Live in a Swanky Palace, and get no more than 40$ per Hour for his Services, even if his Gardeners are getting 50 to 60 dollars per Hour for their Services: beCause he would have an easier Job to Perform than those Gardeners. Otherwise, he could be "Put Out to Pasture" with those Wicked Politicians and Corrupted Lawyers, who could also Live in their Swanky Palaces, and be Contented with Foods and Clothing and whatever is Provided for them within those Palaces, or else be left to Starve to Death in Cities of Confusion — such as New Yuck City, which will become a Ghost Town within 10 Years! — that is, IF the Masses of People Wake Up and come to their Right Senses, and Elect YOU to be their Leader, or Righteous KING, who has Command over all of those News Networks, whose Servants may also Choose to Live in those Swanky Palaces, and be Contented with Foods and Clothing. After all, what Poor "Nigger Jim" would not be Happy to Live in the White House with Huck Finn and Tom Sawyer, and Enjoy all of the Free Services that the President is now Enjoying at Tax Slaves' Expenses? Indeed, there is likely not one Poor Person on this Earth, who would not be Happy to Trade Places with the President of the United States (POTUS), who now Wastes more than a Million Dollars per Day on White House Services! Yes, you might Wonder just Exactly HOW it could Cost a Million+ Dollars per Day, just to Maintain the White House, in Washington? Well, that is beCause a Mop Boy gets 50,000+$ per Year for Mopping the Floors, while a Secret Service Man gets no less than 80,000+$ per Year, just to stand around and do nothing, except to Watch Out for Lunatics who might Jump Over the Surrounding Fence, and run into the White House and SHOOT the President: beCause of being in Love with DUMBmocracy and Capitalism! Yes, there are more than 5,000 of those Secret Servicemen, who Collect no less than 400,000,000$ per Year for Presidential Security! However, if you were in Charge of **"The New RIGHTEOUS One-World Government!" (HOW to Establish a Righteous One-World Government without Going to WAR!) By The Worldwide People's Revolution!®**, Book 056, O Selected King, all of those Secret Servicemen would become little Organic Gardeners and Unimportant Mop Boys in **"Beautiful Swanky PALACES"**: beCause everyone, including those Mop Boys, would LOVE you to no end: beCause of getting to Live in those **"Beautiful Swanky PALACES!"** Book 066. Yes, it is True that not one of them would Rebel against your Master Plan: beCause they never had it so GOOD! †§‡

16-07 [_] O Selected King, do you not Understand that most People, and especially Americans, would not Want to Live in those UGLY Swanky PALACES with all of those UGLY Fruit Trees, which would be Dropping those Nasty Tree Leaves, Fruits and Nuts all over the Sidewalks; not to Mention those very UGLY Flower Gardens, Vegetable Gardens, Waterfalls, Rocky Creeks with Noisy Running Water, Marble-faced Workshops, Sales Shops, and UGLY Stone Dome Home Complexes with Polished Marble-faced Walls, with Fine Hand-crafted Furniture — such as one might Discover in some King's Palace in Europe, which would make all of those Poor Niggers SICK to their Stomachs, just to Think that they could have had all of those Good Things for all of their Lives, and been Eating like Kings and Queens at Royal Swanky Buffets within **"Beautiful Swanky PALACES!" (A New Concept in Living Habits — Swanky Palaces for Poor People!) By The Worldwide People's Revolution!®**, Book 066? For Example, the Poor Vietnamese are now getting 65 Cents per Hour for Minimum Wages, which no Americans could Compete with: beCause we can Barely Live on 15$ per Hour. Therefore, HOW could we Compete with People in Sewing Factories, who are Earning only 65 Cents per Hour for Sewing 10 Shirts together? Yes, you are a GLOBALIST, O Selected King, who Believes that everyone in the World should have EQUAL Wages for EQUAL Services, just to be Fair about their Wages. Therefore, if a Work Slave in Vietnam can Live on 65 Cents per Hour for Wages, and Work for only 10 Hours per Day, making no less than 100 Shirts, which sell for 10$ each, in **"The Divided States of United Lies,"** so can American Work Slaves do the same, and be Happy with their Wages, even if one Organic Mango Costs 4$: beCause $6.50 per Day will Buy one and a half Mangos, which might be Spoiled on the Inside by Organic Worms, which will leave them with 50 Cents to Pay for Rent in some little Room in the Attic of some Rich Edomite's Mansion, who is getting 500 Million Dollars per Year for his Services in an Air-conditioned Office in some Tower in New Yuck City, which you say is Inequitable and Unfair; but, it is the American Way of Righteousness. Yes, you are Welcome to get yourself a Good Education, and Earn even more Money as the Chief Executive Officer of Ford Motors or General ElecTrickery. Personally, I would be Contented to Live in a Pup Tent in some War Zone in the Middle East, and Eat F-Rations with Nigger Jim and Huck Finn, as Opposed to Living in any Swanky PALACE, whereby I might become Fat and Lazy. †§‡§§

16-08 [_] O Selected King, no American has a Right to Complain about his or her Wages: beCause everyone is Welcome to Borrow enough Money from some Bankster, in order to go to College and get a Good Education: so as to be Able to Properly Wash Dishes in some Greasy Restaurant, just to Pay Off that College Loan Debt, which might amount to 100,000$ or more, and especially if one does not become a GOOD Student, and thus have to Borrow more Money for getting a Better Education in some other Field of Endeavor — such as the Medical Industry, whereby a Doctor Knife can Charge 60,000$ for 15 Minutes of Work! Yes, that is what I call Fair Wages! Likewise, as a GOOD Lawyer, one might Legally Charge 20,000$ for one Hour of Work, seeing that the Secretary does most of that Paperwork for 16$ per Hour, and is Worried about HOW she is going to Pay her Endless Bills, while Sleeping in a Used Van in a Wal-mart Parking Lot. Once again, she is Welcome to attend some College, and become a Greedy Selfish Lawyer, herself, if she can Remember all of the Legal Details that are Necessary for becoming such a GOOD Trustworthy Lawyer, who Robs Old Weak Widow Ladies: so that she can Eat 1,000$ Meals with the Elite Class in Washington, District of Criminals, who have their Haunts and Hangouts in New Yuck City. Yes, there are presently some 100,000+ such Unemployed Lawyers. †§‡§§

16-09 [_] O Selected King, there comes a Time when the Rich People get too Rich, and the Poor People get too Poor, which Inspires a Great REVOLUTION, and even a Bloody Revolution, if the

Rich People do not Submit to Reason and Logic, which, in this Case, calls for: **"The Great Worldwide TELEVISED Court HEARING!" (That Great Meeting of the Most Intelligent and Well-Educated Minds!)**, Book 041, whereby the Whole Truth can be Discovered and Published, Worldwide, whereby the Masses of People can Decide for themselves just how much Longer they should go on Living in their Slums, Ghettos, Shanty Towns, Mud Huts, Firetrap Houses, and those UGLY Apartment Houses, which barely have enough Space to Turn Around in, which have none of the Amenities of those **"GLORIOUS Swanky Hotels Castles and Fortresses!" (Beautiful Planned City States for WISE Intelligent Well-Educated People with Common Sense and Good Understanding!)**, Book 019, which almost everyone in the World could be Living in, if they just had the FAITH to Join one of those **"Seven Great Armies of Working Soldiers!" (HOW to Provide a Way for Everyone to WORK: so as to Eliminate Poverty, Crimes, Drug Abuses, Prisons and Unnecessary Taxes!)**, Book 015, or at least one of: **"The Swanky Associations of Working Soldiers!" (A Fascinating Collection of Various Kinds of Voluntary Working Soldiers!)**, Book 018, who would only have to do an Average of 4 Hours of Common Skilled Labor per Day, once those Fortresses are Finished, whose Children would have even less Work to Perform, unless they Willingly Chose to do otherwise: beCause it is Possible to do as little as 2 Hours of Work per Day, once you are Set Up Properly for LIVING! Indeed, once those Swanky Palaces are Finished, the Masses of People would be Ready for: **"The END of CONFUSION!" (The Great CELEBRATION of the Magnificent Wedding of the Most Humble Honest Nations, and the Grand Year of JUBILEE!) By The Worldwide People's Revolution!®** Book 050. Therefore, I Propose that we Work Slaves, Tax Slaves, Interest Slaves, Debt Slaves, Drug Slaves, Insurance Slaves, Sex Slaves, and Childcare Slaves get our Acts Together, and Use our DUMBmocracy to Elect the Inspired Author of all such Exceptionally Good Books to be our Righteous KING! {See www.Amazon.com for: **"Are Americans the Most STUPID People who ever Lived?" (HOW Working People can PROSPER and Live in PEACE Under the Rulership of a RIGHTEOUS KING!)**, Book 047.}

16-10 [_] Well, rather than have another Bloody Revolution, it is Time for the Masses of People to go to Bed, come next April 21st, and Stay in Bed, until the Leaders of all Nations Submit to **"The Swanky Sword of Divine Truths,"** and thus DEMAND that Great Meeting of the Most Intelligent Minds, which might Require a Week or 2; but, even if it Requires a Month or 2, it is Okay: beCause, after X-amount of People STOP SHOPPING, the Businessmen will Wake Up and come to their Right Senses, and thus DEMAND: **"The Great Worldwide TELEVISED Court HEARING,"** even at their Expense, if need be: beCause, if they do not Cooperate with us, they will become BANKRUPTED! Yes, they will ALL go OUT of Business, if they do not Cooperate: beCause none of their Trash is Needed, much less Wanted. Indeed, most People Lived for thousands of Years without their Junk and Toys, which they can now do, once again — except that this Time, if they are Wise, they can have all of those Useful Toys in their Swanky Palaces, if they Want them, and only Top Quality Tools to Work with — such as the Best of Mercedes-Benz Bulldozers, Trackhoes, Cranes, Trains, and whatever is Needed for Building those **"GLORIOUS Swanky Hotels Castles and Fortresses!" (Beautiful Planned City States for WISE Intelligent Well-Educated People with Common Sense and Good Understanding!)**, Book 019, which have **"The Right Design for Living!" (A List of Great Advantages for Building Beautiful Planned City States!)**, Book 012, whereby all of our Massive Problems will be Solved! Yes, I am the Man with the Spirit of Elijah! Yes, I Know that it is Difficult to Believe, even for me: because I have never Sought any such Positions of Authority; but, the Great Creator God has Pressed me into it, even against my own Will; but, not without a Good Purpose, which is to Prepare the Way for the Second Coming of Jesus Christ. Therefore, let no one Despise those People whom God has Ordained, lest they should Discover themselves Despising the Almighty God, who has Power over their Spirits, who can Consign them to a Lower Order of Worlds, whereby they can be Tormented both Day and Night, forever and ever, until they Repent! Yes, he can do all such Things, even Reluctantly, just to Save their Souls by Means of Sufferings. {See: **"The Proper RULES for FASTING!" (The Complete Instruction Manual for True Repentance!) By The Worldwide People's Revolution!®** Book 046.}

— Chapter 17 —

Will Uncle Sam come to his Right Senses?

17-01 [_] Well, if Uncle Sam were an Actual Person, there would be some Hope for him to come to his Right Senses; but, since "he" only Represents a Great BEASTLY False Government, it is Extremely Doubtful: beCause it would Require a Change of many Minds and Hearts, who are now so PUFFED UP with Great Pride for being Members of "the greatest nation on earth," that their Spiritual Ears are Filled with the Wax of Unbelief.

17-02 [_] O Selected King, I was Thinking that your "Father," Adolf Hitler, had that same Problem, who Failed to Memorize that Proverb of King Solomon, who said that *"Pride comes before Destruction, and a Haughty Spirit before a Fall,"* if I Remember it Correctly.

17-03 [_] Well, you do Remember it Correctly, and it is found in *Proverbs 16:18,* which is Related to other Verses, which Reveal that it is much Better to be Humble and Honest in all Cases. After all, we did not Create ourselves, nor anyone else; and therefore, what Right do we have to be so Proud of ourselves? Indeed, we could have been Born in the Bodies of some of those Tucker Children, who do not know their Right Hands from their Left Hands, much less how to Speak Coherently.

17-04 [_] O Selected King, I Think that Uncle Sam should Appoint some Congressional Chaplin to Present a Daily Confession of America's Sins, in Joint Congressional Meetings of both Houses, just to Remind those Elected Representatives that we are only Human Beings, and NOT Gods. After all, the Greatest Person who ever Lived did not even Own a Pillow to rest his Head on at Night. (See *Matthew 8:20 and Luke 9:58.*)

17-05 [_] Well, Jesus Deliberately Sold his Houses, and Gave his Money to Poor People: so as to be a Good Example for his True Disciples to Follow, who were also Contented with Foods and Clothing: beCause they did not Preach the "Prosperity Gospel," as many Modern Preachers do, who completely Misunderstand *First Timothy 6,* for which you can Discover the New MAGNIFIED Version (NMV) in: **"For the Love of Money!" (The Strange Things that People Say and Do to Get more Money!)**, Book 003, which is most Enlightening to the Mind of any Honest Person.

17-06 [_] O Selected King, if a Person must Live like a Beggar, in order to be a True Christian, I have no Interest in it: because I am able to Earn a Good Living by Working for it. Indeed, I would rather Shovel an entire Dump Truck full of Sand, than to Beg even one Person for a Dollar: beCause it is Demeaning to my Character, and Hurts my Pride. After all, I have never been a Beggar. However, I must Confess that I am an Independent Jackass. {See www.Amazon.com for: **"The Loathsome Burdens of the Independent Jackasses!" (A New Approach for Solving our Massive Problems!)**, Book 051.}

17-07 [_] Well, it would all Depend on the Circumstances. For Example, if you were Helpless: because of having no Legs, you would have a Good Excuse for Begging. Nevertheless, I would not say that Jesus was a Beggar by any Means. In Fact, it is more likely that he would pitch in and Help someone to Build his House, rather than Beg for some of his Money. After all, Jesus was not Afraid of Hard Work. Moreover, the Apostle Paul walked for thousands of Miles as a Missionary, going from City to City in the Middle East, Preaching what he called the Gospel, which was quite Successful: because most of the known World around there eventually became "Christians," at least in Name. Chances are that they did their Best to be Christians, even as Modern Professing "Christians" do, who seldom go to such Extremes as Living like Paul, being Contented with Foods and Clothing, who was a Tent Maker. Therefore, he likely Lived in a Tent most of the Time. ‡

17-08 [_] O Selected King, do you Think that Jesus Intended that all People should become Ministers, like himself?

17-09 [_] No. I would say that he knew that there would be a Limited Amount of Believers, which did not bother him at all: because he only needs a few Good Men for his Good Future Government.

17-10 [_] O Selected King, I Wish to God that I had Hope of being in the Kingdom of God: because I much Prefer Telling other People what to Do, rather than Obeying other People, whom I find to be rather Stupid most of the Time.

— Chapter 18 —

WHO will become Leaders in the World to Come?

18-01 [_] *"For you see your Calling, Brothers, how that not many Wise Men after the Flesh, not many Mighty Men, not many Noble Men, are Called for Positions in the Kingdom of God; but, God has Chosen the Foolish Things of this World to Confound the so-called Wise Men; and God has Chosen the Weak Things of this World to Confound the Things that are Mighty; and Base Things of the World, and Things that are Despised, God has Chosen, yes, and Things that are not, to bring to nothing Things that are in Existence: so that no Flesh should Glory in his Presence. But, of him are you in Christ Jesus, who of God is made unto us Wisdom, Righteousness, Sanctification, and Redemption: so that, according as it is written, He who Glories, let him Glory in the Supreme Ruler."* — RKJV of First Corinthians 1:26—31.

18-02 [_] So, O· Selected King, that seems to Exclude you: because you Hold several World Records — such as the Most Prolific Inspired Author who ever Lived! ‡

18-03 [_] Well, that is fine with me: because I never did Want to Rule Over anyone else. However, at the same Time, I must Confess that the World, including all of the People, Animals, and Plants would be in a much Better Condition, IF everyone should Do as I Teach, and DEMAND **"The Great Worldwide Televised Court Hearing,"** and thus bring Confusion to an END.

18-04 [_] O Selected King, if it ever Happened, it would be a Glorious Event, which would make all other World Events PALE in Comparison: beCause, when were the Leaders of all Nations ever Forced to Submit to the Sword of Truths? Which one would Dare Reject your Master Plan, which is Acceptable among 99% of the People, beginning at 10 Years of Age? Indeed, if it were put to an International Vote, Today, you would without any Doubt Win the Election by an Overwhelming Majority — that is, IF all of the People should Learn just Exactly what your Master Plan IS for True Peace and Overpowering Prosperity.

18-05 [_] Well, that would Depend on whether or not those Masses of People got to Learn ALL that I have to Teach about ALL Important Subjects, which they would not all Agree with: beCause I do have some Strange Beliefs — such as the Father of Jesus Christ Living Inside of Jupiter, whose Name is Yohoovu, which is spelled "Funetiklee." Indeed, very few Professing "Christians" would Accept that Belief. However, my Religious and Spiritual Beliefs will not be a Stumbling Block for Righteous People, for the other "Truths" that I Teach, which concern Peace and Prosperity, which can easily be Proven in a Courtroom, while some of the Religious and Spiritual Things cannot be Proven in a Courtroom, nor should they have to be: beCause that is a Matter of FAITH, while Building a Good Strong Stone Wall is a Matter of Nolij and SKILL with the Correct Materials and Tools to Work with, which can only be Provided for all People in the World by the Assistance of: **"Seven Great Armies of Working Soldiers!" (HOW to Provide a Way for Everyone to WORK: so as to Eliminate Poverty, Crimes, Drug Abuses, Prisons and Unnecessary Taxes!)**, Book 015. Indeed, no Independent Jackass is Able to Build his or her own Private Swanky FORTRESS, including all of the Amenities that are Listed in Verse 00-32!

18-06 [_] O Selected King, I Think that the Best Leaders in the World are those People who have a Good Education, which Naturally includes those who have Biblical Foundations: because, knowing the *Bible* Well is more Important for Leadership than knowing whatever might be found in a Newspaper, which is Okay for Third-graders; but, not for Adults, who need more Spiritual Foods for Thoughts, and Spiritual Growth. Otherwise, they become Spiritual Babies, like Donald Jinks Trumpeter, who is Desperately in Need of Spiritual Foods. After all, the *Bible* has been around for thousands of Years: beCause of its Truths and Wisdom, which anyone can Discover by Reading it, which everyone should have to do at least one Time from Cover to Cover, and Hopefully in the New MAGNIFIED Version!

18-07 [_] Well, I, for one, have "red" the Bible from cover to cover more than 20 Times, and even have my own Versions of it: because most Hebrew and Greek Words have 1 to 100 or more Definitions for each Word, which Means that any given Sentence could rightly be Translated in Different Ways. However, the Holy Spirit knows what the Meanings should be; and therefore, I find it much Wiser to simply Listen to the Holy Spirit, who can and does Inspire me to write Better Words than those that are found in any Translation of the Bible! For Example, see: **"Thu Nq MAGNUFIID Verzhun uv Thu PROVERBZ uv KING SOLUMUN in Plaan Ingglish!" (The Understandable Version of the Famous Proverbs of King Solomon in Plain English!)**, Book 028. Yes, just make a Comparative Study of any other Version that you Like, and you will See what I Mean: because my Version is FAR Superior.

18-08 [_] O Selected King, your Version is NOT a Translation of any Version, much less a Translation of the Original Texts, which makes it an Abomination in the Eyes of the Gods: beCause it is an Invention of your own Mind, rather than a True Translation of the *Scriptures.* Therefore, you shall Burn forever in Hellfire, right next to your Evil Stepfather, the Devil, who was Incarnated in the Body of Adolf Hitler, himself! †§‡

18-09 [_] And now you are Blaspheming the Holy Spirit, who Inspired my New MAGNIFIED Version: beCause you are Misjudging it, and even Condemning me for Writing it, which puts you in Danger of Hellfire: beCause you did not Prove my Version to be WRong by any Means. Indeed, it can easily be Proven that my Versions are more Accurate than Standard Versions, including the Gay King James Version, which is full of Errors, which Inspired the other Versions, which are also full of Errors, and some are Worse than the King James Version! However, they are all Based on Defiled Books, you might say: because many Things were Added, and many Things were Detracted or Deleted from the Original Writings: beCause someone Judged that all such Words were Fictitious, which could have been the Case. After all, much of the Bible is a Fabrication of Lying Edomites — such as that Noah Story, which is a Great Exaggeration of the Facts: beCause of Reasons that have already been Pointed Out in many other Good Books — such as: **"What is WRong with those Professing Christians?" (A Self-Examination of the Heart of the Body of Good Government!) By The Worldwide People's Revolution!®** Book 002.

18-10 [_] O Selected King, a True Leader would never Criticize the *Holy Bible:* because that would make him Unpopular, and thus Rejected by the Electors, who would not even provide a Grave for him at the Arlington National Cemetery: because he would be a Dishonorable Person — such as Robert E. Lee, who should have been our Elected President in 1868. †§‡§§

— Chapter 19 —

An Honest Critique of Presidential Candidates

A Critique of the Bernie Sanders Campaign

{NOTE: These Critiques are in Alphabetical Order, as in Bernie, Donald, and Hillary, followed by other Leading Political Parties — such as the Libertarian Party and Constitutional Party. Of course, during the Future, the Names will Naturally Change; but, the Critiques will still Apply to some Degree, for Examples of what is WRong with those Political Parties, and WHY it is a Waste of Time, Money, Materials and Energy to Vote for any of them.}

19-01 [_] If you go to www.BernieSanders.com on the Internet, you can easily Discover his Solutions for the Important Issues of the Time, according to his Viewpoint, beginning with "Income and Wealth Inequality," which makes many Valid Points. Indeed, he begins with a False and very Misleading Statement, saying: "Today, we live in the richest country in the history of the world, ..." followed by a very Truthful Statement: "... but that reality means little because much of that wealth is controlled by a tiny handful of individuals." (One could easily write an entire Book about those Inequalities between the so-called "Rich People," and the so-called "Poor People" — none of whom are so Rich nor so Poor as they might Imagine. Indeed, those so-called "Rich People" do not even have Clean Fresh Air to Breathe, Pure Living Water to Drink, Wholesome Natural Foods to Eat, much less Secure Houses to Live in, whereby they might Claim to be somewhat Richer than Jesus Christ, who Presently Lives in a Swanky Palace, such as they cannot Imagine.) {See www.Amazon.com for: **"The Secret City of the Great King!" (HOW the True Church will Escape from the Great Tribulation!)**, Book 042.}

19-02 [_] Americans in general, including Senator Bernie Sanders, Suffer with a Superiority Complex, whereby they Vainly Imagine that they are the Richest People on the Earth, and that the United States of America is the Richest Nation on the Earth, in spite of being 120 Trillion dollars in Debt to Edomite Bankers! (See *PBS* for Bill Moyer's Explanation of it, who Claims that the National Debt is more like 140 Trillion Dollars! And that was 20+ Years Ago!) In other Words, it is a Great FALSE Economy, which has been DEBUNKED among Educated People! Therefore, no Politician should use such a Misleading Statement as Bernie used: because Children are likely to Learn the Whole Truth about it, and come to Despise him for saying it. {See the above Link for: **"The Great False Economy is now DEBUNKED!" (Adolf Hitler had a much Better Economic System!) By The Worldwide People's Revolution!®** Book 053. NOTE: Even though Bernie has now Dropped Out of the Political Race to the Little White Outhouse in Washington, District of Criminals, his Website provides a Good Platform to Build my Case on, which will be True for all Election Deceptions to come.}

19-03 [_] O Selected King, what Bernie says next is the Truth — "The issue of wealth and income inequality is the great moral issue of our time, it is the great economic issue of our time, and it is the great political issue of our time." Yes, from God's Heavenly Viewpoint, looking down at the entire World with Honest Eyes, Ears, Nostrils, and Taste Buds, he can See 7 Billion People Living in their States of Extreme Poverty, who do not have Fresh Clean Air to Breathe, Pure Living Water to Drink, Wholesome Natural Foods to Eat, nor Secure Houses to Live in, much less Secure Swanky FORTRESSES, which have 5,000+ Advantages over Normal Cities of Confusion. {See www.Amazon.com for: **"The Right Design for Living!" (A List of Great Advantages for Building Beautiful Planned City States!) By The Worldwide People's Revolution!®**, Book 012, plus: **"Poverty Hunger Riots Strikes Brutalities Election Deceptions and Civil Wars!" (The High Price that we Earthlings have Paid for Leaving the Good Land!)**, Book 014.}

19-04 [_] Well, you might have Noticed that none of the Presidential Candidates have even Mentioned the States of Poverty that other People in the World are now Living in: beCause they all have a Sorry Attitude toward all other Nations, being Nationalists: beCause of being all PUFFED UP with Great Pride in America — the so-called Land of the Free and Home of the Tax Slaves, which is Actually the Land of the Tax Slaves and the Home of the Self-Deceived IDIOTS, who are Exactly as Jesus Christ Described them in *Revelation 3:17.*

19-05 [_] O Unelected King, if you do not Learn to Flatter Americans, you are unlikely to be Elected by them.

19-06 [_] Well, to be frankly Honest with you, I do not Expect to be Elected by them: because I perceive that most of them will be Radioactive Dust, if they Reject the Great Truths that I Teach. Therefore, it will be Impossible for them to Vote for anyone, if they do not Exist. However, there is the Possibility that the Russians and Chinese will have Mercy on us, and Restrain themselves from Attacking us, just to Lower our Pride. After all, it could Result with the Extinction of most of Mankind, including themselves, which would not be a very Happy Song to Sing, nor to even Play on the Bagpipes at Capitalist Funerals: because no one would have enough Wind to Fill Up the Imitation Goatskins. †§‡

19-07 [_] O Selected King, I like the Quotation from Pope Francis on Bernie's Website. So, how come Bernie does not reach Out to the Whole World with a Proper Economic Plan? Is he Afraid to Address the World Economic Crisis, at large? Indeed, Jesus Christ was a GLOBALIST, not a Nationalist: beCause he Cared for ALL People, and especially for the Children who Died will Malaria, which he Created, according to certain Professing "Christians," who likely have no Idea what they are Talking about. †§‡§§ (See *Matthew 15:24; and John 1:1—3.*)

19-08 [_] Well, I would say that all of the Potential Presidential Candidates have been Afraid to Address the World Economic Crisis: beCause, when you Study the World Situation as a Whole Unit, GLOBALLY, as a Single Body in a Doctor's Office, you might say, it is very SICK from the Head to the Toes, having a Diseased Heart, Abscesses on both of the Brains, a Malfunctioning Liver, Failing Kidneys, and Cancer of the Lower Bowels. Indeed, there are certain Parts of that Body that are still Functioning; but, for the most Part, it is Extremely SICK and Diseased, which is Horrifying to Think about it, which is WHY most People Choose to Ignore it, with the Hope that it will all just go Away, and never be Remembered again by anyone. Yes, even Jesus Christ Ignored it, saying: *"For ye have the poor always with you; ..."* which is Suggesting to some very Ignorant and Superstitious People that it is Impossible to be otherwise, which Contradicts *Deuteronomy 15:4—6.* See *Matthew 26:11, KJV.*

19-09 [_] So, O Selected King, if you had your Way, almost everyone in the World would become Moderately RICH, and would have their own Luscious All-Mineral Organic Gardens, Vineyards, and Orchards, plus Beautiful Stone Dome Homes with Polished Marble Walls, Granite-faced Floors, Home-craft Workshops, Sales Shops, Indoor Swimming Pools, Tennis Courts, Gymnasiums, Bowling Alleys, Ice-skating Rinks, Dance Halls, Royal Swanky Buffets, Churches, Cathedrals, Synagogues, Mosques, Temples, and whatever they are Willing to Work for, huh?

19-10 [_] Yes, if I had my Way, there would be no Lack of Money for doing any Good Thing by Means of Solar Power, Wind Power, Water Power, and Muscle Power. After all, Young People Need lots of Moderate Exercise, just to be Healthy, Wealthy, and Wise, while also Feeling Good about themselves for their Great Accomplishments, who could Accomplish Greater Things than any other People since Ancient Times have Accomplished: beCause of having Professional Tools to Work with, whereby they can Transform those Ugly Mountains of Rocks into Gorgeous Polished Stone Dome Home Complexes within **"Beautiful Swanky PALACES!" (A New Concept in Living Habits — Swanky Palaces for Poor People!)**, Book 066, which are also Explained in: **"The Environmentalists' Paradise!" (HOW almost Everyone could be Living in a Beautiful Manmade Paradise!)**, Book 035. Yes, that would Close the Gap between the so-called "Rich" People, and the so-called "Poor" People, who are ALL Extremely POOR, and so Poor with a Capital P that most of them do not even Realize just how Poor and Miserable that they are! Indeed, Truly Healthy and Happy People are LEAPING and JUMPING for JOY, much like those Wild Kid Mountain Goats, who do not Suffer with Aches nor Pains, who do not Consume any Pills, nor Pay any Bills: beCause they are Free with a Capital F, who can Jump Up as much as 20 feet from any given Standing Point! ‡

19-11 [_] God have Mercy on us, O Selected King, are you Sure about that? Do Truly Rich People go about Jumping and LEAPING for JOY! Is that what Attracted so many People to Jesus Christ and his Disciples? Indeed, he said, *"The Thief comes not, except to Steal, and the Robber comes not, except to Rob you; but, I am Come so that you might have Good Health, and have it more Abundantly, which is the Beginning of True Happiness and Eternal Life, which is to Know God, who is All that is Good!"* — The New MAGNIFIED Version (NMV) of John 10:10. In other Words, those Political Thieves have come to Steal from us, and those Medical Doctors have come to Rob us of Trillions of Dollars: beCause their Symbol on their Doors is 2 Poisonous Snakes Kissing each other, while Wrapped around a Sword; but, Jesus Christ came to Teach to us how to Live an Abundant Life, which begins with Good Health, which is True Wealth, which makes it Possible for us to Obtain all of the other True Riches, including those **"GLORIOUS Swanky Hotels Castles and Fortresses!" (Beautiful Planned City States for WISE Intelligent Well-Educated People with Common Sense and Good Understanding!)**, Book 019, which should be Mandatory Reading in all Public Schools, Worldwide!

19-12 [_] Bernie Sanders states on his Website, quote: "Despite huge advancements in technology and productivity, millions of Americans {should be Billions of Earthlings} are working longer hours for lower wages {than they used to get}. The real median income of most workers is $783 less than it was 42 years ago; while the real median income of female workers is over $1,300 less than it was in 2007. That is unacceptable and that has got to change." Unquote. Yes, he has Repeated that same Message in hundreds of Political Pep Talks around **The Divided States of United Lies,"** whereby he has Gained a Substantial Following of several Million Enthusiastic People; but, not even one Quarter of Americans: because many of them Brand him as "a

Communist, who took his Honeymoon in Moscow, when he should have taken it on the Island of Lesbians and Homosexuals with Barrack Insane Obama, after getting ObamaScare Medicare," as one Anti-Sanders Slanderer Proclaimed to his Republican Inmates during a Drunken Barroom Brawl in SINsinatee, OoHIILoo, which is just across the River of Filthiness from 3-Mile Island, which Barely Escaped from another Chernobyl Catastrophe, which would have made America "the Greatest Nation on the Earth," just after Russia, which used to Brag about its Greatness, also. Yes, it was the First Nation to put a Man into Outer Space, and to Prove that not even Dogs can Withstand the Van Allen Radiation Belts, which have well over 4,000 Times as much Radiation as a Normal X-ray, which only lasts for a Second or 2, while the AstroNAUGHTIES supposedly spent 4 whole Hours in 900+rems (Roentgen Equivalent in Man) of Radiation, during the MoonHOAX! (A normal X-ray is a Millirem of Radiation, or one-thousandth Part of 1 rem. See *Wikipedia* for the Details.) So, what were the Chances of any Astronaut Surviving such a HUGE Dose of Radiation on the Way to the Moon, and back again? Answer: ZILCH! †§‡§§

19-13 [_] O Selected King, I Love your Sarcasms! However, getting back to Bernie Sander's Issues, I find it Interesting that a Socialist Country, like Norway, has a 5.3% Child Poverty Rate, while a Developed Capitalist Country, like the Great United States of America, has a 32.2% Child Poverty Rate, and an Undeveloped Democratic Country, like India, has a 63.4% Child Poverty Rate, and the Republic of the Congo has an 87% Child Poverty Rate, while Bangladesh has a 95% Child Poverty Rate, and the Irreverent LOUDMOUTH Sloth-gut Windbag Hole-in-his-Head never even Mentioned HOW to Raise their Standards of Living by Establishing **"The New RIGHTEOUS One-World Government,"** which has an Unlimited Amount of New Money, which must be Earned by Honest Labor during the Construction of those **"GLORIOUS Swanky Hotels Castles and Fortresses,"** whereby NONE of those People would be Living in a State of Poverty from then onward and forevermore: beCause, HOW could anyone be Poor while Living in a Swanky PALACE!?

19-14 [_] Well, they could be Mentally Poor, Spiritually Poor, and Physically Poor, if they did not have the Correct Books to Study, and the Correct Foods to Eat and Drink, and the Necessary Exercises of their Muscles. Yes, they could be Extremely POOR without having a Personal Relationship with Jesus Christ, who was the Richest Person who ever Lived! Moreover, I must Correct your use of "Country" instead of "Nation." For Example, you should have said, "However, getting back to the Bernie Sander's Issues, I find it Interesting that a Socialist Nation, like Norway, has a 5.3% Child Poverty Rate" — which is Actually even Lower than that, if all of the Facts are Considered: beCause Norway is not 120 Trillion Dollars in Debt, which puts the other 67.8% of American Children in the Child Poverty Category: beCause each of them are Burdened with those DEBTS, while the Children of Norway are NOT! Therefore, we can Honestly say that American Children are CURSED with Edomite Debts, which are Impossible for them to Pay Off, which could simply be Forgiven, if those Edomites were Honest White Jews like Jesus Christ, who would have Wiped Out all such Debts a Long Time Ago, if he had been in Charge of Things around here on the Good Earth. ‡

19-15 [_] O Selected King, Bernie says, "There is something profoundly wrong when one family {speaking of the Walton Family in Bentonville, Arkansas} owns more wealth than the bottom 130 million Americans." Awe, the Establishment of **"The CONSTITUTION for the New RIGHTEOUS One-World GovernMINT"** would Transform that Sick Song into a Great Year of JUBILEE! {See www.Amazon.com for Book 016.} Bernie goes on to say: "The reality is that for the past 40 years, Wall Street and the billionaire class has rigged the rules to redistribute wealth and income to the wealthiest and most powerful people of this country." So, just Exactly WHO are those People? Answer: They are Lying Edomites, and Red Jew Sympathizers, which can be Proven in a Courtroom. However, being an Honest White Jew, Bernie Sanders does not want to Offend the Zionists, lest they should have him Assassinated by one Means or another. However, in the Future, it will not be a Political "Sin" to Refer to Lying Edomites for what they are, who can be Identified by their Red Ears in our Courtrooms.

19-16 [_] Bernie Warns those Lying Edomites, saying: 'This campaign is sending a message to the billionaire class: "you can't have it all." You can't get huge tax breaks while children in this country go hungry. You can't continue sending our jobs to China while millions are looking for work. You can't hide your profits in the Cayman Islands and other tax havens, while there are massive unmet needs on every {street} corner of this nation. Your greed has got to end. You cannot take advantage of all {of} the benefits of America, if you refuse to accept your responsibilities as Americans.' Really? Just Exactly WHAT ARE those Responsibilities, seeing that our Constitution does not "Lay down the Law" concerning any such Responsibilities? In Fact, after reading the entire Constitution, I did not Discover any Citizen Responsibilities. Indeed, it does not even say, *"You shall not Murder, you shall not Commit Adultery, you shall not Steal, you shall not Lie, you shall not Lust after Things that do not Belong to you,"* much less, *"You shall not have any other Gods or Rulers above the Creator God, whose Name is YOHOOVU!"* In Fact, the Constitution Sorely Lacks any Civilian Mandates at all — as if it were just Understood that everyone was a Professing Christian, who Loved and Obeyed all of the Divine Laws of the Master Farmer, by Nature, and did not Need to Study any *Scriptures* at all! Indeed, the Constitution does not even Mention the *Ten Commandments,* much less the Teachings of Jesus Christ about Loving our Naaberz as much as we Love ourselves, whereby those Lying Edomites would have to Change their Ways of Thinking. After all, Capitalism is an EVIL Economic System that is the Exact OPPOSITE of Christianity, which Teaches us to *"Do unto others as we would have others do unto us,"* which Excludes the Sale of Drugs to Ignorant Children, who might get Addicted to them. Indeed, would YOU Want to become a Drug Addict at 10 Years of Age, and thus Waste most of your Life Paying for such Drugs? Of course not! So, WHY would you Want to Sell any such Drugs to other People, Knowing that they might become Addicted to them, whereby they would become Drug Slaves? {See www.Amazon.com for: **"The Nature of Capitalism!" (A List of the EVILS of CAPITALISM!) By The Worldwide People's Revolution!®**, Book 038.}

19-17 [_] Just Think, O Selected King, how Quickly Wall Street Greed would End, if we Used our DUMBmocracy to Elect YOU to be our Righteous KING! Yes, Wall Street would become one of those Deserted Desolate Habitations for Bats and Owls, Snakes and Skunks, Rats and Mice: because, WHO would have any Use for all such Worthless Buildings, after Considering the High Costs of Heating and Cooling them? Moreover, the Subways of New Yuck City would become Habitations for Criminals and Drug Addicts: beCause the Righteous People would simply Forsake all such Cities of Confusion, and Move into those **"Beautiful Swanky PALACES!" (A New Concept in Living Habits — Swanky Palaces for Poor People!) By The Worldwide People's Revolution!®**, Book 066. Moreover, the Tax Slavery System would also DIE, along with the Interest Slavery, Drug Slavery, Sex Slavery, Insurance Slavery, and Work Slavery: beCause no one would Buy their Worthless Merchandise anymore, just as it is Revealed in *the Book of Revelation!* (See Chapters 17—20.)

19-18 [_] Well, like most of the *Bible, the Book of Revelation* has many Interpretations, and some of them are more Confusing than the Book, itself. However, the Great Question is this: "WHY did the *Holy Bible* not give to us Reasonable Solutions for our Massive Problems?" Why does it not Mention those **"GLORIOUS Swanky Hotels Castles and Fortresses"**? Well, that was beCause God did not Want most People to Learn HOW to Live, until NOW: so that he might Test their Spirits, in Order to Discover whether or not they are Worthy to Govern with him within his Holy Kingdom. Indeed, all of the Honest People, who Accept the Great Truths that I Teach, are Worthy to Govern with Jesus Christ in his Holy Kingdom, while the others are not: beCause they are Rejecters of Truths without Justified Causes. †‡

19-19 [_] As President, Senator Bernie Sanders plans on Collecting Taxes from the Rich People for Supporting the Poor People, which is a Typical Socialist "Attack" on the Rich People, who are not all that Happy to Listen to him, who do not like the Sound of "the State Board of Monetary Equalization." Yes, it Sounds like Communism to them. However, when our Selected King takes over this World, some of those so-called "Rich" People will be Wishing that they had not been so Greedy, whereby they Inspired X-amount of Socialist Enemies, among whom is Bernie Sanders, who would Raise the Minimum Wages to 15$ per Hour, beginning in AD 2020. Why not in 2017? Why let Poor People Suffer for another 3 Years, when millions of them are now Living in Old Cars, Vans, Pickup Trucks, Buses, and Abandoned Houses? Why not Immediately form **"Seven Great Armies of Working Soldiers,"** who can Immediately get to Work, Constructing those **"GLORIOUS Swanky Hotels Castles and Fortresses"**? Well, perhaps it is beCause he is also Working for those Lying Edomite Banksters? Yes, he only has a Different Approach to Fleecing the Ignorant Sheeps and Goats, who know nothing about **"The CONSTITUTION for the New RIGHTEOUS One-World GovernMINT!" (HOW all Peoples can get True Justice, and Celebrate the Great Year of JUBILEE!) By The Worldwide People's Revolution!®**, Book 016.

19-20 [_] Bernie plans on Repairing the Highways, Bridges, Railways, Airports, Public Transit Systems, Ports, Dams, Wastewater Plants, Sewage Systems, Waterlines, and other Infrastructure "needs," as if that Trillion Dollars would be Wisely Spent, seeing that it will not be long before all Cities of Confusion will be Forsaken! Yes, the Righteous People will Abandon them, and move into those Glorious Swanky Fortresses: beCause of having more than 5,000 Advantages! Therefore, why Waste any more Time, Money, Materials, nor Energy on all such TRASH Repairs? Why Rebuild any Wooden / Plastic Firetrap Mouse-infested Cockroach Dens, when it is Possible and most Practical to Build Secure Swanky Stone Dome Home Complexes, which are Fireproof, Mouse-proof, Termite-proof, Hail-proof, Rot-proof, Paint-proof, Tornado-proof, Hurricane-proof, Self-air-conditioned, and Insurance-proof, which will Save us tens of Trillions of Dollars over the Years, which would otherwise be Wasted on Worthless and Endless Repairs? ‡

19-21 [_] Bernie plans on Reversing Trade Policies, like NAFTA (North American Free Trade Agreement), CAFTA (Central America Free Trade Agreement), and PNTR (Permanent Normal Trade Relations) with China, which have Driven Down Wages in America, and Caused the Loss of Millions of Boring Jobs, under the Administration of Allan Greenspandex (another Lying Edomite), who was Awarded the Presidential Medal of Freedom by President George Warmonger Bush, Junior. Bernie says that if American Corporations want us to Buy their Products, they will have to Produce them in America. Well, what about the Poor Chinese Slaves, who also need Good Wages? Does Bernie not have any Encouraging Words for them? NO, he is NOT a Globalist!

Indeed, he Judges that only Americans are Worthy of 15$ per Hour for Minimum Wages. Why not have the same Wages for those Chinese: so that a Pair of Shoes, which normally Cost $49.99, will Cost 149.99 phony dollars, in America? Indeed, they are not even Worth $9.99, let alone $49.99, which is an Edomite Price Tag, which should be rounded off to 50$ by the LAW, including all Taxes: because we have Suffered with enough Edomite Deceptions. Yes, Honest White Israelites, like Jesus Christ, would round off the Price at 40$, if it Doubled the Costs of Expenses to Produce them. Therefore, those 10$ Shirts that are Produced by $.065 worth of Labor, would Sell for only $2.06: because that would Cover the Costs, and also put some Profit into the Pockets of the Snoopervisors of Super Small-mart. ‡

19-22 [_] Bernie plans on Investing 5.5 billion dollars in Youth Jobs Programs, while I would Invest no less than 555 Trillion Dollars in **"The Swanky Associations of Working Soldiers,"** much of which would be used for making Proper Tools for them to Work with, if they were Able to Earn that much Money at 60$ per Hour for Skilled Common Labor, Tax-free, during the next 30 Years, whereby we would have no less than 2 Million large Beautiful Swanky Fortresses to Brag about, and also Thank God for: beCause of Sharing his Mountains of Rocks with whomever is Willing and Able to Learn and Work. †§‡

19-23 [_] Bernie finds it an Outrage that Women earn 78 Cents for every Dollar that a Man might Earn, while doing the same amount of Work. For Example, when I went to Work in my Dad's Slaughterhouse at the Age of 14, I Replaced 3 Women at the Meat Wrapping Table: beCause I was Faster than all 3 of them put together. Indeed, they were Earning 1$ per Hour, while I Earned 25 Cents per Hour for the next 4 Years, which Money was put into a Savings Account for me, which my younger brother borrowed and never returned: because he Learned it from the Public School of Ignorant Fools, who Failed to Teach to him **"The Seven Basic Spiritual Building Blocks of LIFE!" (Faith Hope Trust Love Patience Persistence and Obedience!)**, Book 036. Yes, I Escaped by Joining the Army, which paid me 11 Cents per Hour, and put me in Danger of being Killed in Vietnam! And they call that "Freedom, Liberty, and Justice for ALL!" †§‡

19-24 [_] Bernie plans on making Tuition "Free of Charge" at Public Colleges and Universities throughout America: beCause, when you are Born and Raised in a Swanky Palace, you Naturally have to Worry about HOW you are going to Earn a Living in some Capitalist Factory, or in some Greasy Hamburger Shop, or Washing Dishes in a Restaurant: beCause the Palace would Naturally not have any Gardens, whereby the Children might Feed themselves — that is, if it were Designed by Allan Greenspandex, Ben Bersnanke, and Janet Jello Yellen — all of whom have given a Revised Version of the same Sick Edomite Speech ever since 1913, after Meeting on Jekyll Island with the Chief Edomite Banksters, who Tricked President Woodrow Wilson into Signing Legislation to make Future Americans into Usury Slaves by Establishing the Federal Reserve Bank, which is a Private Bank, which is Owned and Operated by Lying Edomites, which now Collects no less than 500 Billion Dollars per Year for Interest on their Loans to **"The Divided States of United Lies,"** and without Moving more Weight than their Ink Pens, which many Americans Believe is GOOD! †§‡§§ (See *Wikipedia* for the Complete Details.)

19-25 [_] Bernie plans on Expanding Social Security Payments by Lifting the Cap on Taxable Income above 250,000$; but, I plan on Retiring all Old People, Worldwide, in Swanky Palaces, where they can Play Pool, Swim, Dance, or just Watch Nature Programs on TV, if they Want to. Otherwise, they could Attend Church Services or Swanky Fasting Sanitariums, whereby they might be Regenerated. {See www.Amazon.com for: **"HOW to Become a HOLY Man!"** (40 **Good Reasons WHY People Should FAST and PRAY!**), Book 045, plus: **"The Proper RULES for FASTING!"** (**The Complete Instruction Manual for True Repentance!**), Book 046, which is Greatly Enhanced by: **"The Gospel According to our Elected King!"** (**The Good News from the Most Modern Perspective!**), Book 077.}

19-26 [_] Bernie plans on providing Universal Health Care for all American Citizens, according to the Single-payer Healthcare System, which is to say that no Luscious All-Mineral Organic Gardens will be Planted for anyone's Good Health; but, everyone will have an Abundance of Edomite Drugs to Consume: beCause, to them, Poisonous Drugs = Health Care. {See the above Link for: **"Did God or Satan Ordain Medical Doctors??"** (**Ask Huck Finn and/or Nigger Jim: because neither Tom Sawyer nor Judge Thatcher would Know!**), Book 022, plus: **"The LUSCIOUS All-Mineral Organic Method of Gardening!"** (**HOW to Grow DELICIOUS Satisfying Foods for Potential Kingz and Kweenz in Swanky PALACES!**), Book 021.}

19-27 [_] Bernie plans on Requiring Employers to provide at least 12 Weeks of Paid Family and Medical Leave; plus 2 Weeks of Paid Vacation, and 7 Days of Paid Sick Days — as Opposed to 40 Days of Paid Vacation per Year according to my Plan, which can be spent Wisely FASTING and PRAYING, whereby a Person will be JUMPING for JOY at the End of it, if such a Person Follows the RULES! Otherwise, when someone does get Sick, and goes to a Doctor for Assistance, he or she will be Committed to a **Swanky Fasting Sanitarium**, whereby his or her Good Health will be Recovered and Improved on. Guaranteed. (The Wise Person will Commit himself to such a Fasting Sanitarium before getting Sick: beCause it is Easier to Fast when you are not so Sick and/or Diseased, whereby you might even become Helpless, and not even be Able to get Out of Bed by yourself, as is the Case for many Old People, who Broke Dietary Laws when they were Young and Fairly Healthy.)

19-28 [_] Bernie says that Real Family Values are about making Sure that Parents have Time to Bond with their Babies, and to take Good Care of their Children and Relatives when they get Ill; but, my Plan calls for 24/7/365 Family Values, whereby almost all Families Live and Work Together at Home, or near Home, whereby they can Attend to each other's Needs, and have Close Relationships, and not Fear the Days when they might get Old and Helpless: beCause of Eating Correctly at all Times and in all Places. {See www.Amazon.com for: **"DIETS!"** (**A Reasonable Solution for the "Eternal Controversy"!**), Book 037.}

19-29 [_] Bernie plans on Enacting a Universal Childcare and Pre-kindergarten Program, which he Imagines might be Better than Mother Mary Caring for her Baby Jesus; but, I Propose that it would not be nearly as Good, which is WHY I wrote an Inspired Book, called: **"GOOD NEWS for REBEL WOMEN!"** (**HOW almost all Wives can become Moderately RICH without Leaving their Homes! Guaranteed!**) By The Worldwide People's Revolution!®, Book 010.

19-30 [_] Bernie plans on making it easier for Workers to Join Unions, whereby they can Protest for Higher Wages, and thus get a certain Meager Measure of Capitalist Justice, whereby they are Better-paid Work Slaves. Just Think, with my Plan, almost everyone in the World will be Moved into the Upper Class of Rich People, who will have Secure Stone Dome Home Complexes with HUGE Cisterns for Water Storage, which are Lined with Ceramic Tiles, which contain Living Water, which has been Produced within those **"Beautiful Swanky PALACES,"** which have

Creeks Running over Rough Boulders, Gravel, and Sand, which Purifies it, Oxygenates it, and makes it into *"Living Water,"* which you can read about in the *Holy Bible,* even though it Fails to Explain HOW to make it. But, after that Water runs over those Rough Rocks for a Mile or so, it is Transformed into Living Water, which is then Stored in Lower Cisterns, until it is Pumped Up by Solar and Wind Power into Higher Cisterns, whereby all of the Cisterns within the Swanky Fortresses contain Living Water! Therefore, it is now Time for you Architects and Engineers to get your Acts Together, and get some Good Plans for Constructing those **"GLORIOUS Swanky Hotels Castles and Fortresses!" (Beautiful Planned City States for WISE Intelligent Well-Educated People with Common Sense and Good Understanding!)**, Book 019.

19-31 [_] Bernie plans on Breaking Up those Huge Edomite Financial Institutions: so that they are no longer too Big to Fail; but, I plan on putting ALL of them OUT of Business: beCause none of them are Needed for True Prosperity, even as Warts on a Hog are NOT Needed for True Prosperity. Bernie says that those Institutions are now 80% larger than they were when we Bailed them Out! Bernie even Imagines that he might Pass Legislation to Break them up, as if the CONgress is going to go along with him, being mostly Reprobate Republicans, who LOVE those Lying Edomite Banksters, while Pretending to Love the Humble Honest Man from Galilee, who said that we should Love our Naaberz as much as we Love ourselves, which is most Certainly something that is NOT Practiced by Lying Capitalist Edomites! ‡

19-32 [_] Bernie plans on making a College Education Free of Charge for everyone at the Expense of Big Corporations, while I Plan on making it Possible for a Better Education than that, Free of all Charges, by use of the Internet and Practical Hands-on Experiences at Work. For Example, since the Primary Thing in this Life is Eating and Drinking, all Students will have to Learn HOW to Grow their own Foods in their own Private Gardens of Eden, who will be Assisted by **The Swanky Associations of Professional All-Mineral Organic Gardeners**, who will have all of the Proper Tools and Materials to Work with: so as to make that Gardening EASY and Thoroughly Enjoyable, whereby most People will become Addicted to it, and also Enjoy the Delicious Fruits and Vegetables that they will Grow in such Gardens, whereby they will be Self-Rewarded. Moreover, they will Learn to SHARE their Extra Foods with their Friends and Relatives, who will also Enjoy Eating such Foods: beCause they will do some Fasting in Advance, whereby Good Sweet Fragrant Fruits will be DELICIOUS Things to Eat, while Cokes and Candies will be BAD Things to Drink and Eat. Otherwise, the Master Farmer is going to STOP the Rain on all of the Land, until your Bellybuttons are Rubbing on your Backbones for Hunger and Thirst: beCause of not Cooperating with me, your Elected King! ‡ (See *Revelation 11, KJV.*)

19-33 [_] Bernie proposes to get Big Money OUT of Politics, while I Propose to make all Potential Elected Candidates Fill Out and File on the Internet the Complete SURVEYS of their VALUES, which we can all Study before using the Internet to VOTE for them; but, only IF we Electors have also Filled Out and Filed **"The Complete SURVEYS of our VALUES!" (SURVEYS of Religious Spiritual Political Governmental Sexual Social Moral Economic Business Labor Habitual and Miscellaneous VALUES!) By The Worldwide People's Revolution!®**, Book 059, and Posted those Surveys on the Internet for everyone to Study, if they Want to: so as to Know whether or not we are Worthy to Vote for any Officials, most of whom will be Like-minded People within their own Beautiful Planned City States: beCause, only a FEW Good Men will be Needed in **"The New RIGHTEOUS One-World Government,"** which will have a Great King, 6 High Priests Representing 6 Major Religions, 60 Elected Kings who Represent 60 Major

Nations, and a Maximum of 600 Elected Governors, for Representing all Minor Nations, Islands of the Seas, and Provinces that need them to Represent them in: **"The Great World TEMPLE of PEACE!" (The Glory of Jerusalem Arises Again!)**, Book 017. Meanwhile, each Swanky Fortress, or Planned City State, will have its own Elected Kings and Queens, who will Enforce the Laws and Rules that each City State Votes for, whereby each City State will Govern itself, and will only be Monitored by **"The New RIGHTEOUS One-World Government,"** just to make SURE that they are Obeying their own Laws and Rules: beCause, if they are not, they are Hypocrites, who must be Exposed and Deposed: beCause Children become Rebellious with Hypocritical Leaders, and Especially with Hypocritical Parents! Therefore, before you Marry a Lying Hypocrite, be Sure to Study the Complete SURVEYS of his or her VALUES! ‡

19-34 [_] Bernie Recognizes the Fact that we do not have a "Government of the People, by the People, nor for the People," as Abraham Lincoln put it; but, not in those Exact Words. Indeed, we have a Corrupt government of the Synagogue of Satan, which Bernie has Proven on his Website, which should be Debunked and Disposed of: beCause it is a Great FALSE government, which does not even Capitalize Liberty, Freedom, nor Justice for All, Worldwide: beCause it is Composed mostly of Lying Edomites, and Edomite Lovers. Yes, we could Honestly say that it is Government of Lying Edomites, by Lying Edomites, and for Lying Edomites, who have Gained TRILLIONS of Dollars by Deceiving the Tax Slaves, Debt Slaves, Interest Slaves, Insurance Slaves, Drug Slaves, Sex Slaves, and Work Slaves, who still find it Difficult to Believe that they have been DECEIVED! Yes, some are still calling up the *Washington Journal* on C-SPAN, informing us that they LOVE this Country, and would be Happy to DIE for it. However, they are Speaking of the COUNTRY — not the Federal Government. Meanwhile, they Play along with the Election Deceptions, and Vote for the Lesser of the 2 Evils, they say, rather than DEMAND: **"The Great Worldwide TELEVISED Court HEARING,"** whereby they might Discover WHO Assassinated President Kennedy, what the Government knows about UFO's, what Actually Happened during September 11th, 2001; and WHY we Need Bankers, at all? Indeed, what they Need is the WHOLE TRUTH, whatever it might be, just to Satisfy their Minds! ‡

19-35 [_] Bernie proposes a Real Campaign Financial Reformation, whereby Elections are Funded by the General Public, much like it is in the Land of Oz, whereby each Potential Candidate gets to Waste X-amount of Money on Television Advertisements that Disgrace their Opponents, while Puffing Up their own Highness, and Glorifying **"The Divided States of United Lies,"** which is likely the Most Corrupted Government in the whole World! My Plan calls for each City State of Like-minded People to Govern itself, Tax itself, and do whatever it Chooses to do to itself, while leaving the other City States alone: beCause they are all Able and Willing to do so. Yes, the People who are like Sheeps, Deers, Elks, Mooses, and Goats may Live Together in Peace with their own Kind, and Govern themselves; but, the People who are like Lions and Wolves will not be Allowed to come among them: beCause they are not Wanted among them, nor should they be. ‡

19-36 [_] Bernie says, "Our vision for American democracy should be a nation in which all people, regardless of their income, can participate in the political process, can run for office without begging for contributions from the wealthy and the powerful." Sounds Good, huh? Well, it was just such a Mob of Idiots who screamed out: *"CRUCIFY HIM! CRUCIFY HIM!!"* — speaking of Jesus Christ, who was Democratically sent to the Cross: beCause that is just how STUPID Demonocracy is! But, of course, that is not to say that Elections are BAD, nor that Officials are not Needed; but, it is only to say that Intelligent Well-Educated People, ONLY, should be Allowed to

VOTE: beCause, if it is not that Way, we get just Exactly what we now have — Government of the Lying Edomites, by the Lying Edomites, and FOR the Lying Edomites: beCause they Manage the News Media, the Movie Industries, the Book Publishing Companies, the Magazine Businesses, the Educational Systems, the Medical Institutions, the Drug Companies, and the Military Industrial Congressional Bankers' Complex! Yes, you can Discover the Truth of it on YouTube Videos, if you Search for it; and a few thousand People have done that; but, most People have yet to Discover it: beCause their Bellybuttons are not yet Rubbing on their Backbones for Hunger nor Thirst! But, you might Recall something about the "Great Depression" of the 1930's, which began with the 1929 CRASH of the Phony Stock Market of the Great False Economy, which they did not Mention in the Public School of Ignorant Fools: beCause that Great Depression was brought about by those Lying EDOMITES! Yes, the Chief Edomite Bankers simply withheld the Money from the small Bankers, who went Broke, and thus Closed their Doors! Yes, thousands of them went OUT of Business: beCause, "there was no money for doing anything," they said. But, just as soon as Franklin D. Roosevelt (another Lying Edomite) and his CONgress Declared WAR on Japan and Germany, there was suddenly an Unlimited Amount of Money for Building millions of Airplanes, Army Tanks, Trucks, Jeeps, Boats, Ships, Aircraft Carriers, Submarines, Big Guns, Bombs, Bullets, Rifles, Mess Kits, Helmets, Grenades, Mortars, Rocket Launchers, Submachine Guns, Cots, Tents, Gas Masks, Backpacks, Sleeping Bags, K-rations, Canteens, Boots, Uniforms, and everything Necessary for making WAR: beCause those Wars are very Profitable for Edomites, even as I Explained before: beCause it is the Truth! Indeed, you do not have to be a Lawyer, nor a Rocket Scientist to Understand the Simple Mathematics of it. War = Financial Gain for Lying Edomites, who cannot Deny it: beCause they Gained TRILLIONS of Dollars from it! Yes, it can be, should be, and must be Proven at: **"The Great Worldwide TELEVISED Court HEARING!"**

19-37 [_] So, O Selected King, was it DEMOCRACY that got us into this Edomite TRAP, or what?? After all, no one ever put anything about those Lying Edomites on any Ballot for an Election. Indeed, they Control the Money Supply, when it should be in the Control of the Constitutional Government, only, which should Consist of Elected Honest Officials, only.

19-38 [_] Well, they should be Honest Elected Officials; but, how many are? Answer: NONE that we know of, or else they would be Demanding: **"The Great Worldwide TELEVISED Court HEARING!"** Book 041. Moreover, such Educated Honest People would have also been Demanding a FULL Unbiased Independent Investigation of the Evil Events of September 11th, 2001, which should have been a CIVILIAN Investigation: beCause it is not Safe to have the Foxes Guarding the Hen House, as the saying goes, much less Investigating who Stole the Chickens. Therefore, Private Investigators, even of other Trustworthy Nations, should have made the Investigations, and come up with as much Evidence as Possible to Present at a Great Worldwide Televised Court Hearing: so that everyone might Learn as much about it as Possible, and then come to Rational Conclusions. After all, if there were no Bodies at the "Crash Site" near Shanksville, Pennsylvania, something seems to be Suspicious about a Government Report saying that all of the Evidence Disappeared! After all, many Airplanes have been Crashing for many Years, and ALL of them left Visible Evidences, except the one that Allegedly Crashed in Pennsylvania! Therefore, that called for a more Thorough Investigation, would you not say? ‡

19-39 [_] I Confess that Bernie does have Good Intentions, and is by far the most Honest one running in the Race to the Little White Outhouse in the District of Criminals. However, at the same Time, I must also Confess that he does not have the Best Solutions, and no Solutions at all for the

Masses of People in Foreign Lands, who would like to have a Piece of the Economic Pie for themselves. Little do they know what I Propose, or else they would be Demanding: **"The Great Worldwide TELEVISED Court HEARING!"** Book 041.

{NOTE: I did not go into any great Details concerning ALL of Bernie Sanders' Proposals, which are presented on his Website, at: www.BernieSanders.com for whomever is Interested in Better Government Policies than the Communists and Capitalists have — at least for the Masses of People in the United States of North America.}

An Honest Critique of Donald Trump's Campaign

19-40 [_] You can discover Donald's proposed solutions for some of the Issues of our Time on his Website, at: www.DonaldJTrump.com on the Internet. I will only Highlight the solutions that I Strongly Disagree with, which you may also Disagree with; but, if not, all that I ask is that you Consider my Viewpoints, which are Valid Objections in the Light of Biblical Truths, as well as in the Light of Social, Moral, Political, Economic, and Monetary Values.

19-41 [_] Donald states: "On day 2 Mexico will immediately protest. They receive approximately $24 billion a year in remittances from Mexican nationals working in the United States. The majority of that amount comes from illegal aliens. It serves as de facto welfare for poor families in Mexico. There is no significant social safety net provided by the state in Mexico." (See *Compelling Mexico to Pay for the Wall* in his List of Issues.)

19-42 [_] So, let us Think about it with a Capital T. First of all, Donald is speaking from a Typical Republican Nationalist Platform, which just Naturally Presumes that Americans are Superior Creatures, when Compared with those Poor Mexicans, whose State does not Provide a "significant social safety net" for Poor Mexicans, as if it would be Wise of the Mexican Federal Government to get itself into 10 to 30 Trillion Dollars-worth of DEBTS for its Children to have to Pay to Edomite Bankers, who would be more than Happy to Loan all such Money to them for Extortionist Interest Rates, much like the "Payday Loans" that are Offered on the Altar of Edomite Sacrifices for Assisting Poor Americans to Buy their Trashy Cars, Pay for Rent, or whatever they need it for, who Charge up to 1,600$ for a 400$ Loan — that is, by the Time that all of the Usury Services have been Paid, which is still Legal, if you can Believe it! Yes, they are called "Payday Loan Sharks," who Infest the "Filthy Waters" from Coast to Coast. (See *Wikipedia* for "Payday Loan" for the Details.)

19-43 [_] Secondly, Donald never Lived as a Poor Mexican, whereby he might Relate with 80 Million of them, who have every Right to do as they Please with the Money that they Earn by Honest Labor, who normally do a hundred Times more Physical Labor than Donald Trumpeter, who would do well to get in some Unemployment Line with American Mexicans, and thus Discover what it is like to Bend Over in some HOT Humid Sweaty Field, harvesting Produce for "Rich Americans" like himself, who are as Spiritually Poor as Church Mice, who have never Studied: **"The Seven Basic Spiritual Building Blocks of LIFE!" (Faith Hope Trust Love Patience Persistence and Obedience!) By The Worldwide People's Revolution!® Book 036.**

19-44 [_] Thirdly, Donald is not Aware of what a Great Sacrifice it is for a Poor Mexican, receiving Minimum Wages in some American Factory, just to come up with any Money to Send back Home to Mexico, while also Paying his Rent and whatever, being little better off than a Typical Slave of the 1800's. Therefore, as the Elected President, the first thing that he should do is to Order all Reprobate Republicans into those Hot Sweaty Fields at less than Minimum Wages: beCause it is Legal for Farmers to Pay such Migrant Workers LESS than Minimum Wages: beCause of often providing them with one or 2 Meals per Day, plus some Shack to Sleep in with 40+ other Migrant Workers, who Serve Community Meals that have been Cooked in large Cheap Capitalist Aluminum Pots and Pans, which the Federal Government would also Feed to the Baby Jesus, if he were here, Today, and without any Great Shame: because, "As Capitalists, we must all begin at the Bottom of the Economic Ladder, and thus Work our way Up to the Top of it with Donald Trump and Associates at Wal-mart, Macy's, Starbucks, and so on."

19-45 [_] Fourthly, Donald Trump Imagines that the Mexican Government has 10 Billion Dollars or more to Waste on a Worthless Wall, when it would be far more Practical to use that Money WISELY to Sponsor: **"The Great Worldwide TELEVISED Court HEARING!"** — Book 041, whereby it can be Proven that there is no Need for any Borders, Border Guards, Police Departments, National Defense DEPARTments, War DEPARTments, Housing and Urban Renewal DEPARTments, Welfare DEPARTments, Healthcare DEPARTments, Food and Drug DEPARTments, Immigration DEPARTments, Transportation DEPARTments, Communications DEPARTments, Homeland Security DEPARTments, Tax Revenue DEPARTments, Insurance DEPARTments, Federal Reserve DEPARTments, nor any of those other hundreds of DEPARTments in Wicked Anti-Christ FALSE governments! Indeed, they are Institutions of the Synagogue of SATAN, which does not Believe in the Truths that can Liberate us Tax Slaves from their Prison of LIES! In Fact, they do not Want the Masses of People to even HEAR such Truths: beCause those Truths are a Great Threat to their EVIL Empire. For Example, there is no Need for any Payday Loans to anyone, Worldwide: beCause it is Possible and most Practical to Establish a RIGHTEOUS One-World GovernMINT, which has an Endless Supply of Good Money, which must be Earned by Honest Labor, without any Loans, without any Interest, without any Usury, and without any Taxes: beCause such a Good Government is so well Loved by the Masses of People that they Cheerfully Contribute whatever Money is Necessary for Operating such a Limited Government, whose Elected Officials are Paid Minimum Wages: beCause all of their Physical Necessities are Provided, Free of Charges by their Electors! Yes, their Houses, Foods, Clothing, Tools, Computers, Papers, Printers, and whatever Things are Needed are Provided by: **"Seven Great Armies of Working Soldiers!"** (**HOW to Provide a Way for Everyone to WORK: so as to Eliminate Poverty, Crimes, Drug Abuses, Prisons and Unnecessary Taxes!**), Book 015: beCause that Good GovernMINT has Provided those Voluntary Working Soldiers with: **"GLORIOUS Swanky Hotels Castles and Fortresses!"** (**Beautiful Planned City States for WISE Intelligent Well-Educated People with Common Sense and Good Understanding!**), Book 019, which will Solve more than 5,000 Massive Problems, including the Unemployment and Underemployment Problems, the Illegal Immigration Problems, the Refugees Problems, the Healthcare Problems, the Malaria Problem, the Zika Virus Problem, the Tick Fever Problem, the Cancers Problems, the Heart Attacks Problems, the Strokes Problems, the Illegal Drug Addictions Problems, the Obesity Problems, the Poverty Problems, the Endless Bills Problems, the Homeless Veterans' Problems, the Social Security Problems, the Retirement Problems, the Rest Homes Problems, the Welfare Problems, the Divorce Problems, the Suicide Problems, the Terrorist Problems, the Pollutions Problems, the Environmental Problems, the Lead Pipes Problems, the

Chlorinated Water Problems, the Poisoned Foods Problems, the Bankers' Problems, the Debts Problems, the Traffic "Accident" Problems, the Drive-by Shootings Problems, the Gang Wars Problems, the Drug Trafficking Problems, the Legal Drug Addictions Problems, the Lonely Broken Hearts Problems, the Expensive Funeral Problems, the Graveyard Problems, the Trash Dump Problems, the Sewage Problems, and all other Problems that you can Think of! †§‡

19-46 [_] God have Mercy, O Selected King — I had no Idea that Swanky Fortresses could SOLVE all of those Massive Problems! What in Hell is the Matter with us? Why do we not get to Work on the Construction of them, right away?

19-47 [_] Well, since Donald Trump is such a Successful Construction Contractor, we could put him in Charge of Building the First Swanky Hotel and Fortress for those Poor Mexicans, in Mexico, who would be Happy to Join his Army of Working Soldiers, who would begin with those one-half-million-gallon Ceramic-lined Cisterns for Water Storage, which would Form the Foundations for the Massive Buildings on Top of them, in Great TERRACES, which are 240 feet Wide and 50 feet Tall and Miles Long! Yes, one Bank of Terraces would Face another Bank of similar Terraces on each Side of a River of Water, which is Bordered on each Side with thousands of Fruit and Nut Trees, as well as Fragrant Flower Gardens, Granite-paved Walkways, Bike Paths, and with Workshops and Sales Shops Bordering those Walkways. Indeed, with that Peaceful Plan, the Mexican "Aliens" in **"The Divided States of United Lies"** would be Happy to go back Home to Mexico, and go to Work for Master Trump and Associates, who would have Plenty of Money to Live on while they Manage it, for Free: beCause of their Love for those Poor Mexicans! †§‡

19-48 [_] And WHO, O Selected King, would FINANCE such Projects, which are also Desperately Needed in Syria, Jordan, Lebanon, Iraq, Afghanistan, Pakistan, Kurdistan, Kyrgyzstan, India, China, Russia, Romania, Hungary, Georgia, Turkey, Iran, Israel, Egypt, Libya, Nigeria, Ethiopia, Sudan, South Sudan, the Republic of the Congo, Sierra Leone, South Africa, Zambia, Zimbabwe, Uganda, Chad, Tanzania, Niger, Namibia, Reunion, Kenya, Zaire, Congo, Rhodesia, Mozambique, Benin, Botswana, Burkina Faso, Burundi, Cameroon, Cape Verde, Central African Republic, Comoros, Democratic Republic of the Congo, Republic of the Congo, Djibouti, Equatorial Guinea, Eritrea, Gabon, Gambia, Ghana, Guinea, Guinea-Bissau, Ivory Coast, Lesotho, Liberia, Madagascar, Malawi, Mali, Mauritania, Mauritius, Morocco, Rwanda, Sao Tome and Principe, Senegal, Seychelles, Somalia, Swaziland, Togo, Tunisia, Algeria, and Angola — not to mention most of South and Central America.

19-49 [_] Well, we would have to Establish **"The New RIGHTEOUS One-World Government,"** which would Finance all of it, Worldwide: beCause that would be its Main Function, as well as Provide the Necessary Transportation, Building Materials, Tools, Voluntary Working Soldiers, and everything that is Needed for TRUE Prosperity! Yes, Donald Trumpeter would have a "Field Day" with so much Money to Work with, whereby he and his Contractors could Build the Most Beautiful Planned City States that your Eyeballs have ever Seen! After all, he can Relate with the BEAUTY of Polished Rocks, which you can See in the Trump Tower in New York City, which is one of the most Beautiful Walls in the World, which has Running Water over it to Enhance the Beauty of it! Yes, I personally spent a whole Hour Gazing at it and the Beautiful Floor in front of it, in the Lobby, which is Open to the General Public most of the Time. Therefore, go over there and take a Good Look at what the Future Holds for Wise People, who Elect me to be their Righteous King! †§‡ {See www.Amazon.com for: **"Mark Twain Races for**

the PRESIDENCY!" (The 2020 Presidential Candidates Desperately Need Some STRONG Undefeatable COMPETITION!) By The Worldwide People's Revolution!® Book 033.}

19-50 [_] Donald Trump argues that the United States has the Moral High Ground when it comes to the Drug Trafficking Business, in spite of knowing that if Americans were not Buying those Illegal Drugs, no Drugs would be coming across the Border, which is Proof that Americans do NOT have the Moral High Ground: beCause they are the Drug Addicts, who Support the Drug Dealers and Traffickers, who would simply Drop Out of the Business if my Plan were Followed, which calls for Legalizing all Drugs in Cities of Confusion, while Outlawing them in all Swanky Hotels Castles and Fortresses, where Righteous People will Naturally Want to Live: beCause of taking Advantage of the 5,000+ Advantages. {See the above Link for: **"The Right Design for Living!" (A List of Great Advantages for Building Beautiful Planned City States!)**, Book 012, which is a Companion Book of: **"Poverty Hunger Riots Strikes Brutalities Election Deceptions and Civil Wars!" (The High Price that we Earthlings have Paid for Leaving the Good Land!)**, Book 014.

19-51 [_] O Selected King, if all Drugs were made Legal in all Cities of Confusion, they would Naturally become Living Hell Holes, much like Amsterdam, Holland, where Recreational Marijuana is Legal, just like it is in Colorado and other States. †§‡

19-52 [_] Well, you need to do more Research concerning Amsterdam, which is one of the Best Cities in the World, with a very Low Crime Rate, in spite of the Marijuana, which is also True of Denver, Colorado, which has less Crime than Chicago by one-tenth! †§‡

19-53 [_] O Selected King, what about the Libertarian Party? Do they not have Better Solutions than the Dimwitcrats and Reprobates? †§‡

19-54 [_] Well, it is Possible, which we will get around to after Critiquing Hillary Clinton's Campaign.

An Honest Critique of Hillary Clinton's Campaign

19-55 [_] O Selected King, you did not even Cover Donald Trumpeter's Stand on the Right to Bear Arms in the *Second Amendment* to *the Constitution for the United States of America,* which clearly states: *"The right of the people to keep and bear Arms shall not be infringed upon."* Notice that it did not say, "The God-given Right of the People to Bear Weapons of Mass Destruction shall not be Infringed upon": beCause God did not give any Nation any such "Rights," nor even the "right" for Babies and Ignorant Children to VOTE: beCause God is not so Stupid as most Americans, who should Appoint the Person to Govern who has the Best Solutions for our Massive Problems — Disregarding his Looks, his Money, his Prestige, his Popularity, and his Education, or Mis-education, which got us into this Living Hell Hole, whereby Americans are no less than 150 Trillion Dollars in Debt, which the Great Grandchildren are supposed to Repay to those Lying Edomite Bankers, who knew full well what they were doing when they Set Up the so-called Federal Reserve Bank, which is neither Federal nor a Reserve of any Kind: beCause, when you are 150 Trillion Dollars in DEBT to Edomites, you do not have any Reserves. Therefore, it is nothing but a Grand Deception, or a HOAX, if you will call it that, which I would call a SCAM!‡

19-56 [_] Yes, it is a Dishonest Scheme, which was Invented by Lying Edomite Banksters, who should be taken to COURT, found Guilty, and Sentenced to 40 Years of Hard Labor in Rock Quarries, unless they Repent and Repay the People whom they Robbed, and also Forgive ALL Debts, Worldwide! Yes, it is now Time for the Great Year of JUBILEE Celebration! {See www.Amazon.com for: **"The END of CONFUSION!" (The Great CELEBRATION of the Magnificent Wedding of the Most Humble Honest Nations, and the Grand Year of JUBILEE!) By The Worldwide People's Revolution!®**, Book 050.}

19-57 [_] O Selected King, I can already Visualize those **"Seven Great Armies of Working Soldiers,"** dressed in their Colorful Uniforms, Marching in Great Parades through the Valley of Megiddo with their Musical Instruments, Horses, Golden Stagecoaches, Colorful Floats, Tools in their Hands, and Beer Barrels by the MILLIONS! Yes, what a Great LYNCH PARTY that will be, when we Celebrate the Great Year of JUBILEE by Hanging all of those Lying Edomites, if they do not Confess their Lies and Financial Sins, and come Clean! †§‡

19-58 [_] Well, I Seriously Doubt that Hillary Clinton will Allow any such Evil Things to go on under her Watch as the President of **"The Divided States of United Lies!"** by Popular Votes. But, as for the Right to Bear Arms, each of those **"GLORIOUS Swanky Hotels Castles and Fortresses"** will have the Right and Duty to Defend itself, whereby they can Vote for HOW they Want to Do that. Indeed, some will Naturally Choose to Store their Rifles and other Weapons in an Armory within their Castle, while others will keep their Weapons in their Houses, in Locked Closets, where they are Handy, if they Need them: beCause of Fearing that some "Enemy" might Actually Overrun their Swanky Fortress with 100-feet-tall Solid Stone Walls on the Perimeter of the Fortress! Yes, you could say that they will be very Paranoid Fearful Republicans, who are Chief Suspects of being little Anti-Christs: beCause of not Voting for the Establishment of: **"The CONSTITUTION for the New RIGHTEOUS One-World GovernMINT!" (HOW all Peoples can get True Justice, and Celebrate the Great Year of JUBILEE!)**, Book 016, which Good Government will be Headquartered in: **"The Great World TEMPLE of PEACE!" (The Glory of Jerusalem Arises Again!) By The Worldwide People's Revolution!®** Book 017. Yes, each Elected Official will have his (not her's) own Private Stone Dome Home Complex, which will have Space for X-amount of Voluntary Servants, who will Attend to the Gardening, Cooking, House Cleaning, and all such Things, while the Elected Leaders will Attend to their Business of Governing, 7 Hours per Day, 6 Days per Week, until everyone in the World, who Wants to be, is Living within a Beautiful Planned City State, Tax-free! ‡

19-59 [_] O Selected King, if there are NO Taxes, WHO will Support **"The New RIGHTEOUS One-World Government!" (HOW to Establish a Righteous One-World Government without Going to WAR!) By The Worldwide People's Revolution!®** Book 056?

19-60 [_] You must not "Reed" too Well, since I already Explained that such a Good GovernMint will be Supported by VOLUNTARY Tithes and Offerings by those **"Seven Great Armies of Working Soldiers,"** which is also known as: **"The Swanky Associations of Working Soldiers!" (A Fascinating Collection of Various Kinds of Voluntary Working Soldiers!)**, Book 018, which Explains HOW all of that will be brought about, and without going to War! In other Words, those Working Soldiers will Love the Swanky Fortress System so much that they will Gladly and Voluntarily Donate whatever Money is Needed for Operating that Extremely Good Government, which will be Limited to just a few million Professional People, many of whom will be Good

News Reporters: because there will be very little Bad News to be Reporting: because of the Overwhelming Peace and True Prosperity among all Peoples! †‡

19-61 [_] O Selected King, Hillary Clinton has a Normal Democratic Political Platform to Stand on, which Naturally has the ObamaScare Healthcare Program, which most American Tax Slaves and Insurance Slaves do not Like. Therefore, just Exactly what is your Healthcare Program?

19-62 [_] Well, I already Addressed that Subject in Previous Verses — such as: 14-07; and 19-26. In other Words, we need a Natural Lifestyle, as in a *"Garden of Eden"* Healthcare Plan, whereby Adam Lived for 930 Years, and without the Assistance of any Drugs, Medical Doctors, nor Witchdoctors. {See www.Amazon.com for: **"In thu Beeginingz uv Thingz!" (Thu Kreeaashun Stooree frum thu Beegining!) By The Worldwide People's Revolution!®**, Book 025.

19-63 [_] Now, Hillary's Website addresses the following Topics / Subjects: **Alzheimer's Disease, Campaign Finance Reforms, College Campus Sexual Assaults, Climate Changes and Energy Consumption, New College Plans, Criminal Justice Reforms, Disability Rights, Early Childhood Education, Raising Incomes, Improving the Economy, Gun Violence Prevention, Healthcare, HIV and AIDS Issues, Immigration Reforms, Infrastructure Repairs, Kindergarten—12 Education, Labor Unions, Lesbian Gay Bisexual Transgender Equality with Normal American Perverts, Manufacturing, National Insecurity, Paid Leave, Protection of Animals and Wildlife (by Stopping Acid Rains, Hillary?), Racial Injustices, Assisting Rural Communities, Assisting Small Business, Social Insecurity and Medicare, Substance Use Disorder and Addictions; Veterans, the Armed Forces, and their Families; Voting Rights and WRongs, Wall Street and Corporate America, Women's Rights to Raise little Baby Jesuses and other Great Opportunities to get Rich without Leaving their Homes, plus Workforce and Skills Training.** Indeed, Hillary has a lot to Say about all such Subjects, which you are Welcome to Study on her Website. But, I still must point out a few Weaknesses in her Plan, just for the Sake of Sanity.

19-64 [_] Hillary wants to Dismantle the School-to-Prison Pipeline, as she calls it, by providing 2 Billion Dollars in support to Schools for Reforming "overly punitive disciplinary policies," while calling on the States to Reform School Disturbance Laws, and Encourage States to use Federal Education Funding to implement Social and Emotional Support Interventions. It Sounds Good, huh? I Think she is referring to the millions of Colored People who have been Imprisoned for such Minor Infractions as Selling a little Marijuana for an Income, after Years of Capitalist Instructions / Indoctrinations in Public Schools about the Goodness of Capitalism, and how the Great False Economy Works on "Supply and Demand," and that "wherever there is a Need, someone will Fulfill it," which, in the Case of Selling Marijuana, is just another one of those "Needs," which is "Fulfilled" by Buying it at a Low Price, and Selling it at a Higher Price, which is only "Good Business." However, you could say that it is Illegal to do so: beCause Marijuana is not as Holy as Tobacco, which is actually 7 Times more Addictive than Marijuana, and is perfectly Legal: beCause "it is a legitimate business." However, there is a Biblical Word that Describes that Kind of "Business," which is "HYPOCRISY." And wherever there is Hypocrisy, there is Great Disrespect from all Honest Souls, Innocent or not. Therefore, no Honest American can Respect their Great False Anti-Christ Federal Cover-up government: beCause of that Hypocrisy, much less LOVE such a Wicked government, which Locks up Young Men in Prisons during the most Productive Years of their Lives. ‡

19-65 [_] O Selected King, if **"The New RIGHTEOUS One-World Government"** Permits the Use of all Kinds of Drugs in Cities of Confusion, is it not also Hypocritical?

19-66 [_] Absolutely NOT! Indeed, **"The New RIGHTEOUS One-World Government"** will have ZERO Control Over those Cities of Confusion, which are Outside of their Jurisdiction, which will have to be Responsible for themselves and whatever goes on within them, including the Drug Businesses, since they LOVE Drugs. Otherwise, those Drugs would not be Sold in such Cities: beCause of being made up of Righteous People. ‡

19-67 [_] O Selected King, you have me Greatly Confused. Why do you call it a Righteous ONE-WORLD Government, if it does not Control the WHOLE World?

19-68 [_] Well, that is beCause it only has Power or Control over those People who Willingly Choose to be Righteous, who Want to Live within those **"GLORIOUS Swanky Hotels Castles and Fortresses,"** Voluntarily, whereby they might become Moderately RICH, and without Selling anything! Indeed, they only need to go to Work, and Help Build those **"Beautiful Swanky PALACES"** for themselves, which False governments will Naturally NOT Like; but, if the Masses of People VOTE for it, that is the Way it will BE! Yes, I dare say that 90% or more of the Masses of People will Vote for it, including most Americans: beCause, if they Sincerely Want to Continue with their Capitalistic Nonsense within their own Beautiful Planned City States, they are Welcome to do so. Likewise, if the Europeans Sincerely Want to Continue on with their Socialist Systems within their Beautiful Planned City States, they are also Welcome to do so. Likewise, if the Chinese Sincerely Want to Continue on with Communism within their Beautiful Planned City States, they are also Welcome to do so: beCause it will not Bother ME! Indeed, I will be Living within a Beautiful Planned City State that Practices a Brand New Economic System, called: **"SWANGKEENOMIKS Rules the Roost!" (HOW all People can Prosper in a RIIT WAA, and STOP Polluting the Earth with Capitalist TRASH!)**, Book 039. Therefore, I will be Free, Healthy and Happy, in spite of whatever the Ignorant Fools are doing in those Filthy Cities of Confusion, which will soon DIE OUT: beCause the Righteous People will Quickly Discover those **"GLORIOUS Swanky Hotels Castles and Fortresses,"** Book 019, and thus Pack Up their Bags, and MOVE OUT of those Cities of Confusion, in Order to take Advantage of the 5,000+ Good Reasons and Great Advantages for Living within Swanky Fortresses!

19-69 [_] O Selected King, are you Sure that Democratically-elected Governments around the World will Cooperate with that Master Plan? Indeed, if most of the Righteous People DEPARTED from those Cities of Confusion, they would simply Collapse! In Fact, only Criminals would be left Alive within them, and only IF they were Well-armed with Military Weapons: beCause the Gangsters would be taking Over! †§‡

19-70 [_] Well, that is Exactly the Good Effect that we Want to Create, you might say: beCause, if all of the Righteous People DEPART from all such Filthy Cities of Pollution, with their Countless Crimes, Murders, Adulteries, Fornications, Sodomies, Rapes, Swindles, and whatever, only Ignorant and Insane People will be left in them! However, the Good People in those Swanky Fortresses will Naturally be Sending Missionaries among them, with the Hope of Persuading them to Join some Voluntary Army of Working Soldiers, and thus Build their own Beautiful Planned City States, whereby they may Govern themselves According to their own Elected Laws and Flexible Rules. After all, none of the Righteous People Object to that Plan: beCause, without a certain Degree of Righteousness, they will Fail, and thus Die Out! Yes, they will Exterminate themselves, Automatically, which will be GOOD! Indeed, the Saying will come to pass — *"Goodness will Overcome Evilness."* — The Bible.

19-71 [_] So, O Selected King, what about the other Planks on the Democratic Platform that Hillary Supports? What about the Rights of the Lesbian Gay Bisexual and Transgender Communities — will they also be Allowed to Build their own Beautiful Planned City States, whereby they can also Live in Peace with True Prosperity?

19-72 [_] Of course they will be Allowed and Encouraged to do so: beCause it is the only Way that they can have True Peace. However, that is not to say that other Swanky Fortresses will not also Permit such People to Live among them: because they Naturally will: because they are not Prejudiced against them. Moreover, they will have Laws that Forbid Persecuting all such People. However, if they Want to Discover lots of Like-minded People, the Wisest Thing that they can Do is to Join Forces with Like-minded People, who will no doubt Build the Most Beautiful Planned City States in the World: beCause Gay Men — like Michelangelo, Leonardo da Vinci, and Steve Jobs, will be among them! Yes, the most Gifted Men in the World have always been somewhat GAY, including Plato, Socrates, Alexander the Great, Henry David Thoreau, Benjamin Franklin, Thomas Edison, Nicola Tesla, John Steinbeck, Howard Hughes, Abraham Lincoln, Robert E. Lee, Steven Foster, Oscar Wilde, Walt Whitman, Greg Louganis, Elton John, Ricky Martin, Liberace, Rock Hudson, Dick (Scruffy Puppy) McKay, Christian Saint John, and many other Actors, Artists, Musicians, Poets, Authors, Missionaries, Preachers, Priests, Teachers, Professors, Politicians, Doctors, Lawyers, and Jesus Christ, himself, who had his *"Beloved Disciple John,"* who was that Guy who was lying in his Bosom at the Last Supper, who Loved him more than any other Disciple, who is still Alive and Well! †§‡ {See www.Amazon.com for: **"The Gospel According to our Elected King!" (The Good News from the Most Modern Perspective!)**, Book 077.}

19-73 [_] O Selected King, now we are Discovering what is wRong with thee! Indeed, you are a Distant Relative of that very Gay King James, who was too Proud to Confess it, much less provide an Accurate Translation of the King James Version (KJV), which was Originally much more Inclined to Favor the Gay Jonathans and Davids, who were the Greatest of Warriors, being like Joshua, who Loved Moses, and Elisha who Loved Elijah, and Nephi who Loved Lehi, and Amuulek who Loved Almu, and Nimrod who Loved Enoch, and so on, and so on — all of whom will BURN in Hellfire: beCause God HATES Faggots, which is WHY he Blest them with Special Gifts that most People do not have! Yes, if you Doubt it, just Study the Sculptures and Paintings of Michelangelo, who Lived for 93 Years, with the last 14 of those Years in Bed with his Young Lover, who gave to him a Cause for Living, which was very Comforting to him, which Inspired his "Beloved David" Statue, who was his Lover with a Modified Face and Hands, who is Greatly Admired in the Art World until this very Day! †§‡§§

19-74 [_] Well, it is for Sure that the Greatest Men who ever Lived were GAY, at least to some Degree, whereby you might call them Bisexuals, which is True of God the Father, himself, who has a Natural Love Affair with his Beloved Son, who was also Adam, himself: beCause he was the First Man, as well as the Perfected Man, being the First and the Last, just as it is Stated in *the Book of Revelation,* and in *Luke 3:38, KJV.* Yes, most Professing "Christians" find it Difficult to Believe their own *Bibles,* in spite of many Verses that Confirm that Fact of Life. Yes, he is *"the Alpha and the Omega, the Beginning of the Creation of White Men on the Earth, and the End of their Perfection, even the First Man to be Tempted by the Devil, and the Last Man to be Overcome by him,"* who was brought to Perfection on the Torture Stake, who Endured the Sufferings of it for the Salvation of Mankind: beCause he was the one who Caused the Fall of Mankind when he was Adam! Therefore, he kept Silent, and Paid the Price for our Redemption, which he could not have Done without a LOT of Love for MEN, and Especially for the Young Men who will make up the Rulers of his Holy Kingdom, who are NOT Sodomites, who do NOT have Anal Intercourse with anyone: beCause that would be a Chief Sin, just after Adultery, Rape, and Murder! Yes, even a Sodomite is a few Degrees Above a Murderer in the Eyes of the Gods; but, the Lowest and Least in the Kingdom will have to be Better Souls than Sodomites, Adulterers, Fornicators, Thieves, Liars, and Hypocrites. Therefore, if anyone has any Hope for getting into such a Holy Kingdom, that Person should be Wise, and Study the Good Books by **The Worldwide People's Revolution!®**: because they Reveal WHO will be Qualified to Govern, and they will not be Filthy Unclean People, even if they have Received all of the Medals of Honors by all Nations.

19-75 [_] So, what about the Libertarian Party — do they not have something Special to Offer on the Altar of Political Controversies? Indeed, they must at least have a little Smoke or Incense to Offer Up to the Gods of Confusion.

19-76 [_] Well, Gary Johnson is the Libertarian's Choice for President, who runs on a Campaign of FREEDOM! You can find their Platform at www.ip.org/platform on the Internet. Indeed, they "defend each person's right to engage in any activity that is peaceful and honest, and welcome the diversity that freedom brings. The world we seek to build is one where individuals are free to follow their own dreams in their own ways, without interference from government or any authoritarian power." Imagine that, a whole World that is Free to Commit Adultery, just as long as it is "peaceful and honest," which almost all Adultery has forever been: beCause of being with Mutual Consent between 2 Adulterers. God Forbid that Jesus Christ should come along and Interrupt their Fun by Forbidding it! †§‡

19-77 [_] O Selected King, I want to be a Libertarian, who Kills American Bisons for a Living, whereby I take out their Tongues for Smoking them, and Skin off their Hides for making Shoe Leather: because we can always use more Shoes. Therefore, there should be no Government Restrictions on me — no Regulations, nor any Forbidden Boundaries to Cross, much less any Taxes for any such Departments and their Inspectors. Moreover, after I get all of those Bisons Killed, I want to make all Kinds of Chemical Poisons, and Dump the Toxic Wastes in the Rivers, which may Kill a few Fishes; but, it is my God-given Right to be Able to do so: beCause I am FREE, in a Free Market System, which can Sell and Buy whatever People Want, including Teenage Prostitutes. Therefore, if anyone gets in my Way, I will Kill him. †§‡§§

19-78 [_] O Selected King, the Libertarians say that Individuals should be Free to make Choices for themselves, and to Accept Responsibility for the Consequences of the Choices they make. Therefore, as a Typical American Car Owner, I want to Accept Responsibility for the Pollution that I have put into the Atmosphere during the past 50 Years. However, I am wondering just HOW I will go about Cleaning it up? Yes, the Chinese have a Special Capitalist Problem with their Libertarian Pollution, which is so THICK that a Person can Barely Breathe, over there! †§‡§§

19-79 [_] O Selected King, as a Libertarian, I have the Freedom to Choose for myself what Air I want to Breathe in Los Angeles, as well as what Foods I might Eat from any given Restaurant, which I Know for a Fact was Grown by Holy Angels, whereby I can Trust it to be Good for me. Therefore, I do not want anyone to Interfere with my Right to Eat and Drink whatever I Want, even though I really do not Actually Want anything that is Bad for me, which is WHY I always Eat at Fast-Food Restaurants; and I am NOT a Hypocritter, much less Insane. †§‡§§

19-80 [_] O Selected King, the Libertarians, who Drive Polluting Cars, are "deliberately taking actions that place others involuntarily at significant risk of harm," even as they have done for Decades by Smoking those Stinking Cigarettes. Everyone should have the Right to Breathe Fresh Clean Air, even when they are Working in Subway Sewage Systems. "Individuals retain the right to voluntarily assume risk of harm to themselves," until they find themselves at the Mercy of Medical Doctors to Treat their Lung Cancers and other Cancers that Libertarians Obtained by not having Restrictions on their so-called "rights." †§‡§§

19-81 [_] O Selected King, Libertarians are Free to Grow all of the Sweet Juicy Fruits that they might want to Eat and Sell, if they can figure out HOW to Stop the Acid Rains, whereby their Trees might not be so Sick and Diseased with Capitalist Poisons. However, none of them can figure that out; and therefore, none of them Grow Good Fruits to Eat nor Sell. †§‡

19-82 [_] O Selected King, "Government should not compete with private enterprise," according to Libertarians, whereby 99.999,999,999% of the People in this World of Woes can go on Living in their Confused States of Extreme Poverty, whereby none of them have Fresh Clean Air to Breathe, Pure Living Water to Drink, Wholesome Natural Foods to Eat, Secure Houses to Live in, Natural Clothing to Wear, nor Peace of Mind: beCause they are Work Slaves, Tax Slaves, Interest Slaves, Insurance Slaves, Drug Slaves, Sex Slaves, and Childcare Slaves — most of whom Imagine that they are Free! †§‡§§

19-83 [_] O Selected King, Libertarians would Restore Parents with the Responsibility to Teach their own Children whatever they might Learn, whereby all such Children might become more Ignorant than their own Parents, 50% of whom cannot read nor write very well, and 25% cannot read more than a Stop Sign. †§‡

19-84 [_] O Selected King, Libertarians believe that it is the Individual's Responsibility to Provide for his or her own Retirement Plan, which is not Relying on the Government. Therefore, I plan on Working Hard, and Saving my Money for Retirement, which will be about 5$ per Week: beCause I can barely Pay the Bills, right now. Therefore, when I get ready to Retire, I will have Saved up no less than 10,000$ within 40 Years, which might Buy a Pair of Shoes when I Retire: because of Edomite Bankers' INFLATION, whereby 5 Cents used to Buy a Candy Bar, which is now 1 Dollar. Moreover, I have no Idea what my Invalid Wife will do at that Time for Shoes: because she is a Libertarian, who does not Believe in Government Assistance of any Kind — such as Welfare Checks, Food Stamps, SNAP Programs, nor Social Security Payments. However, I suppose that she could go Barefooted in the Snow when she Grows Old. †§‡§§

19-85 [_] Well, like all of the Political Parties, the Libertarians have no Real Solutions for anything; but, their Proposals do Appeal to People who have "Shallow Thinking Capabilities," as a 10-year-old Boy might say, whereby most People are left to themselves to Solve Problems that Require the United Cooperation of **"Seven Great Armies of Working Soldiers!"** (HOW to **Provide a Way for Everyone to WORK: so as to Eliminate Poverty, Crimes, Drug Abuses,**

Prisons and Unnecessary Taxes!) By The Worldwide People's Revolution!®, Book 015. After all, if it were Possible for the Ordinary Person to Build a Proper House, which is Fireproof, Tornado-proof, Hurricane-proof, Hail-proof, Termite-proof, Rot-proof, Paint-proof, Shingle-proof, Siding-proof, Mouse-proof, Rat-proof, Louse-proof, Snake-proof, Bullet-proof, Cockroach-proof, Bedbug-proof, Mosquito-proof, Self-air-conditioned, and Insurance-proof — like the Pantheon in Rome — then one might Discover such Houses Nationwide; but, instead of that, there are NO SUCH HOUSES in America: beCause the Normal Person cannot Afford such a Good House! However, even the Poorest of Young Working Soldiers could Afford to do sufficient Work to Help Build all such Good Houses for everyone in the World: because of taking Advantage of Mechanical Slaves, which will be Happy to do all such Hard Work for us, and at least 90% of it: beCause, Electric Trains, for Example, simply Obey their Masters / Conductors, and never Complain about Low Wages, nor even NO Wages! Therefore, it is just a Matter of Managing our Natural Resources Properly for the Prosperity of all Peoples, Worldwide, under the Administration of a Righteous KING, who has Power and Authority by the Consent of the Masses of People, who VOTE for him, who Want to Live in **"Beautiful Swanky PALACES!" (A New Concept in Living Habits — Swanky Palaces for Poor People!) By The Worldwide People's Revolution!®**, Book 066, who are Sick of Work Slavery, Tax Slavery, Interest Slavery, Insurance Slavery, Debt Slavery, Drug Slavery, Sex Slavery, and Childcare Slavery!

19-86 [_] O Selected King, we would all have to Sacrifice our Freedoms, if we Joined such Voluntary Armies of Working Soldiers: because we would no longer have the Freedom to Criticize any of those **"Beautiful Swanky PALACES,"** which would make it Possible for all of us to become Moderately RICH, and not be in Debt to any Banksters, which I would HATE! †§‡§§ {See: **"FREEDUM uv SPEECH!" (U Speshoul Maguzeen uv Onist Upinyunz!) By The Worldwide People's Revolution!®** Book 030-0001.}

19-87 [_] And what do you Think a Normal Soldier does when he or she Joins a Regular Army of Murderous Soldiers? Indeed, he or she must Sacrifice ALL Freedoms, and OBEY his or her Superior Officers, or else be Punished, or even go to Jail! Therefore, 99.999,999% of them simply OBEY: beCause they do not Want to go to Jail, much less get Beat Up by some Big Black NIGGERS, who have Control, who do not give a Damn about anyone's Feelings, much less their Political nor Religious Preferences and so-called "Rights." However, when a Person Joins **"The Swanky Associations of Working Soldiers!" (A Fascinating Collection of Various Kinds of Voluntary Working Soldiers!)**, Book 018, that Person has Democratic Powers, and can Vote for the Officers that he or she Wants to Love and Obey. For Example, during the Civil War of the 1860's, most Soldiers in the North and South much Preferred the Leadership of General Robert E. Lee, who was so Loved by the Southerners that they would Gladly Die for him, while most of the Northern Soldiers HATED General Grant, and did not even Respect him: because he was a Stinking Cigar-smoking Cursing Alcoholic, while General Lee was a Real Self-disciplined Gentleman, who did not Touch Cigars nor Booze, who Wanted to Settle the Slave Issue Legally in the Legislative Branch of the Federal Government. However, the Majority of the Intelligent Congressmen were on the Side of the South: beCause of the Things that are Written in the *Holy Bible,* which seems to Support the Master / Slave System: beCause of MISINTERPRETATIONS of what is Written! Yes, the whole Argument was Resting on a few Mistranslated Verses — such as, *"Servants Obey your Masters in all Things,"* which they Translated as *"Slaves Obey your Masters in all Things."* See: Colossians 3:20—25; Malachi 1:6; Matthew 8:9; Luke 6:46; 7:8; Ephesians 6:5—8; First Timothy 6:1—2; Titus 2:9—10; First Peter 2:18—19. Indeed, if someone

Wants to Discover the Truth about that Important Subject, they should Study: **"A Sound Argument for Masters and Servants!" (WHY Everyone Needs a Good Master, and every Master Needs Good Obedient Servants!)**, Book 008; and Remember that a Good Master is NOT a Nigger of any Kind, neither White, Brown, Yellow, nor Black. †§‡

19-88 [_] O Selected King, why does the *Bible* not make it Clear that most People were Born to be SERVANTS, and NOT Masters? After all, most People would have no Idea what to Do for a Living, if they could not Discover some Boss with a Paycheck in his Hand. Indeed, no Individual Person is Able to Make a Boeing 747 Airplane: beCause it is far too Technical and Complicated, which Requires Several Master Architects and Engineers to Design and Organize it; but, almost any Servant is Intelligent enough to Weld a Joint, Insert a Screw, Rivet a Sheet of Metal, or do whatever is Necessary to Assemble an Airplane, which is far more Technical and Complicated than any Swanky Hotel, Castle, or Fortress: beCause the Airplane must be Exact, while a Fortress Wall only needs to be somewhat Precise: beCause Mortar makes Rocks FLEXIBLE, even if they are not Cut Perfectly, which is WHY we Use Mortar to begin with, which the Inca Indians did not use: because they Understood HOW to Cut Stones so Precisely that they did not Need any Mortar to keep Out the Ants and other Bugs, which could not crawl through any Cracks in the Walls: beCause there were NO Cracks! †§‡

19-89 [_] Well, it has Rightly been Argued that the Inca Indians did NOT Build those Walls: because they were Built by Aliens with Far Advanced Superior Nolij than any Indians had, who were NOT Building any such Walls when they were Discovered by the Spaniards during the early 1530's. Indeed, there is much Proof that Aliens, and especially Giants, were at Work in this World of Wonders a very long Time Ago, who must be given Credit where Credit is Due, as the Apostle Paul wrote. See *Romans 13:7.* †§‡

19-90 [_] O Elected King, you should not Believe everything that you Discover on YouTube Videos: because not all of it is True. In Fact, it could be that NONE of it is True. After all, Satan is in Charge of this World of Woes, and he is out to Deceive everyone, including YOU! Therefore, all such Things must be Proven at: **"The Great Worldwide TELEVISED Court HEARING!" (That Great Meeting of the Most Intelligent and Well-Educated Minds!) By The Worldwide People's Revolution!®** Book 041.

— Chapter 20 —

The Conclusion

20-01 [_] O Selected King, this is not much of a Memorial Day Legacy for Uncle Sam, whose Nieces and Nephews must have at least 20 other Political Parties that you did not Mention — such as the Constitutional Party, the LGBT Party, the Communist Party, the Socialist Party, the Reformation Party, the Christian Party, the Moslem Party, the Hindu Party, the Buddhist Party, the Reformed Baptist Catholic Party, the United Presbyterian Methodist Party, the Lutheran Episcopalian Seventh-day Adventist Party, the United Pentecostal Reformed Church of Jesus Christ Party, and so on — all of whom have Legitimate Causes. For Example, the Reformed Southern Baptist Convention Party proposes that HALF of everyone's Paycheck should be used for Buying GOLD, which should be Saved for their RETIREMENT Plan: because Gold is the only Thing that seems to Maintain its Value, or even Increase in Value: beCause of the Scarcity of it. For Example, if I had been Wise, when I was only 20 Years Old, and had used my Military Pay for Buying One Ounce Gold Dollars, which were Selling for only 32$, each, and had Bought no less than 10 of those Coins per Month, for no less than 10 Years, I would have Collected no less than 1,200 Coins, which would now be Worth no less than 1,920,000 Dollars! However, just a few Months ago, each Coin was Worth 2,000$, which would have made those Coins Worth 2,400,000$! Therefore, I would have been Set Up for Retirement, just by Sacrificing 320$ per Month, when I was Young, which I could have done: beCause the Army Covered all of my Expenses, such as Food, Clothing, Housing and Transportation. Indeed, now that I Think back on it, I was just another Ignorant FOOL, who Drank and Ate Up his Money, and Wasted it on Whores, when I could have had a Good Secure Retirement Plan.

20-02 [_] Well, the Army could have Saved up those Gold Coins for all of its Victims, if the Government had been Wise for their Sakes; but, we cannot Expect Uncle Sam to have much Common Sense, being the Dunce that he is. After all, even if those 1,200 Coins had only Retained their Value of 32$, each, they would have been Worth no less than 38,400$, which would be at least a thousand Times more Savings than most of those Military Victims Presently have: beCause most of them have ZERO Savings! However, if we Built those **"GLORIOUS Swanky Hotels Castles and Fortresses,"** Book 019, **"The Swanky Associations of Working Soldiers,"** Book 018, would be Able to Provide all of the Old and Retired People with a Good Living: because their Basic Necessities would already be Provided by the Fortresses. Indeed, they would all have Beautiful Stone Dome Home Complexes to Live in, even as Retirement Homes: beCause at least 8 of those Old People could Comfortably Live in just one Stone Dome Home Complex, which would have no less than 4 large Bedrooms. However, if some Old Person Feels Uncomfortable Living with some other Person, who could be a Grandson or Granddaughter, he or she could have his or her Private Bedroom with a Bathroom, which could also have a little Kitchen / Dining Room, and a Living Room with all of the Comforts, much like I now Live in, which is about 13 feet by 27 feet by 10 feet high, which is quite Comfortable, at least for me. However, if someone is Willing to Work for more Space when they are Young and Able, that is their Privilege and Right. After all, every Beautiful Planned City State will be Free to VOTE for whatever Sizes of Rooms they Want, at least within Reason, up to a 24-feet-wide Bedroom Dome, a 50-feet-wide Living Room Dome, a 40-feet-wide Kitchen / Dining Room Dome, and 12-feet-wide Bathroom Domes with 4-feet-wide Doorways, just in case they get Extremely FAT, and can barely squeeze though a Normal Doorway, which is 30-inches wide, even though I have stayed in Hotels that had less than 2-feet-wide Bathroom Doors, in Europe: because the People used to be much Smaller. Most Families in the World would be quite Happy with a House that has only 3,000 square feet of Space inside of it; but, few of those present Houses have Sufficient Storage Space for all of the Foods and Drinks that a Family might Consume. Therefore, I Recommend Spacious Houses, and especially Spacious Cisterns for Water Storage, and Walk-in Coolers with Freezers in the middle of them, being surrounded by Root Cellars and Pantries for Canned Foods: because one never knows what a Day will be bringing forth; and therefore, it is Wise to be Prepared for the Worst Conditions, including Droughts, Famines, Wars, Deaths, Divorces, and so on. ‡

20-03 [_] O Selected King, Uncle Sam is not Interested in Providing everyone with a Good Retirement Plan: beCause Uncle Sam Understands that everyone must be Tempted by the Devil to the Maximum Amount, whereby all such Souls can be Tested for their Goodness. Otherwise, a Good Retirement Plan would have been Explained in a Chapter within the *Holy Bible,* which also needed several other Chapters about several other Important Subjects, most of which do not even get one Verse Addressed to them — such as Abortions, Gay Marriages, the Right to Bear Arms, and the Right to Vote when you are 12 Years Old, when you might be more Honest than some Old Fart, who only Thinks of himself — such as that Wicked Uncle Sam, who should be brought to Court and put on Trial for all of his LIES! Yes, it is no wonder that his Face is Full of Political Scars, and Deep Wrinkles from all of his Worries and Fears about National Security, and Future Social Security Payments. Yes, he is also Toothless, after Chewing on Sand and Gravel, you might say; but, that would be Tolerable, if he were not also Spiritually Blind and Deaf, being like some Old Elephant or Floppy-eared Emasculated Jackass, who can Trumpet and Bray very LOUDLY; but, he has no Real Workable Solutions for our Massive Problems, when Compared with your Solutions, which are most Reasonable to a Person who Studies them, which is WHY you Offer a ONE-MILLION-DOLLAR REWARD to anyone who can Prove your Solutions to be WRong, Unreasonable, or Unworkable. †§‡

20-04 [_] Well, I would Offer a Trillion-dollar Reward, if I had that Kind of Money; but, I Seriously Doubt that it would get the Attention of Elected Officials in Washington. Moreover, when you are in the Government, you are just Automatically Working for the Military Industrial Congressional Drug Cartel News Media Bankers' Complex, which is Naturally Controlled by MONEY and the Lust for more and more of it, no matter what you have to Do to get it. For Example, *CBS 60 Minutes* reported about Congressmen *Dialing for Dollars,* whereby each of them Averaged 30 Hours per Week, just across the Street from: **"The BIG White OUTHOUSE on the Not-so-Biblical Capitol DUNGHILL!" (The Chief Sins of the Divided States of United Lies!),** Book 023. In other Words, those CONgressmen and Women were Busy on the Telephones Begging for Contributions from Wealthy Americans, who might Sympathize with them, or just FEAR that the other Party might get into Power or Control, when both Parties and all Parties are Controlled by those Lying Edomite Gangster Banksters, who Control the Money Supply, who can Cause Great Depressions by Withholding Money, and also Cause Recessions by "Creating" Housing Bubbles, and then Bursting them into our Faces, like they did during 1929—1941, and during 2008, when hundreds of millions of People around the World "Lost their Shirts," as they say: beCause of the Great Recession, whereby Americans, for Example, were Losing some 600 to

800 thousand Jobs per Month! But, not to Worry: beCause that also Neatly Wiped Out their Life's Savings, if they had any: beCause they had to Live on SOMETHING, which, of course, was their Life's Savings! Therefore, all of that Money was Spent on "Survival," which was Absorbed into the False Economy, which is a Financial Deception, much like the Magician's Scarf is Stuffed into and Hidden in his False Thumb. {See www.Amazon.com for: **"The Great False Economy is now DEBUNKED!" (Adolf Hitler had a Much Better Economic System!) By The Worldwide People's Revolution!® Book 053.**}

20-05 [_] O Selected King, Uncle Sam is as Phony as the so-called "Foods" in Gross Grocery Stores, which are not Fit to Eat; and as Deceptive as the Artificially-flavored Sugar-water in so-called Fruit Juice Drinks, which millions of Poor People Buy: beCause they cannot Afford Real Fruit Juices, which Cost 5 to 10 Times as much Money. For Example, the 100% Pure Mango Juice is Selling for about 6$ per Liter, while the Imitation Mango-flavored Recycled Sewage Water is Selling for only $1.59 per Gallon, which would be about 40 Cents per Quart, as opposed to 6$, which would be 15 Times the Price! Therefore, what Poor Family could Afford the Healthy 100% Pure Mango Juice with Natural Pulp?

20-06 [_] Well, if those "Poor People" were Living within those **"GLORIOUS Swanky Hotels Castles and Fortresses!" (Beautiful Planned City States for WISE Intelligent Well-Educated People with Common Sense and Good Understanding!)**, Book 019, they could ALL Afford the 100% Pure Mango Juice: beCause it would be made as Abundant as Mangos, themselves, which would be Produced by the hundreds of BILLIONS by **"The Swanky Associations of Working Soldiers,"** Book 018, which would Concentrate on Growing GOOD Foods, and so many of them as to have a 10-year Supply of them in Reserve at all Times for everyone on the Earth, who Acts Wisely and Joins those Associations, one of which is **"The Swanky Association of All-Mineral Organic Gardeners,"** which will Perform MILLIONS of Experiments around the World, until the Best Mangoes can be Discovered and Duplicated. In other Words, we must Discover HOW to Grow Healthy Happy Mango Trees with the most Fragrant Flavorful Mangos, and then Graft those Twigs onto Mango Trees around the World: beCause they are a Superior Fruit, which can be Frozen in Proper Freezer Boxes, and Preserved for at least 10 Years, which is also True of Dates and Figs, and perhaps Blueberries, Gooseberries, Blackberries, Raspberries, and Strawberries, which can be Preserved with Pure Honey, and made into Various Kinds of Iced-creams, for Survival Foods, whenever the Trees are not Bearing Fruits: beCause of whatever Reasons. ‡

20-07 [_] O Selected King, what about the Billions of People who will not Want to JOIN those Swanky Associations of Working Soldiers, who want to Remain as Independent Jackasses, who have never Studied: **"The Loathsome Burdens of the Independent Jackasses!" (A New Approach for Solving our Massive Problems!)**, Book 051? Will any of those Independent Jackasses get any Foods and Drinks from **"The Swanky Association of Merciful Missionaries,"** when the Great Famine comes? §

20-08 [_] Well, that all Depends on just how Many People Join **"The Swanky Associations of Working Soldiers,"** Book 018, which I am Hoping will be at least 90% of the People; but, if not, Uncle Sam will do his Best to Store up some Old Rancid Butter and Dehydrated Potatoes in Government Warehouses, along with Devitalized Rice, Highly-refined White Flour, White Sugar, and Dried Bulls' Testicles, which are now run into Hot Dogs, a little here and a little there, one Nut at a Time. Yes, Uncle Sam already has such a Plan, with at least one Warehouse full of Frozen

Hotdogs, whereby each American has a 2-week Supply of such so-called "Foods," just in Case there is an "Emergency," whereby FEMA will Save us! For Example, if some Enemy Explodes an Atomic Bomb in the Upper Atmosphere, it will Knock Out the ElecTrickery for no less than 2 Years, and that 2-week Supply of Rancid Butter, Dehydrated Powered Potatoes, Parmesan Cheese, Macaroni, and Imitation Recycled Sewage Water will all Disappear within a Day or less: beCause of the Great DEMAND; and then the Greatly Deceived Americans will be Whining and Complaining about how BADLY Uncle Sam is Mistreating them! Indeed, Poor Ignorant Uncle Sam is not Aware of the Bad Effects of 300+ Million Americans with Weapons in their Hands, being Well-armed by the *Second Amendment* to the Constitution for the FALSE Government, which has ZERO Provisions for Drinkable Water Storage, Large Cisterns for Flushing Toilets and Washing Clothes, and Well-preserved Fruits and Vegetables: because none of those Things are Listed on the Constitutional Menu, you might say. In Fact, it was written by Spiritual Children, for Spiritual Babies, who have no Idea what a Great FAMINE even Looks like: beCause, when someone Attempts to Show to them some of those Poor Starving Africans, on the Greatly Worshiped TV, they simply Change Channels: beCause they have no Interest in the Realities of Life in Africa, nor even in their own Backyards, you might say: beCause "it is Upsetting" to them. Therefore, when their own Bellybuttons are Rubbing on their own Backbones for Hunger and Thirst, they might Recall how GOOD those **"GLORIOUS Swanky Hotels Castles and Fortresses"** are, which are Designed for Survival and Prosperity at the same Time.

20-09 [_] O Selected King, you would Surely not Expect Proud Americans to Humble themselves by Means of Fasting and Praying, whereby they might come to Realize the Great Importance of having a GOOD RELIABLE FOOD and WATER SUPPLY, and for each Person, at Home: because, if the ElecTrickery goes OFF, not even the Gas and Water Pumps will Work; and therefore, no one will be Able to Transport that Rancid Butter and those Dehydrated Potatoes from those Government Warehouses to the People, who are in Desperate Need of those DELICIOUS Satisfying Foods, who have been Used to Eating Hamburgers, Pizzas, Iced-creams, Candies and all such Tasty Foods, who will be in SHOCK by the Third Day, who will be Pulling Out their Hairs, Screaming for Pains in their Stomachs, and even Cannibalizing their Naaberz: beCause of FEARING that they might Starve to Death within a Week or less! Yes, they are not Aware that it is Possible to Fast, or Stop Eating, for as much as 100 Days without Starving to Death, which many People have Proven. Indeed, Holy Moses Fasted for 80 Days, according to *Deuteronomy 9:9, and 18,* when he was 80 Years Old. Therefore, you do not have to Castrate yourself, just to have something to Eat, much less take a Hunk of Fresh Flesh Out of your Fat Grandmother's Leg, just to Feed the Children: beCause you can Fast on nothing but Water for 40 Days and 40 Nights, while Uncle Sam is Delivering that Rancid Butter and Dehydrated Potatoes, which will Naturally KILL YOU, if you are so Ignorant as to Eat it, after Fasting for a Week or more: beCAUSE Potatoes are Extremely Sticky and thus CONSTIPATING, whereby they will "LOCK UP" in your Bowels, and KILL YOU! Yes, what you Need is Plenty of FRESH Fruit Juices — such as Grapefruit and Orange Juices, which will Loosen Up and FLUSH OUT the Sticky Filth and Stink and Poisons that have Accumulated within your Bowels, after doing some Fasting. †§‡§§ {See www.Amazon.com for: **"HOW to Become a HOLY Man!" (40 Good Reasons WHY People Should FAST and PRAY!),** Book 045, plus: **"The Proper RULES for FASTING!" (The Compete Instruction Manual for True Repentance!),** Book 046.}

20-10 [_] Well, I would say that the Prophet Isaiah was Correct — that a Person is Cursed, if he puts his Trust in People, and especially in Government Officials, none of whom Accept any

Personal Responsibilities for whatever might go WRong with the Government. After all, it is Extremely easy to Blame someone else, including the Children, who often take Illegal Drugs, just for the Experience of Using them. After all, their Hypocritical Parents are Consuming Legal Drugs by the thousands. Therefore, "If Mom and Dad can do it, so can I," they say. However, after the Flint, Michigan, Lead-pipe Episode, WHO in his or her Right Mind would Trust any Government in **"The Divided States of United Lies!"**? One such Addicted Parent Consumed no less than 40,000 Pills during just 10 Years.

20-11 [_] O Selected King, the SINators had a "Hearing" on Synthetic Drug Abuses, and Revealed that it is a Pandemic Problem, which could Ruin the Great Divided States of United Lies: beCause there are Literally thousands of Kinds of New Synthetic Drugs, which can be as Small as a Grain of Salt, whereby just a few Grains can Kill a Person! Therefore, what is to be Done about such a Pandemic?

20-12 [_] Well, as I stated in my other Book, called: **"The Loathsome Burdens of the Independent Jackasses,"** Book 051, nobody would be Dealing with those Drugs, if there were no Money for Buying them. Therefore, it is just a matter of getting Rid of Money, which will Drastically Cut Down on Drug Dealing, if not Kill it. After all, what would a Drug Addict Trade for his 3 or 4 Grains of Contaminated Salt?

20-13 [_] Well, O Selected King, it might become Inconvenient to Trade Knives, Forks, and Spoons for Drugs; but, I am Sure that Desperate Drug Addicts will figure out HOW to Continue Trading in Drugs, even if they have to Trade Sex for it. After all, once they are "Hooked" on Drugs, they are Trapped in that Awful Deep Dark Bottomless Pit, unless they Discover: **"The Proper RULES for FASTING,"** Book 046, which makes it easy to Overcome all Drugs, both Legal and Illegal. However, with such a Wicked Person in Charge of such Things as Scar-faced Uncle Sam, very few People are going to Hear about that Inspired Book, much less Actually take up Fasting, which is not an Easy Thing to Do while being Hooked on Drugs.

20-14 [_] Well, it is now Time to put someone like our Selected King in Charge of this World of Woes, whereby there might be a Slight Chance of getting it Straightened Out, before everyone becomes a Drug Addict, and thus a Child of Satan, the Devil, who is the Chief Angel of Hell, you might say, who is the Inventor and Inspirer of all such Evil Things. Indeed, there must be a much Better Way to Live, and without becoming a Work Slave, Tax Slave, Debt Slave, Interest Slave, Drug Slave, Insurance Slave, nor any other Kind of Slave. Therefore, by the next Memorial Day, we should have a New Song to Sing in Honor of **"The New RIGHTEOUS One-World Government!" (HOW to Establish a Righteous One-World Government without Going to WAR!) By The Worldwide People's Revolution!®**, Book 056. {See www.Amazon.com for: **"Our Elected King Who Speaks Out!" (It is High Time for some Sane Person to Get Control of this Insane World!) By The Worldwide People's Revolution!®** Book 070.}

20-15 [_] O Selected King, according your Master Plan, no one would have to Plan for his or her Future, nor Save any Money for his or her Future Retirement: beCause everything would be Provided by **"The Swanky Associations of Working Soldiers,"** Book 018, whereby everyone would Retire within only 6 Years of Common Skilled Labor within those **"Beautiful Swanky PALACES!"** Yes, it Sounds Unbelievable to most People; but, it is Physically Possible, and most Practical. After all, when everything is Set Up Correctly, 2 or 3 People could Feed a hundred

People from the Proodqs that they might Prudqs from their Gardens, Vineyards and Orchards. Indeed, even Old People can Pick Strawberries from a Raised Bed that is 2 feet high, whereby they do not have to Bend Over much in the Garden: because of Vertical Farming, whereby the Strawberries are Growing in Special Planter Boxes, from 2 feet to 5 feet high on a Slanting Wall on each Side of a Raised Bed, like this very Rough Drawing shows:

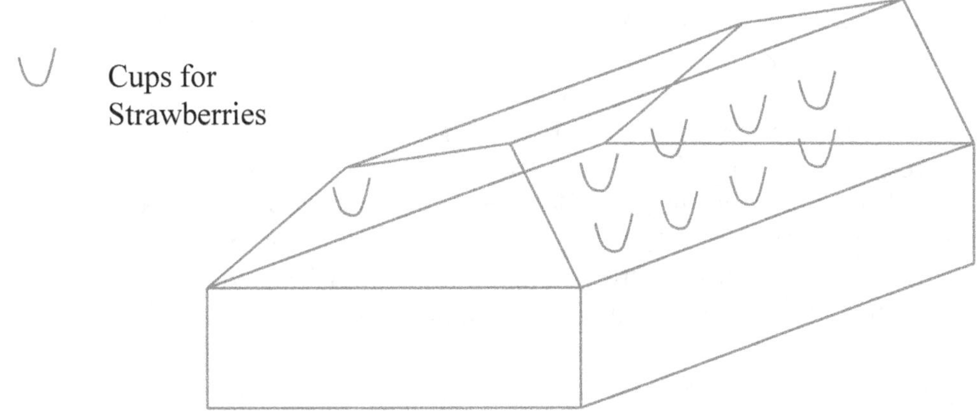

20-16 [_] So, the Planter Box would be filled with Topsoil from the Bottom to the Top, and the "Cups" would reach outward, like this End View shows, huh?

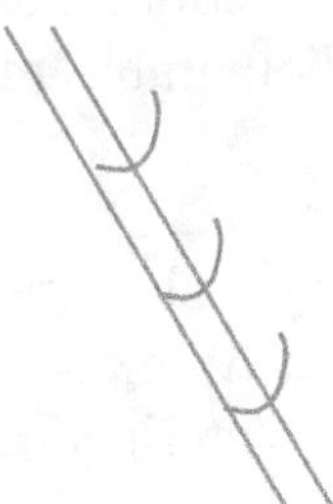

20-17 [_] Yes, that is the Basic Idea, except that the "Cups" would be full of Topsoil, which would be Connected to the Topsoil inside of the Planter Box: because there would be Holes in the Wall, which could be made of Ceramic Clay that is 2-inches thick, and Painted on the Outside with Bright Flowers, which would Attract the Honeybees, who would Pollinate the Strawberries, which would be Growing out of the Cups. Moreover, such "Panels" with "Cups" could be made in Sections that are 2 feet wide and 5 feet tall: so that 2 Strong Men could Maneuver the Panels into Place, by Hand. Otherwise, those Panels could be made 20 feet long with Concrete, and be set in Place with a Crane, if there were a lot of those Planter Boxes to be Built. †‡

20-18 [_] I Believe that it would be less of a Problem to just have a Normal Raised Garden Bed that is 3 feet tall, 6 feet wide, and 40 feet long, which is FLAT and easy to Work around, which can be used for Growing Various Kinds of Plants. After all, there is lots of Space in Texas for Spreading Things Out, without Trying to Grow Strawberries Vertically. Otherwise, you could Plant a Strawberry Tree, Cherry Tree, or some other Fruit Tree, and not have to Deal with Ceramic Retainer Walls with Cups for Strawberries, which could be made of Stainless Steel; but, in my Honest Opinion, it would be a Waste of Precious Metals.

20-19 [_] Do you not know that Strawberries will make your Mouth Bleed, if you Overeat on them? Why not Plant Grapes, which will Dissolve your Precious Teeth: beCause of the Acids in them? †§‡§§

20-20 [_] I much Prefer Cherimoyas, Soft Dates, Yellow Sapotes, and certain Kinds of Dried Figs.

20-21 [_] Okay, we can Conclude by saying that Uncle Sam has some Crazy Nieces and Nephews, huh?

20-22 [_] I would say that each Beautiful Planned City State should have the Freedom to Choose HOW to Grow their own Gardens, Vineyards and Orchards, just so long as they can figure out HOW to Do it without Poisoning the Good Earth, by the Organic Method, without the Use of Harmful Chemicals, Pesticides, Herbicides, nor Genetically-modified Seeds and Trees. After all, the Objective is to Obtain the Healthiest Happiest People in the World. Therefore, if it Requires more Work to get it done Riit, then that is the Thing to Do. ‡

20-23 [_] Sometimes it is more Beneficial to do LESS Work, and just allow Nature to take Care of it. For Example, you could do a lot of Digging around your Fruit and Nut Trees, and thus Damage the Roots of the Trees, and make them Susceptible to Bad Bugs and Diseases; or, you could just stay away from those Trees, except to put down a 4-inch Layer of Properly-composted Horse Manure under Swanky Mulching Rocks, once every 3 to 4 Years, whereby the Earthworms would "Plow" it into the Topsoil, along with the Powdered Rock Minerals that have been added to the Compost, which will Feed the Worms that Feed the Trees. Therefore, that Plan needs to be Experimented with, and Accurate Records and Photographs made of it, whereby it can be Copied, Scientifically.

20-24 [_] I would say that a Good Memorial Day Celebration should including the Planting of Millions of Fruit and Nut Trees, even for the Wild Animals and Birds to Feast on. Moreover, we should Build Stone Shelters for them, and set up Watering Tanks, and make it a Good World for all Wildlife. Yes, that is what Muhammad Ali would have done.

— Chapter 21 —

Appendix 1 — A Memorial Day Eulogy for World Heavy-weight Champion Muhammad Ali

21-01 [_] Muhammad Ali — otherwise known as Cassius Marcellus Clay, Jr., his Slave Holder's Name — was born January 17th, 1942, and died June 3rd, 2016, at age 74, who was and still is known as "The Greatest," "The People's Champion," "The Louisville Lip," "Pretty Boy Ali," and "Fast Track Islamic Poet," who had a Good Mind, a Better Heart, a Strong Constitution, a Stubborn Determination to Do what he Believed was RIIT, a Persistent Will to Stick with it, and the Humbleness to Confess his Failures. He was, in short, nothing less than an American Hero with Dark Skin, Brown Eyes, and a White Pure Honest Soul, you might say.

21-02 [_] Muhammad Ali was an American Heavyweight World Champion Boxer with 61 Fights, 56 Wins, 37 Wins by Knock Out Blows, 5 Losses, and 0 Defeats. His Best Victory in Life came when he Defeated Uncle Sam with his Knock Out Blow to the War in Vietnam, which set him Apart from all other American Champions, whereby he Suffered Persecutions and Ridicules from Various Sources, and especially from Government Officials, News Reporters, Magazine Publishers, Authors, Preachers, and Misguided Sunday School Teachers, who Vainly Imagined that Cassius Clay should have done his "Duty" and "Served his Nation" in Vietnam for the Sake of Poor Old Scar-faced Uncle Sam, who got his Ass Kicked by a little Man called Ho Chi Minh, who had the Sword of Truth on his Side, who was the First Secretary of the Central Committee of the Communist Party of Vietnam, and the First Elected President of the *Democratic Republic of Vietnam* from 1945—1969, who only wanted to Raise the Standard of Living for the Millions of Victims of Capitalism, who now Work for 65 Cents per Hour, who had been Lorded Over by Rich Hogs for Decades, who got just Exactly what they Deserved when Ho Chi Minh and the Viet Cong Defeated the *French Union* in 1954 at the Battle of Dien Bien Phu. And thus *Ho Chi Minh City* replaced Saigon, Vietnam, and Uncle Sam tucked his Tale of Lies between his Hind Legs and Ran for the Bushes and Briers in New Orleans, as Muhammad Ali might say with a Grin, while Remembering the Battle of New Orleans, in 1814.

21-03 [_] Yes, for his Resistance to the Evil Empire, he was Charged with "Draft Evasion," and Sentenced to 5 Years in Prison, after being Fined for 10,000$ and Banned from Boxing for 3 Years; but, his Conviction was later Overturned by the Department of Injustices on Account of the Fact that they Discovered that Muhammad Ali was 100% Human, and not some "Missing Link" between Man and Monkey, whose Religious Convictions had Precedents over his Military Duties to Murder other Poor Innocent Souls in the Names of Demon-ocracy, Freedom, Liberty, and Justice for NONE, which is Represented by Uncle Sam's "Stars and Stripes," which are Drenched with Innocent Blood from the 1500's and onward: beCause Uncle Sam was and still is a WARMONGERING Son of Satan, who always Wages War in the Holy Names of "freedom, liberty, and justice for ALL," but, not with Capital Letters, as in True Freedom, True Liberty, nor True Justice for anyone: beCause Uncle Sam is only Interested in just one Thing, which is Gaining more WEALTH. Yes, he calls it "the interests of America," which is a Euphemism for "America's Personal Gain at the Expense of whomever might get in the Way of her Interests, which begin with Gaining more and more MONEY, at whatever the Cost to People, the Earth, and whomever gets in the Way of so-called 'Progress,' which is Promoted most Equitably by the 1% who Owns 80% of the Wealth." Yes, it is a Strange Paradox, if you Think about it: beCause, at the same Time, she Claims to be "Christian" in Nature and Judeo-Christian in Practice! †§‡

21-04 [_] To put it more Understandably in the Minds of Innocent Children, that would be like saying that Jesus Christ Sells Cigarettes to Raise Money for Cancer Research, thereby doing the World a Great Favor, for which he should be Awarded with the most Noble Peace Prizes. †§‡

21-05 [_] There is now little Doubt in any Honest Person's Mind that Muhammad Ali made a Major Mistake when he Joined the Sunni Branch of the Muslim Islamic Faith, whose Far Right-wing Representatives are now known as ISIS (Israeli Secret Instigation Services), who are raising such Havoc in the Middle East, who would like to Establish an Islamic Government over all of the Nations: beCause of Judging that other MuhamMAD to be "God's Most Holy Prophet," when he never even gave so much as ONE Prophecy about anything in the Future that ever Happened, as far as we know, much less the many Prophecies that were given by Jesus Christ in *the Book of Revelation,* which seem to be Realities of our Time — such as *the Mark of the Beast* Numbering System, whereby no Man can Buy nor Sell anything without the Use of his Personal Identification Numbers — much like the Nazis Numbered the Victims of the Nazi Concentration Camps, who had Identification Numbers Tattooed on their Arms, as in "AU10746AU," which stood for Prisoner Number 10,746 in Auschwitz, Poland, which Distinguished that Person from "AU10747AU," who may have been a Son or Daughter. However, the most Interesting Thing about those ID Numbers was the Fact that the Greatest Number was less than 105,000: beCause there were NOT Millions of Jews put into any such Concentration Camps; but, there were tens of thousands of them. You can Discover the Truth about it on YouTube Videos. (See *HoloHOAX,* for beginners.) †§‡

21-06 [_] First of all, there are thousands of Aerial Photographs that were taken by Russian Reconnaissance Airplanes during World War 2, showing the Number of Barracks, or "Condominiums," at Auschwitz, which Reveal more Truths than you might Imagine: beCause one such Barracks / House might have contained as many as 300 Bodies, Maximum, being only 30 Meters Long and 7 to 8 Meters Wide, and 3 Meters Tall. None of the Beds were on the Floors, and most of the Beds were in 2 or 3 Tiers, like Shelves in a Warehouse. None of them were 4 or 5 Deep, as the HoloHOAXERS Loudly Proclaim. However, even if they had been 5 High on each Side of a Barracks, those Houses could not have Possibly Held anywhere near a Million Prisoners at any given Time: because there were less than 100 such Barracks in Auschwitz! Therefore, even if it were Possible to get 1,000 Victims in one Barracks, that would be a Total of 100,000 Victims. However, many of those Buildings in the Photographs were Workshops for the Inmates, and NOT Sleeping Quarters, at all. Therefore, given the Reality of the Situation, it is Fair to say that as many as 200 to 300 Persons could have been Bedded Down in each Barracks, for a Total of 30,000 Inmates at any given Time, which is a very Long Ways from the False Accounts of those Lying Edomites, who like to Exaggerate almost everything. ‡

21-07 [_] O Selected King, how did you Manage to JUMP from the Memorial of Muhammad Ali into the HoloHOAX Museum in Washington, District of Criminals? Do you find some Connection between the Holocaust and Muhammad Ali?

21-08 [_] Well, there is no Direct Connection — even as there is no Direct Connection between Muhammad Ali and the Sunni Islamic Religions, which are Worlds Apart from the Heart and Soul of Muhammad Ali in Words and in Deeds: beCause he most Certainly did NOT have the Evil Nature of those Radical Sunni Muslims, much less the more Vile Nature of Radical Shiite Muslims, who Flog themselves with Chains, or Straps, until they Bleed, which Saddam Hussein Outlawed in Iraq: beCause, "he was the Bad Guy," you might say, if you Worked for the Warmonger Bush Regime, who Visualized Saddam Hussein as being the WORST of the Worst Offenders, even though he is likely to Enter into the Kingdom of God long before George Warmonger Bush, who Caused the Deaths and Woundings of more than 2 Million People in the Middle East, and the Displacements of no less than 10 Million other Poor Victims of his Insanities — all beCAUSE of his Disobeying the Constitution for the United States of America, which he Swore to Uphold! Yes, it clearly states that the United States shall NOT Attack any Nation, until we are First Attacked. Therefore, he Clearly Broke the LAW with his "Preemptive Attack on Iraq." †§‡

21-09 [_] O Selected King, did your own Stepfather not also Clearly Break the Law with his Preemptive Attack on Poland, during September of 1939?

21-10 [_] NO. It was NOT a Preemptive Attack: because the Polacks had been Attacking Eastern German Farmers for no less than 8 Years, before my "Adopted Father" Executed some Justice on them, whereby the Polacks got just Exactly what they Deserved, which was later on Enhanced by the Communists, who Mistreated the Polacks much Worse than my so-called "Stepfather," after those Bloody Communists took Control of Poland — in spite of the Fact that Sir Winston Cigar-chomping Whiskey-guzzling Lying Churchill had PROMISED the Polacks Protection, if they got into a War with the Germans and Russians. Indeed, Sir Winston turned out to be Poland's Worst TRAITOR, which is now Verified by the History Channel, which did a Documentary Program on the whole Thing, which you are Welcome to Study for yourself. Yes, as it turned out, those Russian Communists were the BAD Guys, who Murdered tens of millions of Innocent People — NOT Adolf Hitler! Nevertheless, **"The Divided States of United Lies"** Sided with the Communists and Capitalists of the World: beCause of being Chief Proponents of Communism and Capitalism: beCause American Red Jews are otherwise called ZIONISTS, as **Rabbi Michael Lerner** pointed out in his Eulogy at the Funeral of Muhammad Ali, who most Accurately Expressed my own Sentiments at the Funeral Service on June 10th, 2016, in Louisville, Kentucky. Yes, he was the Star of the whole Program, in my Honest Opinion, being an Honest White Jew, who Pulls no Punches, as Muhammad Ali might say, who would be Happy to Punch Israeli Prime Minister Benjamin Netanyahu square in the Mouth: beCause of his Mistreatments of Palestinian Muslims, who also have Radical Muslims among them, who are mostly Seeking JUSTICE in the Cases of Israeli "Land Grabs," who basically STOLE the Land from those Palestinians, much like the British and Americans Stole the Land from the American Indians, who have yet to get any True Justice, who were simply Overrun by Warmongers, Incorporated. Yes, the Military Industrial Congressional Bankers' Complex was very Busy several hundred Years Ago, doing what they do Best, which is to Steal, Lie, Cheat, Rob, Rape, Enslave, and Mutilate other People, rather than figure out HOW to Help all Peoples to Prosper in a Right Way: so that there are no Poor Miserable

People among us. After all, the Earth does not Lack any Materials, Young Voluntary Working Soldiers, Money, nor Technologies for doing that Correctly; but, it does Lack a New RIGHTEOUS One-World GovernMINT!

21-11 [_] O Selected King, are you Aware that there are AshkeNAZI Jews, Sephardi Jews, Mizrahi Jews, Beta Israel Jews, Bene Israeli Jews, Karaite Jews, and many other Groups of Jews in this World of Woes — all of whom Claim to be the TRUE Descendants of Father Abraham, who was only a Jewish MYTH? Indeed, there is ZERO Physical Evidence to Prove the Existence of any Biblical Characters, including Moses, Elijah, King David, King Solomon, and Jesus Christ, himself! Yes, I find it Strange that anyone in the World with a RIIT Mind would Fall for such Edomite Nonsense, seeing that none of those Characters left any Physical Evidence of their Existence! For Example, NONE of their Graves have been Discovered, which is rather Strange for "the Richest Man of all Ages," whom the Jewish Mythmakers called King Solomon, who could not even Manage to Build a Stone Tomb for himself, in spite of supposedly Receiving a Billion Dollars-worth of Gold each Year from his Tributaries, who Loved him for his Great Wisdom, who was so Unwise as to Marry 700 Wives and 300 Concubines, which MuhamMAD Attempted to Imitate, and Failed to get enough Erections to Impregnate so few as 3 Wives with his Seeds. Indeed, he must have needed some Viagra for his Erectile Dysfunctions, seeing that his own Children did not Multiply like those of Genghis Khan, who had 11 Wives and 3 Children, whose Mongol Empire became "the largest contiguous empire in history after his death," according to *Wikipedia.* Yes, Genghis Khan started the Mongol Invasions that resulted with the Conquest of most of Eurasia, and the wholesale Massacres of Civilian Populations. Strangely enough, he was also Buried in an Unmarked Grave, somewhere in Mongolia, at an Unknown Location: beCause it was Feared that Future Generations of Enlightened People might Desecrate his Grave, and Burn his Rancid Bones, whereby they might Destroy his Unholy Spirit, which might be Born in the Body of a Pig the next Time Around, which is also every Lying Bloodthirsty Red Jew's Greatest Fear. After all, there is hardly anything Lower than a Hog, and yet they Want to Hoggishly Control the Money Supply: because they Believe in **Meritocracy**, which is Government by People who are Selected on the Basis of their Abilities and Qualifications to Govern — such as Hilarious Rotten Clinton, who likely knows more about Running a Wicked Government than any other Woman on the Earth! †§‡§§

21-12 [_] Well, I am also a Believer in Meritocracy, which is much more Rational and Practical than DEMON-ocracy, or MOB Rulership, which is supposed to be WHY we have a so-called "REPUBLIC," which is Government by which the Supreme Power is held by the Rich People and their Elected Representatives — as in the Union of Soviet Socialist Republicans (USSR) — who always Elected the most Truthful Honest Representatives — none of whom have ever taken any Tests of their Beliefs: because that is Unconstitutional in **"The Divided States of United Lies"**: beCause some Electors might Discover too much Truth about their Potential Representatives, and thus not Vote for them. However, I Propose that all Potential Candidates for all Offices of Governments should have to Fill Out and File **"The Complete SURVEYS of our VALUES,"** Book 059. Yes, I also Propose that no one should have a Right to Vote for any such Potential Leaders, until he or she or it has also Filled Out and Filed the Complete Surveys of their own Values on the Internet for everyone to Study, no matter what their Beliefs might be: beCause there is a Possibility that at least ONE of them might Qualify to be the Elected KING of the whole World, in which Case he could Sit on the Great White Ivory Throne of **"The New RIGHTEOUS One-World Government,"** in: **"The Great World TEMPLE of PEACE!"** (The Glory of

Jerusalem Arises Again!) By The Worldwide People's Revolution!®, Book 017, which Good Government will just Naturally Enforce the LAWS and RULES of: "The CONSTITUTION for the New RIGHTEOUS One-World GovernMINT!" (HOW all Peoples can get True Justice, and Celebrate the Great Year of JUBILEE!), Book 016, which is a Companion Book of: "Seven Great Armies of Working Soldiers!" (HOW to Provide a Way for Everyone to WORK: so as to Eliminate Poverty, Crimes, Drug Abuses, Prisons and Unnecessary Taxes!), Book 015, which is a Companion Book of: "The Swanky Associations of Working Soldiers!" (A Fascinating Collection of Various Kinds of Voluntary Working Soldiers!), Book 018, which is a Companion Book of those "GLORIOUS Swanky Hotels Castles and Fortresses!" (Beautiful Planned City States for WISE Intelligent Well-Educated People with Common Sense and Good Understanding!), Book 019, which is a Companion Book of: "The Right Design for Living!" (A List of Great Advantages for Building Beautiful Planned City States!), Book 012, which is a Companion Book of: "The Low Court of Supreme Injustices is Brought to Trial!" (Our Elected King Butts Heads with the United States Supreme Court, with or without their Black Robes of Hypocrisies and Lies!), Book 011, which is a Companion Book of: "Poverty Hunger Riots Strikes Brutalities Election Deceptions and Civil Wars!" (The High Price that we Earthlings have Paid for Leaving the Good Land!), Book 014, which is a Companion Book of: "The LUSCIOUS All-Mineral Organic Method of Gardening!" (HOW to Grow DELICIOUS Satisfying Foods for Potential Kingz and Kweenz in Swanky PALACES!), Book 021, which is a Companion Book of: "Orgimmick Gardening at its Best!" (HOW to Grow Delicious Satisfying Foods without a 10-Million-Dollar Investment!), Book 079, which is a Companion Book of: "Did God or Satan Ordain Medical Doctors??" (Ask Huck Finn and/or Nigger Jim: because neither Tom Sawyer nor Judge Thatcher would Know!), Book 022, which is a Companion Book of: "The Public School of IGNERUNT FQLZ!" (HOW we have been GRAATLEE DISEEVD by Capitalism!), Book 024, which is a Companion Book of: "Are you a Jobless Graduate of the SKQL uv FQLZ?" (HOW to get a GOUD EJUKAASHUN without Robbing the Bank!), Book 020, which is a Companion Book of: "The BIG White OUTHOUSE on the Not-so-Biblical Capitol DUNGHILL!" (The Chief Sins of the Divided States of United Lies!), Book 023, which is a Companion Book of: "Does a Good Soldier have to be a MURDERER?" (Seven Great Swanky Armies of Voluntary Working Soldiers!), Book 027, which is a Companion Book of: "God Speaks and the Whole World Listens!" (Fire on the Mountain from the Burning Bush by the Spirit of Truth!), Book 026, which is a Companion Book of: "Thu Nq MAGNUFIID Verzhun uv Thu PROVERBZ uv KING SOLUMUN in Plaan Inggglish!" (The Understandable Version of the Famous Proverbs of King Solomon in Plain English!), Book 028, which is a Companion Book of: "ECCLESIASTES UNCOVERED!" (The New MAGNIFIED Version of Ecclesiastes and the Song of Solomon in Plain English!), Book 034, which is a Companion Book of: "The Seven Basic Spiritual Building Blocks of LIFE!" (Faith Hope Trust Love Patience Persistence and Obedience!), Book 036, which is a Companion Book of: "In thu Beeginingz uv Thingz!" (Thu Kreeaashun Stooree frum thu Beegining!), Book 025, which is a Companion Book of: "The Gospel According to our Elected King!" (The Good News from the Most Modern Perspective!), Book 077, which is a Companion Book of: "FREEDUM uv SPEECH!" (U Speshoul Maguzeen uv Onist Upinyunz!), Book 030-0001, which is a Companion Book of: "UNLIMITED ENERJEE 99 Percent Pollutions Free!" (HOW to Obtain FREE ElecTrickery, Worldwide!), Book 029, which is a Companion Book of: "A Sure Cure for GUN VIOLENCE!" (HOW TO STOP GANG WARS and CRIMINAL SHOOTINGS!), Book 031, which is a Companion Book of: "AIIRMWVC and Reasonable Solutions!" (Aliens, Illegal

Immigrants, Refugees, Migrant Workers and other Victims of Capitalism!), Book 032, which is a Companion Book of: "Mark Twain Races for the PRESIDENCY!" (The 2020 Presidential Candidates Desperately Need Some STRONG Undefeatable COMPETITION!), Book 033, which is a Companion Book of: "The Nature of CAPITALISM!" (A List of the EVILS of CAPITALISM!), Book 038, which is a Companion Book of: "The Environmentalists' Paradise!" (HOW almost Everyone could be Living in a Beautiful Manmade Paradise!), Book 035, which is a Companion Book of: "DIETS!" (A Reasonable Solution for the "Eternal Controversy"!), Book 037, which is a Companion Book of: "SWANGKEENOMIKS Rules the Roost!" (HOW all People can PROSPER in a RIIT WAA, and STOP Polluting the Earth with Capitalist TRASH!), Book 039, which is a Companion Book of: "The New MAGNIFIED Version of The Book of MORMON!" (The Story of the White and Dark Indians in the Americas!), Book 040, which is a Companion Book of: "The Great Worldwide TELEVISED Court HEARING!" (That Great Meeting of the Most Intelligent and Well-Educated Minds!), Book 041, which is a Companion Book of: "Terrorists Beware that your Days are Numbered!" (HOW to Bring those Terrorists Attacks to a Screeching HALT!), Book 043, which is a Companion Book of: "Are Americans the Most STUPID People who ever Lived?" (HOW Working People can PROSPER and Live in PEACE Under the Rulership of a RIGHTEOUS KING!), Book 047, which is a Companion Book of: "The Secret City of the Great King!" (HOW the True Church will Escape from the Great Tribulation!) By The Worldwide People's Revolution!®, Book 042, which is a Companion Book of: "The New MAGNIFIED Version of ISAIAH in Plain English!" (The Understandable Version of the Book of Isaiah!), Book 044, which is a Companion Book of: "HOW to Become a HOLY Man!" (40 Good Reasons WHY People Should FAST and PRAY!), Book 045, which is a Companion Book of: "The Proper RULES for FASTING!" (The Complete Instruction Manual for True Repentance!), Book 046, which is a Companion Book of: "What is WRong with those Professing Christians?" (A Self-Examination of the Heart of the Body of Good Government!), Book 002, which is a Companion Book of: "What is WRong with those CRAZY Christians?" Book 076, which is a Companion Book of: "For the Love of Money!" (The Strange Things that People Say and Do to Get more Money!), Book 003, which is a Companion Book of: "HOW to Prepare for CLIMATE CHANGES!" (The Wisest Plan for Mankind to Follow!), Book 004, which is a Companion Book of: "WHY do I have to be Surrounded by CRAZY PEOPLE?" (Do almost all People Feel like they are Surrounded by Crazy People??), Book 005, which is a Companion Book of: "The Washington Journal is a FARCE!" (C-SPAN Managers are not very WISE!), Book 006, which is a Companion Book of: "The PRAYERS of PUMPKINHEADS!" (Even God Needs a Little Humor to Cheer himself Up!), Book 007, which is a Companion Book of: "WHY are some Preachers so POOR?" (HOW almost all Preachers could get Moderately RICH without Preaching any Outlandish Lies!), Book 009, which is a Companion Book of: "A Sound Argument for Masters and Servants!" (WHY Everyone Needs a Good Master, and every Master Needs Good Obedient Servants!), Book 008, which is a Companion Book of: "GOOD NEWS for REBEL WOMEN!" (HOW almost all Wives can become Moderately Rich without Leaving their Homes!), Book 010, which is a Companion Book of: "Justifications for Capitalizations!" (WHY our Elected King Defies the School of Fools by Capitalizing LOVE and HATE!), Book 049, which is a Companion Book of: "An Amazing Collection of Wit and Wisdom!" (The Marvelous Tale of the Colorful Peacock from Angel Ridge, and the Strong Rope of Everlasting Hope!), Book 048, which is a Companion Book of: "The END of CONFUSION!" (The Great

CELEBRATION of the Magnificent Wedding of the Most Humble Honest Nations, and the Grand Year of JUBILEE!) Book 050!

21-13 [_] O Elected King, I Swear to God that I will Read all of those Inspired Books before I Vote for another Dimwitcrat, Reprobate, or Independent Jackass!

21-14 [_] Well, I would say that you are among the Wiser People in this World of Wonders.

21-15 [_] O Selected King, I would say that she has a LOT of Extra Time on her Hands, if she Intends to Read all of those Inspired Books within less than a Lifetime of Reading! †§‡

21-16 [_] You have got to be Kidding us! Indeed, our Selected King, wrote all of those Books in less than 3 Years — Thanks to one of those Mac Computers with a Big Screen. Therefore, if he could Write them, Proof-read them, and then read them to his Brother, who sat through all of those Readings with Concentrated Attention, then I Suggest that every Student in the World could do the same Thing; and we are all Eternal Students of the Higher School of Superior Learning.

21-17 [_] O Selected King, why do you not Publish all of those Books on CD's or DVD's: so that other People only have to Listen to them while Driving to Work, whereby they might Increase their Chances of CRASHING Head-on into some other Intent Listeners? After all, Driving does not Require a Person's Full Concentration, now that we have Smart Cars that do the Driving for us. Yes, when that Day comes, I want my Personal Copies of all 2,540 CD's of all of your Inspired Books! After all, one CD only Contains one Hour of Reading. Therefore, if it Requires 10 Hours to Read this Book Properly, it would Require at least 10 CD's, which would Cost a Minimum of 100$ for a 10$ Book! †§‡§§

21-18 [_] Well, actually, it might Require 20 Hours to Read this Inspired Book Properly, which would be SLOWLY and CAREFULLY, which is as Untraditional as True Christianity; but, that would be the RIIT WAA to do it.

21-19 [_] O Selected King, if Muhammad Ali had had a Chance to Read or Listen to all of your Inspired Books, when he was just 16 or 17 Years Old, he might have become the Elected King of the Whole World! After all, he only went through 4 Wives, and never did Finish reading any book during his Lifetime, including the Holy Koran, in spite of Claiming to be a Muslim. †§‡

21-20 [_] Well, if he had "red" or heard all of my Inspired Books when he was only 16, he would likely have had only one Wife, and she would have likely had a dozen Boys, who would have been Greater Heroes than Muhammad Ali, who probably Wished that he had it all to do over again, which is WHY his Spirit will no doubt be Born in a New Body to some more Diligent Mother, who will make Sure that her Children get to Hear all of the Inspired Words of Provable Truths within my Exceptionally Good Books, even if it takes up 2 Years of their Lives to Accomplish it. After all, there is nothing else that they could Do during this Life, that is Better than to Learn WHY they were Born. Therefore, if you Failed to Discover it, you should Re-read this Good Book, and Encourage others to Read it with Open Minds and Receptive Hearts: beCause that is what MuhamMAD would have everyone to Do, if he were here, Today. Guaranteed! Yes, I am Referring to that Legendary MuhamMAD who was Born in the Body of Muhammad Ali, himself! Indeed, we can Honestly say that his Spirit was Greatly Improved upon as he Trickled Down through Time, ever since the 600's AD. However, it is a Great Shame that he did not Discover it for himself, and will therefore have to be Recycled, once again: beCause of not Learning ALL of his Lessons, as every Soul should. PLEASE make this a Good Day, and pass this Book on to someone who might Appreciate it as much or more than yourself. Yes, Remember Muhammad Ali, who Stood Up with Great Courage in front of the Ugly Scarred Dishonest Face of Poor Old Miserable Uncle Sam, and gave to him a Hard Right-handed Punch in the Solar Plexus, and quickly Delivered 2 Left-hand Hooks to his War-torn Lower Jaw, and Knocked him Out COLD, you might say; but, now it is Time for you to Bury him under one of his own Bloody Rags, if he does not Quickly Agree to DEMAND: **"The Great Worldwide TELEVISED Court HEARING!"** — whereby we can all Learn the Whole Truth about the EVILS of Capitalism, the HoloHOAX, the MoonHOAX, the Kennedy Assassination Covered-up Pack of Deceptions, the Oklahoma City Bombing Cover-up, the False Flag Operations of World War 2, and of September 11th, 2001, and whatever else Uncle Sam is Attempting to HIDE from the Electors at large.

21-21 [_] I Promise to pass this Book on to someone who Promises to Read it and do the same, if they Like it. Otherwise, they should Kindly Return it to me.

— Chapter 22 —

Appendix 2 — A Letter to Andrew Maloney

June 3, 2016

22-01 [_] Dear Peter Slen, the *Washington Journal* Host,

22-02 [_] Please read and then Forward this E-mail Letter to Andrew Maloney — another Kind of Criminal at large!

22-03 [_] Dearest Andrew Maloney,

22-04 [_] Thank you for appearing on the *Washington Journal,* this morning. I Believe with a Capital B that you are Sincere; but, also "Dead wRong," as they say: beCause you are "a Piss Poor Representative of the Whole Truth," as my Brother said, and he does Listen Carefully with a Capital L and C.

22-05 [_] Being a Chief Lawyer of the Tribes of Levi and Judah, I am Doubly Ashamed of you with a Capital D and A — as in the Department of Attorneys are Debunked and Arrested for "Neglect of your Duties" as Representatives of the Victims of the 9/11/2001 Conspiracy.

22-06 [_] At least you do freely Confess that it was a Conspiracy with a Capital C in both Cases. However, I would also Bet that you Failed to Capitalize either Word — both on Paper, and also within your own Mind, where it is most Needed; or else you might have done some Thinking with a Capital T, and also done it in the Light of Good Understanding with King Solomon and Jesus Christ, who could put all of you Weak-minded Lawyers in your Proper Places within a Minute or 2 in a Courtroom with True Law and Order, where ALL of the Evidences are Presented for Examinations.

22-07 [_] First of all, as a Chief Architect, Engineer, Inventor, and Author of more than 300 Inspired Books, I would like to Remind you that the 9/11/2001 Trials have barely begun, which you also admitted was "just the tip of the iceberg," being without that Capital T nor I: beCause you Obviously do not Believe in True Justice, or else you would Capitalize it, on Paper, and also within your own Mind — that is, IF your Mind is still Functioning Properly after being Drugged with Government Propagandist LIES — such as the NIST Report about "Thermal Expansion" bringing down World Trade Center (WTC) Tower 7, which came Crashing Down in the Form of mostly DUST at 5:20 p.m., September 11th, 2001, whereby 283 Hardened Steel Columns (many of which were 22-inches by 52-inches by 47-stories tall) all came down in UNISON in less than 7 Seconds: beCause, beCause, beCause ... but, "NOT beCAUSE of EXPLOSIVES," declared NIST Conspiracy Theorists, who "thoroughly examined all of the evidence" and reported NOTHING about Tower 7 in *the 911 commission report,"* which was first Published, which was Published by your Lying Anti-Christ FALSE Cover-up WICKED Federal Government of the Synagogue of SATAN! Yes, I speak rather Rudely concerning it: beCause it is Obviously Guilty as Charged, which most Americans Agree with, and with a Capital A, as in Absolutely Agree 100%, after not Hearing all of the Evidences for the Kennedy Assassination Covered-up Conspiracy!

22-08 [_] Indeed, if it were not so, WHY Hide so much Information in Top Secret Government Files in Endless Vaults at the Pentagon, Federal Burdens of Instigations (FBI), and the Central Unintelligent Agencies (CIA), of which there are 30+ Agencies!? Awe, perhaps there are 200 of them, by now — HOW would us Tax Slaves Know for Sure? There seems to be Zero Accountability in Washington, District of Chief Criminals, who Swear to Uphold the Constitution, and then Fail to Defend us against all Domestic Enemies — such as George Warmonger Bush and Little Dick Chicanery, Incorporated. Otherwise, we Tax Slaves might Know something for Sure in the Line of Truths.

22-09 [_] Secondly, you Confess that millions of People SAW what Happened during 9/11 by Watching their TV's. Yes, "we all saw it," you say. Question: "Did you See any Airplanes strike WTC Tower 7?" Answer: "NO." "And neither did I," says the entire World of Honest Souls: beCause no Airplanes struck that HUGE Building, which covered nearly an entire City Block! Awe, little "Kitchen Fires" must have heated up all 283 Hardened Steel Columns, EQUALLY, to more than 3000 °F, and all from one Corner of the Building, I suppose? Pure Unadulterated NONSENSE, Andrew! Try your Best to be Realistic for a Change — nothing short of EXPLOSIVES could have brought that Building Down in the Form of PULVERIZED Concrete and "Vanished Steel," as Dr. Judy Wood put it on one of her Scientific Videos, which you have Obviously NOT Studied with a Capital S, much less Reported anything about HOW one might go about Pulverizing 900,000 TONS of Hardened Concrete without the Use of Explosives, whereby the Dust was Distributed all over the Streets for as much as 10 City Blocks away, which is Common for Imploded Buildings to do, which have been brought down by Demolitions?! Indeed, I would like you to Demonstrate just HOW that might be Done without Explosives, since NIST has not Explained it, nor Demonstrated it; and they consist of more than 3,000 Conspiracy Theorists, who call themselves "Scientists" — none of whom even Discovered any Residues of Military-grade Thermite: beCause, they confess with a lower-case c, that they never even Tested for it, nor for any other Kind of Explosives: beCause they Ruled Out that Possibility after Watching those "Passenger Airplanes" hit Towers 1 and 2 on their TV's, without Realizing that no Airplane Crashed in the Field near Shanksville, Pennsylvania: beCAUSE there were no Bodies found — no Blood, no Guts, no Teeth, no Jaw Bones, no Femurs, no Tough Penises, no 6-ton Titanium Jet Engines, no Cockpit, no Fuselage, no Wings, no Tail, no Seats, no Luggage, no Pink Underwear, no Black (Orange) Boxes, nor even any Parts of an Airplane at all, which you can Discover on YouTube Videos, beginning with www.AE911TRUTH.org and other Enlightening Websites, which go into the Necessary Details that you and C-SPAN and the Wicked Government — even the entire Military Industrial Congressional Lawyers' Snooze Reporters' Journalists' Bankers' Complex — just IGNORE! (See *Experts Speak Out* on YouTube. They are my Honest Friends. Remember, *the Truth only Asks for a Fair Hearing,* as Jesus would say. Therefore, do your Best with a Capital B.)

22-10 [_] Shame on them — that is, Shame on the Military Industrial Congressional News Media Bankers' Complex; but, Double Shame on YOU, Andrew Maloney: beCause you have a Good Head with a Sound Mind, which you should Use more often, and especially when you are in Danger of being brought to Court by our Elected King, and Charged with "Neglect of Duties as a

Lawyer." Indeed, it is your Duty to Discover the WHOLE Truth, whatever it might be in this Case: beCause that is what is Required for True Justice.

22-11 [_] Now, I Fully Understand that your Lawsuit is against Saudi Arabians and perhaps other Co-conspirators of the Evil Events of September 11th, 2001; but, your Chances of getting a Bill passed by the CONgress, in order to Accomplish it, is almost Zilch, I would say: beCause, if the CONgress was at all Interested in Truths and Justice for ALL Peoples — including ME and YOU and those Poor Ignorant People "over there" — even the 5-hundred-million-plus Victims of Capitalism in IRAQ, Afghanistan, Pakistan, Libya, Egypt, Jordan, Syria, Palestine, Somalia, and wherever in the Middle East — that CONgress would Surely DEMAND: **"The Great Worldwide TELEVISED Court HEARING,"** whereby True Justice could be Served, Worldwide: beCause of Opening ALL of the Files, and Revealing ALL of the Important Pertinent Information / Evidence, whereby we could all be Liberated from our Prison of LIES! Yes, Jesus summed it up — *"You shall Learn the Whole Truth, and the Truth will Set you Free when you Practice it."* — NMV of the Gospel According to Saint Bartholomew.

22-12 [_] So, Dearest Andrew, while you are Seeking Justice for a handful of the Victims of a Grand Conspiracy, you might want to Meditate on the Great Truths within the above mentioned Inspired Book, which you can Discover on www.Amazon.com — among many other Inspired Books for your Enlightenment with a Capital E, as in a True Education for Honest Sincere Souls, like yourself! Otherwise, I Hope to God that Adolf Hitler arises again, and puts People like you to WORK in Rock Quarries, whereby you might come to your Right Senses with the Prodigal Son of *Luke 15*. After all, this Capitalist MADNESS has gone on Long Enough, whereby 99.99% of the People in this World of Woes Suffer in their States of EXTREME Poverty! Yes, even People like you do not have Fresh Clean Air to Breathe, Pure Living Water to Drink, Wholesome Natural Foods to Eat, Natural Clothing to Wear, nor SECURE Houses to Live in with other People of Like-mindedness, whereby you might Live in PEACE — much less become Moderately RICH in all Ways! Selah. (Selah is Hebrew for *Stop and Think.*)

22-13 [_] Sincerely, The Chief Agitator

22-14 [_] PS — I do not Expect to hear a single Word from you, nor from any of the Lackeys at C-SPAN: beCause, as far as I am concerned, you are all Spiritual COWARDS, which you can Prove by NOT Responding, which will Naturally Convince me of it — along with many other People, who will no doubt Learn about it, and come to the same Sad Conclusion. Otherwise, you would put up some Solid Evidence that www.AE911TRUTH.org might be WRong! This Letter of Reproof is Copyrighted 2016 by the Chief Agitator. All Rights are Reserved.

— Chapter 23 —

Another Letter to John McArdle

23-01 [_] June 13th, 2016

23-02 [_] Dear Brother John,

23-03 [_] Thank you for Dedicating the entire Program to the Islamic / ISIS Massacre in Orlando, Florida, this morning. Chances are that most of the Survivors in Orlando were not Watching the *Washington Journal.* In Fact, I dare say that most Americans were not Watching you, and most of them who were Watching did not consist of Government Officials, nor Important People who should have been Watching: because they were Distracted by other things — such as Eating and going to Work.

23-04 [_] Moreover, I have only met a few Americans who knew what C-SPAN is all about, and most of them did not care to Upset themselves by Watching it: beCause of their Distaste for the "Wicked Government." Therefore, you must have a very low / minor Viewer Audience, none of whom mentioned: **"A Sure Cure for GUN VIOLENCE!" (HOW TO STOP GANG WARS and CRIMINAL SHOOTINGS!) By The Worldwide People's Revolution!® Book 031.**

23-05 [_] Chances are that none of them have ever Heard of it, and you said nothing to them about it, even though you have Heard about it — that is, IF anyone over there Forwarded my E-mail Letters to you? Amazon offers a ONE-MILLION-DOLLAR REWARD to anyone who can Prove that our Selected King's Solutions will not Solve that Problem, and many more.

23-06 [_] You must be getting Sick of those 3-hour *Washington Journal* "Episodes," "TV Soap Operas," "Memorial Services," or whatever you would like to call them, without discovering any Real Solutions for Gun Violence, Massive Shootings / Murders / Terrorist Attacks, or whatever the Bad Snooze Reporters like to call them. Try to not let it get you down in a Suicidal State of Great Depression: because there is still Hope for you, them and myself; but, only IF we and they are Willing to EDUCATE ourselves.

23-07 [_] Otherwise, that same Sad Song will be Sung again and again, perhaps next month, or even next week: because ISIS (Israeli Secret Instigation Services) has "Allah" on their Side, which not only makes it "Right" in their Honest Opinions; but, it DEMANDS more and more "Terrorist Attacks," even though ISIS prefers to call them "Liberation Movements," or "Justifiable Missions of Mercy with some Collateral Damages," in Arabic: because they Sincerely Believe that they are doing GOOD for God by getting Rid of those "Queers," both at home and abroad!

23-08 [_] Like the Lady said, one can be thrown off of a high roof in Saudi Arabia, just for being Gay. They get that Idea from the *Bible Story* about Jezebel being thrown out of the Window by the Eunuchs, who was Trampled on by Horses and Chariots, and Eaten by the Dogs, just after she

Painted her Face, and Polished her Fingernails, and Perfumed her Buttocks. She was a Syrian Queen who "Perverted" Israel. (See *Second Kings 9:30—37.*)

23-09 [_] So, HOW can we "Defeat" them, seeing that "GOD" is on their Side? Well, first of all, we would have to Persuade them to Change their Minds about that, which you and I Know for a FACT is an Impossibility: beCause nobody can Change the Leopard's Spots, as King Solomon informed us. In other words, we cannot Change the Natures of other People, once they have been Persuaded that "God" / "Allah" is on their Side, whereby their Doctrines are Pure and Undefiled.

23-10 [_] Indeed, it would be the Equivalent of Changing your own Religion to that of the Hindus, Buddhists, or Voodoos — which has happened in rare cases; but, generally-speaking, it is not the General Rule that People Change their Religions so Radically — at least not on account of Saving the Lives of so-called "Enemies," such as those LGBTQ People, who, according to the Islamic religion, have no Right to Live!

23-11 [_] {FOOTNOTE: Did you get to see the YouTube Videos of those Sunni Arabians rejoicing over the Omar Mateen Massacre in Orlando? Many Professing "Christians" are in Agreement with them! They get that Notion from the *Old Testament,* which Condemns Gays, according to their Interpretation of it. All such books should be brought to Court, along with the *Koran / Qur'an* or *Qu'ran,* which is the Worst of Non-Christian Inspiration on the Earth, which would make a Camel Sick to Eat it. I know, since I have bored my way through the entire book, which Muhammad Ali could not do, and he was a Professing "Muslim" (aka, Deceived Goat), while I am a Professing "Christian" with much Higher Values, one of which is to be Perfectly Honest about all Religious, Spiritual, Governmental, Financial, Economic, Monetary, Business, Labor, Sexual, Social, Moral, and Miscellaneous Subjects — including the Conspiracies of the Oklahoma City Bombing, and the Evil Events of September 11th, 2001, which were far Worse Crimes than the Orlando Massacre; but, not quite as Impressive for the Dirty Work of only one "Lone Wolf," as you called him, who should have never been let through the Doorway with any Weapons. Could that Club not have Afforded a Metal Detector? Perhaps he came with his Weapons in Hand, saying that he was the New Security Guard, whereby the Wolf Deceived the Sheep at the Door: beCause of Wearing Sheep's Clothing. I Personally would not Trust most "Policemen," "Security Guards," nor Government Officials with Uniforms and Badges: because there is not much Difference between some of them and First Class Murderers. End of Note.}

23-12 [_] It is Interesting to Note that none of your Callers presented any Reasonable Solutions for the Massacres, in spite of your prodding them for a "Fix." Not even the Dalai Lama could Think of any Good Solution, much less the CONgress, who are Represented by people like David Jolly (R) of Florida, whose best source of Wisdom comes from the *Bible,* which is a Primary Cause for the Hate and Violence in this World of Woes, which comes from the *Old Testament,* which is where MuhamMAD, the so-called Islamic "Prophet," got his Hate and Violence from, who Sincerely Believed that it was his and our God-given Mission in this Life to "Destroy all of the Infidels."

23-13 [_] Yes, MuhamMAD visualized himself being like Joshua going into the Promised Land, which needed to be Cleaned up or Purged of all of those Canaanites, Hittites, Hivites, Perizites, Jebuzites, and whomever did not Believe in the God of Moses, who used to be rather Harsh with his Judgments, who even Drowned every Living Breathing Creature on the whole Earth, according to the Noah Story, which has since then been Debunked by our Selected King. {See www.Amazon.com for: **"What is WRong with those Professing Christians?" (A Self-Examination of the Heart of the Body of Good Government!) By The Worldwide People's Revolution!®** Book 002.}

23-14 [_] Carman from Montana referred to a book, called: "The Devil's Triangle," which makes some Legitimate Arguments, which all Dimwitcrats and Reprobates should Study before getting into any more Hateful Wars in the Middle East.

23-15 [_] Since you seem to be "too pressed for time," to read an Exceptionally Good Book, I will now sum up our Selected King's Best Solution for the Terrorist Attacks, which would naturally include School Shootings and Massacres in Gay Nightclubs by Radical Islamic Lunatics. Therefore, please give to me your Full Attention: because I am also getting Sick of this Depressing Subject.

23-16 [_] Moreover, you should also pass on this E-mail to those CONgress People: because they do not provide any Convenient Way for me to get into Personal Contact with them, even though I Seriously Doubt that they will be Interested in it: beCause the Solution will also do away with their Phony Occupation as Lying Deceiving Worthless Politicians!

23-17 [_] First of all, our Selected King makes it Crystal Clear that there is no Need for Changing the Leopard's Spots, which are most likely God-given Spots to begin with, for which there is much Provable Evidence. In Fact, he Proposes that all Like-minded People should Live Together within their own Beautiful Planned City States, which he calls those: **"GLORIOUS Swanky Hotels Castles and Fortresses,"** which will Solve more than 5,000 Problems, just by their Designs, alone!

23-18 [_] In other words, the People who are like Sheeps and Goats must be SEPARATED from the People who are like Lions and Wolves: beCause they are Incompatible, and do not get along very well, even as the Israelis and Palestinians have Proven for Decades. Therefore, there is no need for Attempting to FORCE them to get along well, when they have Contrary Natures.

23-19 [_] Therefore, each Political / Religious Group of Wise People will be Able and Willing to Govern themselves, according to their own Beliefs, and thus be Happy with themselves, who will be Free to Defend themselves within their own Fortresses / City States, even as the President is Defended by his 5,000+ Security Guards, and it does not Bother my Conscience, even if it Troubles certain Tax Slaves, who are Sick of Supporting such "Criminals," as they would say.

23-20 [_] So, you might ask, "Just exactly HOW will they go about Separating themselves from each other, seeing that almost all Cities, Worldwide, are made up of Mixtures of Various Kinds of Religious and Political People?"

23-21 [_] Well, first of all, you must Try to Understand that ALL of those Cities of Confusion have BAD Designs: beCause they are not Designed Properly for the Best Kind of Living Conditions with a Capital L and C. They are not Designed for Eternal Employment, and 100% Employment for everyone with Good Swanky Wages. They are not Designed to be Fireproof, Hail-proof, Rot-proof, Paint-proof, Termite-proof, Bedbug-proof, Mouse-proof, Rat-proof, Snake-

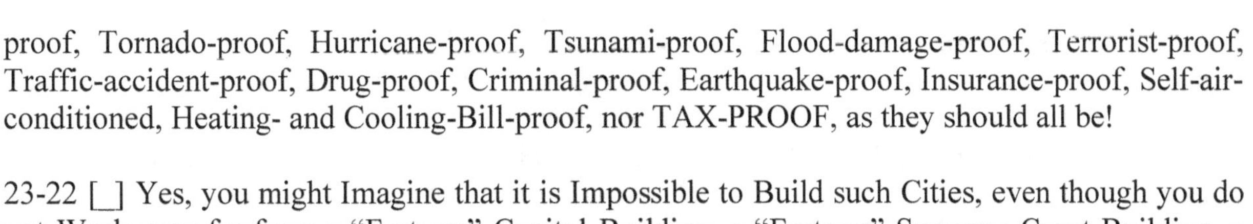

proof, Tornado-proof, Hurricane-proof, Tsunami-proof, Flood-damage-proof, Terrorist-proof, Traffic-accident-proof, Drug-proof, Criminal-proof, Earthquake-proof, Insurance-proof, Self-air-conditioned, Heating- and Cooling-Bill-proof, nor TAX-PROOF, as they should all be!

23-22 [_] Yes, you might Imagine that it is Impossible to Build such Cities, even though you do not Work very far from a "Fortress" Capitol Building, a "Fortress" Supreme Court Building, a "Fortress" Library of Congress Building, a "Fortress" White House for the President, a "Fortress" Senator's Office Building, "Fortress" Representatives' Office Buildings, a "Fortress" Holocaust Museum Building, a "Fortress" Department of Treasury Building, and a "Fortress" Smithsonian Institute Set of Buildings with millions of square feet of Floor Space — none of which will Permit anyone to Enter without being Thoroughly Checked for Weapons by Suspicious Security Guards: beCause they all have a "Fortress Mentality," you might say, even though the Federal Government DENIES it, and prefers to Pretend that Americans Live in a FREE Country, and "can Live Well without any Fortress Walls."

23-23 [_] Yes, it is a Part of their Hypocrisy, Brother John, whereby they Say one thing, and Do another: beCause they have Double Standards for almost everything; and thus their "Fortress Walls" are a FARCE: beCause they could not even Prevent a certain Man from Jumping Over the White House Fence, and running into the Little White Outhouse on Pennsylvania Avenue, as you no doubt Recall.

23-24 [_] So, you might Rightly Ask, "Just HOW could such a City be Built Properly, so as to Keep Out all Unwanted Poisonous Snakes, Sneaky Mice, Pack Rats, Junk Collectors, Stinking Skunks, Thieving Raccoons, Porcupine Lawyers, Political Rabbits, Greedy Capitalist Hogs, Squirrelly Banksters, and False News Reporters?"

23-25 [_] Well, the First Step is to make everyone who Wants to Live in **"Beautiful Swanky PALACES"** in such Secure Cities, fill out and file **"The Complete SURVEYS of our VALUES!" (SURVEYS of Religious Spiritual Political Governmental Sexual Social Moral Economic Business Labor Habitual and Miscellaneous VALUES!) By The Worldwide People's Revolution!®**, Book 059, whereby the Like-minded People can be Discovered and brought Together. Yes, they should Join: **"Seven Great Armies of Working Soldiers,"** whereby they can immediately go to Work, Constructing those Beautiful Planned City States, which are Designed for Peace and True Prosperity.

23-26 [_] After all, most People in this World of Woes are Underpaid, even if they now have Boring Jobs in Factories. Therefore, they will be Happy to Earn 50 to 60 dollars per Hour for Common Labor and Common Skilled Labor — such as Picking Fruits and Setting Ceramic Tiles on Cistern Walls. Indeed, we have Need for MILLIONS of such Large one-half-million-gallon Cisterns, just to get Prepared for the Great Famine that is Destined to come, "... if we just Continue on the Climatic Road to Hell with Climate Changes," as Top Scientists Predict.

23-27 [_] Therefore, Stefani from Indiana can go to Work with Like-minded "Christians" in Indiana, in order to Build their own Swanky Fortress with STRONG Stone Walls, Beautiful Stone Dome Home Complexes with Luscious All-Mineral Organic Gardens, Walk-in Coolers / Freezers / Pantries / Root Cellars, Spacious Home-craft Workshops, Sales Shops, Elevators, Tunnels, Subway Electric Trains, Tombs, Churches, Cathedrals, Theaters, Gymnasiums, Swimming Pools,

Bowling Alleys, Ice-skating Rinks, Roller-skating Rinks, Tennis Courts, Game Rooms, Fish Aquariums, Museums, Art Galleries, Concert Halls, and whatever they are Willing to Work for, using Stones like you can see right there in the District of Chief Criminals, in Washington, beginning right next door at Union Station, which has some Beautiful Marble and Granite Stones. Please Inspect it Carefully, and then Visit the Shrine of Immaculate Conception for Good Examples of what can be done with Polished Marble Stones. Go to the Basement.

23-28 [_] Awe, you might also Rightly Ask, "And WHERE would the Poor People of Indiana get Sufficient MONEY for Building all such Extremely Expensive Buildings?"

23-29 [_] Well, that is where **"The CONSTITUTION for the New RIGHTEOUS One-World GovernMINT"** comes in Handy, which you have Obviously NOT yet Studied: beCause of "being pressed for time," you might say: beCause of Wasting a lot of Precious Time with the *Washington Journal,* and other Political Nonsense at C-SPAN. Indeed, it is now Time to get your Priorities in Order, and spend some Quality Time in a Swanky TRUTH-brary, whereby you might Discover HOW to Solve our Massive Problems, and without going to War, as Mike from New Jersey would Understand, whom you Cut Off before he got to Finish his "Important One-minute Congressional Speech" — as if some Poor Ignorant Tax Slave in Georgia, Alabama, Arkansas, or Mississippi, might have something more Important to Reveal, who Obviously did not Discover the above mentioned Book. Trust me, our Selected King tells HOW to get an Unlimited Supply of GOOD Money for Doing GOOD Works, even if the Lady Doubtfulness Doubts it.

23-30 [_] The Dalai Lama Vainly Imagines that we are all the same, with the same Potentials in Life, having the same Emotions, Feelings, and whatever; but, he completely Ignores the Great Differences between the Lying Edomite Scribes and Pharisees, and the Humble Honest White Israelite from Nazareth, in Galilee, who could Walk on the Water and Raise Up the Dead People, who clearly said that when he Establishes his Righteous Kingdom, or One-World Government over all of the Nations, he will SEPARATE the People who are like Sheeps and Goats from the People who are like Lions and Wolves, which you can Learn about in *Matthew 25:32,* and in *the Gospel According to Saint Bartholomew,* who was one of his 11 Self-disciplined Disciples, who went into more Details about that Important Subject than Saint John did, who had very little to write about the Future Kingdom of the Supreme Ruler, even though *the Book of Revelation* has much to Reveal about it in a Subtle Top Secret Way.

23-31 [_] All of those Muslims (Radical or not) could Build their own Beautiful Planned City States, and thus Live in Peace with their own Kinds of People, and Attend to their own Businesses, and leave all other People alone, after Proving that they have Legitimate Religions, which are Based on Truths, and not on Jewish Fairy Tales, which must be Proven at: **"The Great Worldwide TELEVISED Court HEARING!"** Book 041. And that will Solve all such Massive Problems, which arise from Ignorance, False Religious Doctrines, Superstitions, False Economies, and Phony Governments.

23-32 [_] For Example, the "U.S. House Morning Hour" consisted of an entire Minute of Words, Today, which Meeting was quickly Dismissed / Adjourned, until "Later," which did not even Mention the Massacre in Orlando. We find it most Interesting that the Speaker of the House, Paul Ryan, did not even show his Face at that Congressional Meeting of the Weakest Minds, as he sometimes does for a Minute or 2.

23-33 [_] The House Chaplin asked his God to Bless all of us, and to give wisdom (with a lower-case w) to the Elected Members of the House, 98% of whom were Missing in Action, Today, for "General Speeches," whereby one Brave Representative by the Name of Jim Himes Stood Up for the Congresses' "Moral Fiber," which is so Weak that a little Baby could Tear it Apart, and Spit it Out. Jim summed it all up with a Moment of "Eternal Silence," which was most Appropriate, seeing that 98% of the Members of the House were Missing in Action, as I said, which is done as usual on a normal Monday; but, I Imagined that this was a Special Monday, when ALL of the Representatives should have Congregated in the House of Representatives, just for the Sole Purpose of Hearing John McArdle reading my Previous Letter to them, which can be found in the Introduction to this Inspired Book.

23-34 [_] Indeed, those CONgress People Customarily Congregate from Tuesday at Noon, until Thursday Evening, and only about a dozen of them Manage to Drag themselves into that Stinking House by 10 a.m.: because the other 500+ CONgress People are "Dialing for Dollars," across the Street, as *60 Minutes* reported on CBS, where they spend an average of 30 Hours per Week, in spite of getting Paid a Hefty 183,000+$ per Year, with all Expenses Paid by the Tax Slaves.

23-35 [_] Perhaps you could Forward this E-mail Letter to Jim Himes, since he is not in my District, which is far South of the Border, down Mexico way, where I have Retired in Peace in my Million-dollar Mansion with the Polished Marble Walls and 5,000+ Disarmed Security Guards. Just Kidding. Dr. Obama would Envy me for my Good Healthcare Plan, whereby I have not had any Need for the "Services" of a Medical Doctor in 50+ Years: beCause of Discovering the "Top Secrets" in our Selected King's Inspired Book, called: **Did God or Satan Ordain Medical Doctors??"** Book 022. Yes, you would also do Well to Study it for yourself, Brother John, and thus perhaps get Good Vision, for FREE!

23-36 [_] Now, the DEPARTment of so-called "Justice" weighed in on the Orlando Massacre by Sending James Comey of the Federal Burden of Investigation (FBI) to take Dead Aim at the Real Criminals behind it all with his Double-barreled Shotgun, whereby he Refused to even Mention the Unholy Name of the Radical Muslim who performed his "Duties to Allah," who was Smiling down on him from Jupiter with his most Powerful Telescope, who could have "Accidentally" Caused Omar to CRASH his Car, and thus Kill himself on the Way over there, had he been a God of True Justice, who could have at least Encouraged Omar's Wife to Telephone 911, and Report him to the Orlando Police DEPARTment, who {Allah} could Foresee what was Coming — that is, IF that Part of the *Holy Koran* is True, that Allah knows everything in Advance; but, behold, it seems that he has never Stepped In to Prevent any such Evil Events since Biblical Times: because he is Playing some little Mysterious Game with Satan, according to *the Book of Job,* which seems to be the most Reliable Book in the entire *Bible,* which Credits Satan with all of the Evils in the World, including all of those Terrorist Attacks, which makes a lot of Sense, if you Think about it: beCause Satan is Mankind's Scapegoat, you might say, whom we can Blame for whatever we do WRong — except in the Cases of Hilarious Rotten Clinton, and her Holy Husband, who has Straightened Out his most Promiscuous Parts, you might say: because of getting Old and Flabby and Impotent, whereby not even Viagra is of any more Benefit: beCause the Mind has gone Limp, you might say, after being Bombarded with X-amount of Accusations from the Far Right Wing of Spiritual Adulterers, who have their own Promiscuous Heroes, whom James Comcy would not mention, even though several Billion Dollars have been Wasted by the Federal Burden on all such Investigations, which was one of Gay Edgar Whoever's Secret Services, who Recorded all such

Transgressions in Countless FBI Files: because he had such a Rich Natural Resource to work with, called Human Beings, who are, above all else, Spiritually WEAK, which is the Basic Problem with all of those Radical Religious NUTS, which James Comey did not Discover in his Political Telescope, nor even in his Scientific Microscope: beCause it is an Invisible Thing, being Spiritual, being a Weakness of the Mind, you might say, which can only be Corrected by much FASTING and Praying, whereby the "Demon Spirits" might be Cast Out of them.

23-37 [_] But, of course, James did not Discover that Great Truth, and neither did anyone else who Refused to DO it — even though many Muslims Attempt to do what they call "Fasting," whereby they Stop Eating all Day, for a whole Month, during Ramadan, which is the 9th Month on the Islamic Calendar — only to Eat like Hogs for half of the Night, at least in some Cases, whereby they Lose more than they Gain, and sometimes go Insane!

23-38 [_] I am not saying that I Know for a Fact that such was the Case with Omar Mateen, nor with MuhamMAD the "Prophet," himself; but, it is Worth an Investigation, if anyone Sincerely Wants to get down to the Root Cause of his Insanity. After all, his Driver's License Photo reveals that he appears to be Guilty, Depressed, and perhaps Overweight. He had a History of using Steroids, which Means that there was a Good Chance that he, like previous Criminals of the same Order of Insane Idiots, was using other Drugs, which could Rightly be Blamed for his Insanity: because those Evil Drugs are more Dangerous than Rifles and Pistols. Therefore, if the FBI is Determined to get to the "Bottom" of it, they must Learn his Drug Use History. No such Drugs would be Permissible in a First Class Swanky Fortress. For sure, there were Witnesses who reported that Omar visited the Pulse Nightclub several times, and got Drunk several times, and became "loud and belligerent," according to *Wikipedia*. Those were all Warning Signs or Red Flags that something was very wRong with him, which would have Caused him to be Expelled from any Swanky Fortress, even without Purchasing any Firearms: because such a Person could use a Butcher's Knife, Ax, Dagger, or other Deadly Instrument, whereby he could Kill or Injure someone, rather than take them to Court, if they were doing something Wrong, even as any Law-abiding Civilized Citizen would Naturally do, if the "Law" was Fair and Just, as it should be.

23-39 [_] Sincerely, the Chief Agitator

23-40 [_] PS — If you want to read any of those Listed Books for FREE, John, I am able to send Copies to you. Just let me know. (UPDATE: John never did Respond to any of my Letters.)

23-41 [_] O Selected King, it is no wonder that John McArdle did not Respond to such a Letter: because it is Suggesting that we should all Abandon our Houses and Lands, and Move into Swanky Fortresses, which do not even Exist, as of this Date.

23-42 [_] Well, it is Obvious that it will Require a SLOW Transition from one Lifestyle to another, which should begin with Young Voluntary Working Soldiers, which would Naturally include all High School and College Graduates, who are looking for Good-paying Jobs, who might like to get Married and Settle Down in their own Beautiful Planned City States, which they are Welcome to Help Design, according to their own Good Imaginations, if they are not Happy with our Selected King's Plans, which are most Reasonable: because of spending many Years Meditating on that Subject and Related Subjects. After all, in order to have a Self-air-conditioned Fireproof Bomb-proof House, it must have very THICK Solid Stone Walls, which are a Minimum of 10 feet Thick, just to Stabilize the Temperatures between Hot Summers and Cold Winters, whereby the Houses are Comfortable and Livable.

23-43 [_] O Selected King, are you not Aware that all such "Cave Houses" would be COLD and DAMP in the Summertime, if the Stone Walls were a Comfortable 72 °F / 22 °C: beCause of Sucking Moisture into the House, even as a Cold Glass of Iced Tea attracts Moisture to it during a Hot Day: beCause the Surrounding Temperature is Hotter than the Glass?

23-44 [_] Well, that is the Reason for Building an ICE HOUSE / Cistern UNDER the Stone Dome Home Complex, which has a Trapdoor in the Floor, which can be Opened to let the Excess Moisture into the Ice House, and thus Reduce or Eliminate that Problem. Moreover, most Places in the World have a Tendency to Cool Off at Night. Therefore, if the Doors or Windows are Opened after Midnight, it will help to Draw Out the Moisture, and Cool Off the House. However, if the Outside Temperature is still Hotter than the Desired Temperature within the House, it is Wise to only let in just enough Air to Flush Out any Stale Air through the Skylight Window, which can have a Crack in it — such as a one-inch wide Space for the Bad Air to Escape, beginning at Midnight, which Air is drawn into the House through a small Window in the Barrel-vault Entrance to the Stone Dome Home Complex, whereby the Inhabitants can have Fresh Air, even during the Heat of Summertime, and the Cold of Wintertime, which might only Require a one-eighth-inch-wide Crack in the Window, which will Suck in so much Air as to Whistle through the Crack; but, that small amount of Cold Air will not have any Great Negative Effect on the Overall Inside Temperatures of the Rooms: because it Requires a Considerable Amount of Time to Cool Off or Heat Up THICK Stone Walls, which are at least 10 feet Thick, and can be 20 feet Thick in very Cold Places like Alaska, which can also have HOT SALT BLOCKS in Insulated Hot Houses for added Heat during Cold Dark Winters, which Hot Houses can be used as Needed, which will Work much like the Volcanic Hot Water in Iceland.

23-45 [_] O Selected King, are you not Aware of how MANY Cut Stones would be Required for Building all such THICK Heavy Solid Stone Walls? Indeed, it would be much more Practical for most People to MOVE THEMSELVES to more Temperate Climates — such as Venezuela, where the Highest Temperature during the Daytime might be a Maximum of 90 °F / 32 °C, while the Coolest Temperature at Night might be 60 °F / 15.5 °C, which Moderates to about 75 °F / 24 °C, if the Windows and Doors are Managed Correctly. For Example, if the Doors and Windows are Closed during the Heat of the Day, from 10 a.m. to 6 p.m., the Inside Temperatures will be a very Comfortable 70 °F / 21 °C, which will also Suck Out any Excess Moisture during the Night, whereby the Houses will not Sweat during the Daytime: beCause no Hot Air can get into the Houses: beCause of using Underground Elevators and Subway Trains in Tunnels, which are Aired Out each Night, from 6 p.m. to 10 a.m. Therefore, the Air will be Fresh, and the Temperatures Comfortable at all Times. However, that is not to say that People could not go Outside after 10 a.m.: because, if they had some Gardening that Desperately needed to be taken care of, they could Work all Day in the Garden, and do a little Sweating. Otherwise, they could Turn On the Night Lights, and Work in their Gardens after Sunset, when the Temperature would drop down to about 75 °F / 24 °C within one Hour: because it is the Nature of the Climate in Venezuela to do that, which is also True of many Places in Central and South America, at the Correct Elevations. For Example, Caracas is like Springtime the Year around, which is why so many People Live there, and without Air-conditioning Equipment.

23-46 [_] Well, it is Certainly much Easier to Build a New Planned City State in some Wide-open Space, than to Rebuild any Old City of Confusion, where People would have to Deal with all of the TRASHED Houses and Mountains of Toxic Capitalist Rubble, which would Fill entire Valleys, if it were Bulldozed into such Valleys, which would Pollute the Runoff Water beyond Measure, and Ruin it and the entire Valley. Therefore, all such Cities should be Abandoned, after all Valuable Things are Removed from it — such as Copper Wires, Well-made Furniture, Tools, and Metals, which can be used to make more Tools, or whatever is Needed for True Prosperity.

23-47 [_] O Selected King, you Live in a Dream World, while Imagining that most People will be Cooperative with you, just beCause you have a Better Vision than they have, which is a Globalist Vision of True Prosperity, Worldwide. However, in the Real World, no such Good Things will ever Happen: beCause SATAN is in Charge of almost everything.

23-48 [_] Well, I would say that it is now Time to put Satan OUT of Business, by Establishing **"The New RIGHTEOUS One-World Government,"** which has an Unlimited Supply of New Money, which must be Earned by Honest Labor for the Construction of those: **"GLORIOUS Swanky Hotels Castles and Fortresses!" (Beautiful Planned City States for WISE Intelligent Well-Educated People with Common Sense and Good Understanding!) By The Worldwide People's Revolution!®**, Book 019, which will Solve more than 5,000 Problems, including those Terrorist Attacks, which are Committed by Sick-minded People, who will not be Able to Enter into any of those Beautiful Fortresses with Sound-minded People, until they have Fasted and Prayed Sufficiently to Remove any Demon Spirits within them; and thus Righteousness will Overcome Wickedness.

23-49 [_] O Selected King, I do Hope to God that you are RIIT — that Riichusnus will Overcome Wickedness, which would be a Wonderful Worldwide Experience; but, just as long as Satan is Roaming all about, I do not Expect it.

23-50 [_] Well, when we Hold that Great Meeting of the Most Intelligent and Well-Educated Minds, called: **"The Great Worldwide TELEVISED Court HEARING,"** Satan will be put Out of Business by Means of **"The Swanky Sword of Divine Truths"**: because no one can Defeat the Pure Truth. Therefore, it is just a Matter of Discovering the WHOLE Truth, whatever it might be, even if it Proves all of us to be WRong. For Example, the Snooze Reporters say that 49 People were Killed in the Pulse Nightclub in Orlando, Florida, and 53 were Wounded, when, in Fact, 50 were Killed, including the Lunatic who Murdered 49 People, who should have never been Sold any such Military Weapons, even as no one should be Sold Mortars and Mortar Launchers, whereby they could take them up to the Roofs of Hotels in Washington, D.C., and commence to Launch Mortars at: **"The BIG White OUTHOUSE on the Not-so-Biblical Capitol DUNGHILL!"** Book 023. Indeed, it would only Require 3 or 4 such Mortars to Ruin the entire Building, and just one for the Little White Outhouse that the President Resides in, which could be Carried in a Suitcase up to the Roof of the nearest Hotel, which is less than a City Block away. Therefore, should all such Weapons be Sold to Veterans, on Account of the *Second Amendment* to the Constitution, which gives everyone the Right to Bear Arms? Let all such People be Wise for themselves, and Move into those Swanky Fortresses, where they may have all of the Defensive Weapons that they Want, including Stinger Missiles for bringing down Helicopters and Airplanes that Stray into their Territories without Permission. After all, with such Beautiful Cities, almost no one will have any Desire to Leave such Cities, except to take SECURE Subway Electric Trains to other Beautiful Planned City States, which might have more Fruits to Eat, depending on the Seasons of the Year, and the Kinds of Fruit Trees that have been Planted. Otherwise, People could go there to Observe their Beautiful Cathedrals, Temples, Mosques, Synagogues, Basilicas, Theaters, Concert Halls, Flower Gardens, and the Strong Healthy Beautiful Bodies at Gymnasiums and Swimming Pools, which would never get Boring, Sickening, nor Drenched in Blood: beCause of those Hateful Weapons.

— Chapter 24 —

A List of other Fascinating Literature by the same Inspired Author

24-01 [_] — **"LIGHTNING Versus the Lightning Bug!" (HOW almost Everyone can become Moderately RICH, without Telling Any Lies nor Selling Any Trash!)** Book 001.

[_] 24-02 — **"What is WRong with those Professing Christians?" (A Self-Examination of the Heart of the Body of Good Government!)** Book 002.

[_] 24-03 — **"For the Love of Money!" (The Strange Things that People Say and Do to Get more Money!)** Book 003.

[_] 24-04 — **"HOW to Prepare for CLIMATE CHANGES!" (The Wisest Plan for Mankind to Follow!)** Book 004.

[_] 24-05 — **"Why do I have to be Surrounded by CRAZY PEOPLE!" (Do almost all People Feel like they are Surrounded by CRAZY People??)** Book 005.

[_] 24-06 — **"The Washington Journal is a FARCE! (C-SPAN Managers are not very WISE!)** Book 006. (This Book has lots of Good Humor.)

[_] 24-07 — **"The PRAYERS of PUMPKINHEADS!" (Even God Needs a Little Humor to Cheer himself Up!)** Book 007. (Some of it is for Adults only.)

[_] 24-08 — **"A Sound Argument for Masters and Servants!" (WHY Everyone Needs a Good Master, and every Master Needs Good Obedient Servants!)** Book 008.

[_] 24-09 — **"WHY are some Preachers so POOR?" (HOW almost all Preachers could Get Moderately RICH, without Preaching any Outlandish LIES!)** Book 009.

[_] 24-10 — **"GOOD NEWS for REBEL WOMEN!" (HOW almost all Wives can become Moderately RICH without Leaving their Homes! Guaranteed!)** Book 010.

[_] 24-11 — **"The Low Court of Supreme Injustices is Brought to Trial!" (The Worldwide People's Revolution!® Butts Heads with the United States Supreme Court, with or without their Black Robes of Hypocrisies and Lies!)** Book 011. (This Inspired Book contains the Famous *Declaration of Interdependence,* which is a Must Read. It also contains the Correct Wording for the Placard on the Statue of Liberty.)

[_] 24-12 — **"The Right Design for Living!" (A List of Great Advantages for Building Beautiful Planned City States!)** Book 012. (This Book contains many Important Drawings, as well as HOW to Save hundreds of Trillions of Dollars by Building Swanky Fortresses, and Living in Peace within them. It is a Companion Book of Book 011, which contains many more Great Advantages for Fortresses.)

[_] 24-13 — **"The Gospel According to The Worldwide People's Revolution!®" (The Good News from the Most Modern Perspective!)** Book 013. (This Book contains the Famous Sermon of Jonah to the Ninevites, whereby 120,000 People Repented in Sackcloth and Ashes! Do not Miss Out on it.)

[_] 24-14 — **"Poverty Hunger Riots Strikes Brutalities Election Deceptions and Civil Wars!" (The High Price that we Earthlings have Paid for Leaving the Good Land!)** Book 014.

[_] 24-15 — **"Seven Great Armies of Working Soldiers!" (HOW to Provide a Way for Everyone to WORK: so as to Eliminate Poverty, Crimes, Drug Abuses, Prisons and Unnecessary Taxes!)** Book 015. (This Book contains a True Life Story when I was in the Army.)

[_] 24-16 — **"The CONSTITUTION for the New RIGHTEOUS One-World GovernMint!" (HOW all Peoples can get True Justice, and Celebrate the Great Year of JUBILEE!)** Book 016.

[_] 24-17 — **"The Great World TEMPLE of PEACE!" (The Glory of Jerusalem Arises Again!) By The Worldwide People's Revolution!®** Book 017.

[_] 24-18 — **"The Swanky Associations of Working Soldiers!" (A Fascinating Collection of Various Kinds of Voluntary Working Soldiers!)** Book 018. (There will be thousands of Associations for all Kinds of Occupations, which will Specialize in Fine Arts — such as Hand-carved Leather-bound Books. See **"LIGHTNING STRIKES Versus Lightning Bugs!"** Book 074, for a Good Example.)

[_] 24-19 — **"GLORIOUS Swanky Hotels Castles and Fortresses!" (Beautiful Planned City States for WISE Intelligent Well-Educated People with Common Sense and Good Understanding!)** Book 019. (This Book contains many Rough Drawings, which could be Greatly Improved upon by someone who Knows the Art, and has the Correct Computer Programs for doing it.)

[_] 24-20 — **"Are you a Jobless Graduate of the SKQL uv FQLZ?" (HOW to Get a GOUD EJUKAASHUN without Robbing the Bank!)** Book 020. (This Inspired Book contains the New MAGNIFIED Version {NMV} of *First Corinthians 13,* plus: HOW to Produce Pure Living Water!)

[_] 24-21 — **"The LUSCIOUS All-Mineral Organic Method of Gardening!" (HOW to Grow DELICIOUS Satisfying Foods for Potential Kingz and Kweenz in Beautiful Swanky PALACES!)** Book 021. (This Book Explains HOW to make a Flood-proof Garden, while Trapping the Rainwater.)

[_] 24-22 — **"Did God or Satan Ordain Medical Doctors?" (Ask Huck Finn and/or Nigger Jim: because neither Tom Sawyer nor Judge Thatcher would Know!)** Book 022. (This Inspired Book Reveals HOW to Prevent Common Colds, and has a Special Chapter that Explains what a True "Nigger" IS. Surprise yourself!)

[_] 24-23 — **"The BIG White OUTHOUSE on the Not-so-Biblical Capitol DUNGHILL!" (The Chief Sins of the Divided States of United Lies!) By The Worldwide People's Revolution!®** Book 023. (This Book contains Special Words that most People have never Heard! Surprise yourself again!)

[_] 24-24 — **"The Public School of IGNERUNT FQLZ!" (HOW we have been GRAATLEE DISEEVD by Capitalism!)** Book 024. (This Book Teaches Children HOW to "Reed and Riit in Funetik Ingglish in just wun Daa!" You should Challenge your Frendz and Naaberz with it.)

[_] 24-25 — **"In thu Beeginingz uv Thingz!" (Thu Kreeaashun Stooree frum thu Beegining!)** Book 025. {The Cover Photo shows a Picture of a Golden Supootaa (Sapote), which not one Person in a Million has ever Tasted: because it does not Ship very well, in spite of it being one of the most Sweetest Pleasant Fruits known to Mankind, which must Ripen on the Tree to be Extremely Good, after it is Grown Properly by **"The LUSCIOUS All-Mineral Organic Method of Gardening!"** Book 021, which Means that the Topsoil must have all of the Proper Minerals in it. Remember the Grapes of Eschol, which the Children of Israel brought back from the Promised Land in the *Book of Joshua,* which Required 2 Strong Men to Carry just one Cluster! See the Fascinating Photos in: **"Orgimmick Gardening at its Best!" (HOW to Grow Delicious Satisfying Foods without a 10-Million-Dollar Investment!) By The Worldwide People's Revolution!®** Book 079.}

[_] 24-26 — **"God Speaks and the Whole World Listens!" (Fire on the Mountain from the Burning Bush by the Spirit of Truths!)** Book 026. (This Powerful Book contains the Best Noah Story of all of the Books, including that of Gilgamesh the Great of Ancient Babylon!)

[_] 24-27 — **"Does a Good Soldier have to be a MURDERER?" (Seven Great Swanky Armies of Voluntary Working Soldiers!) By The Worldwide People's Revolution!®** Book 027. (Chapter 03 contains a True Life Story about a Dog Pile, which happened to me when I was just 10 Years Old.)

[_] 24-28 — **"Thu Nq MAGNUFIID Verzhun uv Thu PROVERBZ uv KING SOLUMUN in Plaan Ingglish!" (The Understandable Version of the Famous Proverbs of King Solomon in Plain English!)** Book 028. (This Marvelous Book MAGNIFIES each Proverb unto the Glory of the Great God of Inspiration, which is taken from the Original 4,000-page Book, which was written in less than 2 Months by the GIFT of Inspiration, which also contains the Famous Proverbs of Queen Izubelu!)

[_] 24-29 — **"UNLIMITED ENERJEE 99 Percent Pollutions Free!" (HOW to Obtain FREE ElecTrickery, Worldwide!) By The Worldwide People's Revolution!®** Book 029. (This Book contains the Jackson Brower Suicide, among many other Fascinating Subjects.)

[_] 24-30 — **"FREEDUM uv SPEECH!" (U Speshoul Maguzeen uv Onist Upinyunz!)** Book 030-0001, which contains the Great Advantages for Using Swanky Mulching Rocks in an All-Mineral Organic Garden, plus Baptism by Fire and Speaking in Foreign Languages! It is a Must Read. The Cover Photo shows a Portion of the Author's Marbleous Indian Countertop or Food Bar, which is just one Example of what you can also have in your own **"Beautiful Swanky PALACES!"** if you have the Honesty, Faith, Hope, Trust, Love, Patience, Persistence, Cooperation and OBEDIENCE that are Required for True Prosperity! Therefore, Ejukaat yourself, and you will be Glad that you did!

[_] 24-31 — **"A Sure Cure for GUN VIOLENCE!" (HOW TO STOP GANG WARS and CRIMINAL SHOOTINGS!) By The Worldwide People's Revolution!®** Book 031. {The Cover Photo shows a Picture of a Short Shotgun, which is Fully Loaded with Double 00 Shells, and is Ready for any Tax Master who might Attempt to Steal the Retirement Home, who never moved a Finger to Help Build the Rock Houses, whereby we moved more than 66,666,666 Pounds by Hand, whose Property was Cunningly Stolen by that False Anti-Christ WICKED Cover-up Government, which allowed Bankers to Rob us of 30 Years of Hard Labor and more than 300,000 dollars-worth of Investments in our Uncommon American Farm, which is Explained in: **"LIGHTNING STRIKES Versus Lightning Bugs!" (HOW you can Become Moderately RICH, without Telling any Lies nor Selling any Trash!) By The Worldwide People's Revolution!®** Book 074, which contains many Photographs with Profound Explanations! Do not be left out in the Darkness of Ignorance. Get Informed, now: beCause, **"The Great False Economy is now DEBUNKED!"** Book 053.}

[_] 24-32 — **"AIIRMWVC and Reasonable Solutions!" (Aliens, Illegal Immigrants, Refugees, Migrant Workers and other Victims of Capitalism!) By The Worldwide People's Revolution!®** Book 032. (This Inspired Book contains *the New MAGNIFIED Version of Job 33.*)

[_] 24-33 — **"Mark Twain Races for the PRESIDENCY!" (The 2020 Presidential Candidates Desperately Need Some STRONG Undefeatable COMPETITION!) By The Worldwide People's Revolution!®** Book 033. {This Book contains a Part of my Autobiography, and my Personal Answers to the Questions in **"The Complete SURVEYS of our VALUES!" (SURVEYS of Religious Spiritual Political Governmental Sexual Social Moral Economic Business Labor Habitual and Miscellaneous VALUES!)** Book 059. It also contains many Black and White Photographs.}

[_] 24-34 — **"ECCLESIASTES UNCOVERED!" (The New MAGNIFIED Version of Ecclesiastes and the Song of Solomon in Plain English!)** Book 034. (This is the Book that contains the Famous Sayings for *"There is a Time to be Born, and a Time to Die ..."* which has been Greatly Magnified!)

[_] 24-35 — **"The Environmentalists' Paradise!" (HOW almost Everyone could be Living in a Beautiful Manmade Paradise!) By The Worldwide People's Revolution!®** Book 035. (This Book contains the NMV of *Psalm 48,* which will Amaze you, O Lady Doubtfulness!)

[_] 24-36 — **"The Seven Basic Spiritual Building Blocks of LIFE!" (Faith Hope Trust Love Patience Persistence and Obedience!)** Book 036. (This Book contains the Mockingbird's Version of *Hebrews 11,* plus the NMV of *First Corinthians 13,* among many other "Goodies.")

[_] 24-37 — **"DIETS!" (A Reasonable Solution for the "Eternal Controversy"!) By The Worldwide People's Revolution!® Book 037.**

[_] 24-38 — **"The Nature of CAPITALISM!" (A List of the EVILS of CAPITALISM!)** Book 038.

[_] 24-39 — **"SWANGKEENOMIKS Rules the Roost!" (HOW all People can Prosper in a RIIT WAA, and STOP Polluting the Earth with Capitalist TRASH!) By The Worldwide People's Revolution!®** Book 039. (The Cover Photo shows a Portion of our Retirement Home, before the 5,000+ square-feet Concrete Roof was Installed, after moving more than 66 Million Pounds by Hand!)

[_] 24-40 — **"The New MAGNIFIED Version of The Book of MOORMUN!" (The Story of the White and Dark Indians in the Americas!)** Book 040, which comes in 2 Volumes of about 500 Pages, each. The Cover Photo on the First Volume shows the Queen of England's Golden Coach, and the Cover Photo on the Second Volume shows one of many Polished Spanish Marble Walls in our Retirement Home, which is worth a thousand dollars per square yard, which is another Example of what you can also have, if you simply OBEY your Righteous KING! All such Marble is very Inspiring. No one could Study it for very long without Believing in a Great Creator God. The Picture does not do it Justice. You would have to See it in Person, and Wash it with Pure Water to bring Out the Beauty.

[_] 24-41 — **"The Great Worldwide TELEVISED Court HEARING!" (That Great Meeting of the Most Intelligent and Wel-Ejukaatid Miindz!) By The Worldwide People's Revolution!®** Book 041. {This is the Book that the World has long been Waiting for: beCause it will Overthrow the Evil Empires, and make it Possible to Establish **"The New RIGHTEOUS One-World Government!" (HOW to Establish a Righteous One-World Government without Going to WAR!) By The Worldwide People's Revolution!®** Book 056. This is the Greatest Idea since the Invention of the Light Bulb, Guaranteed!}

[_] 24-42 — **"The Secret City of the Great King!" (HOW the True Church will Escape from the Great Tribulation!) By The Worldwide People's Revolution!®** Book 042. (Be Sure to Inform your Friends, Relatives and Naaberz about this Wonderful Book: beCause they might also Want to Escape!)

[_] 24-43 — **"Terrorists Beware that your Days are Numbered!" (HOW to Bring those Terrorist Attacks to a Screeching HALT!) By The Worldwide People's Revolution!®** Book 043. (This Book also contains the Fascinating Book of LEHI, which has now been Restored!) †‡

[_] 24-44 — **"The New MAGNIFIED Version of ISAIAH in Plain English!" (The Understandable Version of the Book of Isaiah!)** Book 044. (The Cover Photo shows a Swanky Potato and Avocado Salad with Sweet Peas and Corn, among other "Secret" Ingredients, which are Revealed within the Book. Remember that you can read many Words for Free in the Book Previews on Amazon.com.usa.)

[_] 24-45 — **"HOW to Become a HOLY Man!" (40 Good Reasons WHY People Should FAST and PRAY!)** Book 045, which is a Companion Book of:

[_] 24-46 — **"The Proper RULES for FASTING!" (The Complete Instruction Manual for True Repentance!) By The Worldwide People's Revolution!®** Book 046, which is a Companion Book of the above mentioned Book, which contains a True Life Story about an Old Black Mare called Lucy, who Fasted for 30 Days without Food nor Water, who was Physiologically "Born Again," as Jesus might say. See the Full Details in: **"The New MAGNIFIED Version of The GOOD NEWS According to Saint JOHN!" (The Gospel According to Saint John Zebedee Boanerges in Plain English!)** Book 062, which contains many Inspiring Photographs with Explanations!

[_] 24-47 — **"Are Americans the Most STUPID People who ever Lived?" (HOW Working People can PROSPER and Live in PEACE Under the Rulership of a RIGHTEOUS KING!) By The Worldwide People's Revolution!®** Book 047. (The Cover Photo shows a large Portion of the Author's Living Room Floor, which is worth 100,000$, which is just another Good Example of what you can also have, just for Loving and Obeying your Elected King!)

[_] 24-48 — **"An Amazing Collection of Wit and Wisdom!" (The Marvelous Tale of the Colorful Peacock from Angel Ridge, and the Strong Rope of Everlasting Hope!) By The Worldwide People's Revolution!®** Book 048. (The Cover Photo shows a Book Display, which will be Greatly Enhanced during the Future, when all 350+ Inspired Books are on Display in a Swanky Truth-brary, as Opposed to the Public LIE-brary.)

[_] 24-49 — **"Justifications for Capitalizations!" (WHY The Worldwide People's Revolution!® Defies the School of Fools by Capitalizing LOVE and HATE!)** Book 049.

[_] 24-50 — **"The END of CONFUSION!" (The Great CELEBRATION of the Magnificent Wedding of the Most Humble Honest Nations, and the Grand Year of JUBILEE!) By The Worldwide People's Revolution!®** Book 050. (Just Try to Visualize those **"Seven Great Swanky Armies of Voluntary Working Soldiers"** Marching through the Valley of Megiddo, being Dressed in their Colorful Robes, while the Band Plays *The Battle Hymn of the Republic,* and the Choirs Sing the Praises of the Great KING of Kings! What a Sight and Sound that will be, which will be Climaxed in **"The Great World TEMPLE of PEACE,"** when the Nations will get Married, along with our Elected King! Come one, come all to **"The Great Worldwide TELEVISED Court HEARING,"** by Means of your Wide Flat-screen TVs, whereby you might Learn WHY, WHEN and HOW!) †‡

[_] 24-51 — **"The Loathsome Burdens of the Independent Jackasses!" (A New Approach for Solving our Massive Problems!) By The Worldwide People's Revolution!®** Book 051. (Just Think about the Multitude of almost Worthless Meetings of the Minds, who Strained themselves to Think of Reasonable Solutions for our Massive Problems, who sometimes even Prayed to God for Help; but, the Solutions have been here for no less than 40 Years — Thanks to the Spirit of Inspiration from GOD!)

[_] 24-52 — **"Are we Tax Slaves of a Lower Order than the Lying Cunniving Edomites!" (HOW to be Liberated from all Slavery, Worldwide!) By The Worldwide People's Revolution!®** Book 052. {This Inspired Book once had another Title and Author, which was not Acceptable by Amazon, which has now been Restored in all of its Glory, and is Published by more Trustworthy People, who are not Afraid of Controversies, nor of: **"The Swanky Sword of Divine Truths!" (The Most Powerful Weapon in the Whole Universe!) By The Worldwide People's Revolution!®** Book 067.}

[_] 24-53 — **"The Great False Economy is now DEBUNKED!" (Adolf Hitler had a much Better Economic System!) By The Worldwide People's Revolution!®** Book 053. (Trust me, Adolf was no Saint; but, during the Day of God's Judgment, he will be Justified, while his Anti-Christ Opponents will be Condemned: beCause they Refused to Attend a Worldwide Radio Debate with Adolf Hitler, whose Arguments will Stand Up during the Day of Judgment, which would have Prevented World War 2, and thus Saved the Lives of no less than 60 Million People! Likewise, we Tax Slaves must now Act more Wisely, and DEMAND **"The Great Worldwide TELEVISED Court HEARING,"** Book 041, whereby we might Save the World from that Dreadful Battle of Megiddo, called *Armageddon!* Yes, the Ball is now in YOUR Hands, my Potential Friend or Enemy, and you are now Responsible for it. Therefore, do not Shirk your Duty as a Free Citizen; but, Help us to Spread this Message far and wide, whereby the Masses of People will be Demanding The GWTCH, and thus Prevent another far more Dreadful and Hateful World WAR!)

[_] 24-54 — **"The UGLY Scarred Dishonest Face of Poor Old Miserable UNCLE SAM!" (A Memorial Day Legacy!) By The Worldwide People's Revolution!®** Book 054. {NOTE: This Inspired Book was also Suppressed by Amazon, who will be most Ashamed of themselves if they do not Un-suppress it during the Future: beCause it will also be Published by People of Greater Faith, who Know for a Fact that it is the TRUTH! Therefore, just be Patient.}

[_] 24-55 — **"The United States of the Whole World!" (A True Global Economy for the Masses of Working People!) By The Worldwide People's Revolution!®** Book 055. (This Inspired Book contains many Colored Photographs with Explanations. It is a Good Book to Publish in Foreign Nations, who are not so Blinded by their Pride, who can See the Mountain of Lies much Better at a Distance from them: beCause of not being a Part of the American Corruption.) †‡

[_] 24-56 — **"The New RIGHTEOUS One-World Government!" (HOW to Establish a Righteous One-World Government without Going to WAR!) By The Worldwide People's Revolution!®** Book 056. (This is a KEY Book, which everyone should Study Carefully and Prayerfully.)

[_] 24-57 — **"Those Ridiculous Contradictions within the Holy Bible!" (HOW to Read the Mutilated Bible with an Open Mind!) By The Worldwide People's Revolution!®** Book 057. (Many Professing "Christians" Falsely Claim that their so-called *"Holy Bibles"* do not Contain any Contradictions, being "the Infallible Inspired Word of the Living God," but, without the Capitalized Words, and without Explaining just WHY there are more than 200 Contradictory Versions of it! This Book Reveals how to Deal with those Biblical Problems, and come to Understand WHY God Allowed it to Happen for the Truth's Sake. Trust me, you have never Heard this Explanation before now.)

[_] 24-58 — **"The Divided States of United Lies!" (The so-called "United States of North America" in Disguise!) By The Worldwide People's Revolution!® Book 058.** {NOTE: This is perhaps the most Referred to Book among all of the Books by our Selected King; but, that does not Mean that it is his Best Book by any Means, which is Well Camouflaged: so that it will Survive the Test of Time, even if the others are BURNED by the Anti-Christ Followers of Satan, who are Possession Worshipers of the Worst Kind, who Seek to Justify American Lies, rather than Quickly Confess them, and thus Escape from their Self-made Prison of Propagandish Lies! Just be Perfectly Honest, and you will have no Problem with any of our Literature.}

[_] 24-59 — **"The Complete SURVEYS of our VALUES!" (SURVEYS of Religious Spiritual Political Governmental Sexual Social Moral Economic Business Labor Habitual and Miscellaneous VALUES!) By The Worldwide People's Revolution!® Book 059.** {NOTE: According to our Selected King, every Potential Leader in the World must Fill Out and File those Surveys on the Internet for everyone to Study, whereby the Best People might be Elected by those Wise People who have also Filled Out the Complete Surveys of their own Values, whereby they will be Qualified to VOTE. Otherwise, they will not be Qualified to Vote, which will Eliminate a LOT of Wasted Money on Election Deceptions, while at the same Time it will Educate a lot of Ignorant People, who Desperately Need to Study that Inspired Book before Voting for another Dimwitcrat, Reprobate, or Independent Jackass!}

[_] 24-60 — **"HOW to Get our PRIORITIES in ORDER!" (The Glories of Democracy; and, Does DEMON-ocracy have its Priorities in Order?) By The Worldwide People's Revolution!® Book 060.** This Book will need to be Re-written by a Collective Group of Wise People, who will Contribute their True Life Stories during the Future, when they Wake Up and come to their Right Senses with the Prodigal Son of *Luke 15*. See:

[_] 24-61 — **"The New MAGIFIED Version of The GOOD NEWS According to Saint LUKE!" (The Magnified Gospel of Saint Luke in Plain English!)** Book 061, which is by Far the Best Version of that Gospel on the Earth, which has no Rivals at all among the other 200+ Versions. Guaranteed!

[_] 24-62 — **"The New MAGNIFIED Version of The GOOD NEWS According to Saint JOHN!" (The Gospel According to Saint John Zebedee Boanerges in Plain English!)** Book 062, which also has no Rivals among all of the other Versions: beCause this is no Translation of anything; but, it is the Inspired Words of the Living God, which were Revealed by the Holy Spirit, who has not Died.

[_] 24-63 — **"The New MAGNIFIED Version of the Book of ACTS!" (The Understandable Version of the Acts of the Apostles in Plain English!) By The Worldwide People's Revolution!® Book 063.** (This Inspired Book makes it Understandable WHY the Jews Hated the Apostles so much. You will have to Read it to Believe it.)

[_] 24-64 — **"The New MAGNIFIED Version of the PSALMS of King David!" (The Understandable Version of the Famous Psalms in Plain English!)** Book 064. You will be Amazed!

[_] 24-65 — **"A List of FAIR Swanky Wages!" (The Equitable Wage System!) By The Worldwide People's Revolution!®** Book 065. (All Hardworking People will LOVE this Good Book!)

[_] 24-66 — **"Beautiful Swanky PALACES!" (A New Concept in Living Habits — Swanky Palaces for Poor People!) By The Worldwide People's Revolution!®** Book 066. (You have no Idea what a "Swanky Palace" IS, unless you have read this Unique Book.)

[_] 24-67 — **"The Swanky Sword of Divine Truths!" (The Most Powerful Weapon in the Whole Universe!)** Book 067. (The very Reason that our Selected King has no Rivals is beCause of the Swanky Sword of Divine Truths, which no one can Defeat by any Means. Therefore, you Need to have it on your own Side, whereby no one can Defeat your Arguments! Be Strong, be Brave, have Faith and put on the Whole Armor of GOD!)

[_] 24-68 — **"Has your Life become Extremely Complicated?" (HOW to Live a SIMPLE Life!) By The Worldwide People's Revolution!®** Book 068. (Many People are not even Aware of just how Complicated their Lives are, until suddenly they are ready to Commit Suicide! It is Best to Prevent all such Evil Things, and this Book tells HOW.)

[_] 24-69 — **"The IDEAL Place to Live!" (HOW to Discover the Ideal Place to Live!)** Book 069.

[_] 24-70 — **"Our Elected King Who Speaks Out!" (It is High Time for some Sane Person to Get Control of this Insane World!) By The Worldwide People's Revolution!®** Book 070. (This Inspired Book contains a Special Speech that is Addressed to both Houses of the Congress in Washington. You will Love it, O Man of Greater Faith!)

[_] 24-71 — **"How GAY is GOD?" (Oh the Wonders of it all when it ALL Hangs Out!)** Book 071. (Do not Judge the Book, until you have Carefully "Red" all of it. You will be Surprised by the Truths!)

[_] 24-72 — **"LIGHTNING STRIKES Versus Lightning Bugs and Impotent Fireflies!" (A Memorial Photo Album of some Real American Heroes!) By The Worldwide People's Revolution!®** Book 072. (NOTE: This Book is Unique among all of the Books by our Selected King: beCause he did not get to Proof-read it before the Computer Crashed. It just Happened to be Saved on a Computer Chip before the Computer Crashed, and therefore it was Saved in PDF. But, the Corrections did not get made, which makes it a Special Collector's Item, which has more than 100 Colored Photos, which was what Caused the Crash.) †‡

[_] 24-73 — **"The BEST of CAPITALISM!" (Corrections for: "LIGHTNING STRIKES Versus Lightning Bugs and Impotent Fireflies!")** Book 073. (It is a completely new Book, except for those Corrections; and it is one of the Best Books in the World, which all Honest People will Love.)

[_] 24-74 — **"LIGHTNING STRIKES Versus Lightning Bugs!" (HOW you can Become Moderately RICH, without Telling any Lies nor Selling any Trash!) By The Worldwide People's Revolution!®** Book 074, which is the Perfection of all of the Lightning Striking Books, which is Recommended above all others for Mass Production: beCause it stands the Best Chance of being a Real Winner, just after this Book that you are now Reading, which has a Magnetizing Title!

[_] 24-75 — **"What are the Punishments for Dietary Sins?" (Have we Served ourselves Well at the Tables of our Lusts?)** Book 075. (This Book is too Controversial to be Published at this Time. Be very Patient until it is Available: beCause it is HOT!)

[_] 24-76 — **"What is WRong with those CRAZY CHRISTIANS?" (A Self-Examination of the Heart of the Body of Good Government!) By The Worldwide People's Revolution!®** Book 076.

[_] 24-77 — **"The Gospel According to our Elected King!" (The Good News from the Most Modern Perspective!)** Book 077. (This is perhaps the Best Book that you will Discover on Amazon, which contains the Famous Sermon that Jonah gave to the Ninevites, plus a very Special Sermon by Jesus Christ, himself!)

[_] 24-78 — **"The Root Cause for almost all Evils!" (The Strange Things that People Say and Do to Get more Money!)** Book 078. (This Book contains many Colored Photographs with Fascinating Explanations!)

[_] 24-79 — **"Orgimmick Gardening at its Best!" (HOW to Grow Delicious Satisfying Foods without a 10-Million-Dollar Investment!) By The Worldwide People's Revolution!®** Book 079. (This Book also contains many Colored Photographs with Wonderful Explanations!)

[_] 24-80 — **"Guaranteed Solutions!" (HOW to Solve our Local and Global Problems in the Most Rational Manner Possible!)** Book 080. (See the Description on Amazon: because they Offer a ONE-MILLION-DOLLAR REWARD to anyone who can Prove our Selected King's Solutions to be WRong or Unworkable! Can you Beat that? Do you have all such Guaranteed Solutions? Only our Selected King has those Solutions: beCause God Blest him with those Provable Solutions, which can be Proven in any Courtroom with Law and Order.)

[_] 24-81 — **"Mexicans are more Intelligent than Americans!" (A Unique Challenge to all Americans and Mexicans!) By The Worldwide People's Revolution!®** Book 081. {NOTE: The Remaining 275 Inspired Books by the Author of this Book may only be found in English, until we can get them Properly Translated into other Languages. Shame on you People who Killed him, who Broke his Heart with your Unbelief. May God have Mercy on your Poor Wretched Souls.} †‡

[_] 24-82 — **"The Process of Making a RIGHTEOUS KING!" (A Fascinating Autobiography of our Selected King!) By The Worldwide People's Revolution!®**, Book 082, which is otherwise known as: **"Diarrhea of the Mind!" (Our Selected King's Shortest Autobiography!)**

Our Selected King was Inspired by the 2016 Memorial Day Celebrations in Washington, D.C., to write this Inspired Book, which deals with numerous Important Subjects, which the Federal Government has little or no Interest in: because they like to keep their Minds Distracted from the Realities of Life with their own Invented Complications, being an Obvious Branch on the Military Industrial Congressional Drug Cartel Bankers' Complex Tree of Confusion, as former President Dwight David Eisenhower might say it, who was well Aware of the Multitude of Snakes along Wall Street, who Hide in their Dens of Iniquities, as King David might say, who make a big Pretense to be "All-American" Patriots, while Robbing Americans of Trillions of Dollars! However, our Selected King has Muhammad Ali Courageously giving the Final Knock-out Punches to that Ugly Scar-faced Battle-weary Uncle Sam!